American Indian Lives

Thęwǫnya?s ("Chainbreaker" or "Awl Breaker"), known to whites as
Governor Blacksnake. A daguerreotype made late in his life (later
published in Donaldson 1892, facing p. 28). Governor Blacksnake was
estimated to be 106 years of age when he died in 1859.

Chainbreaker

*The Revolutionary War Memoirs
of Governor Blacksnake*

as told to Benjamin Williams

Edited and
with an introduction and notes
by Thomas S. Abler

University of Nebraska Press
Lincoln and London

Manufactured in the United States of America
The paper in this book meets the minimum requirements
of American National Standard for
Information Sciences—Permanence of Paper for Printed
Library Materials, ANSI Z39.48-1984.
Library of Congress Cataloging-in-Publication Data
Blacksnake, Governor, ca. 1753–1859.
Chainbreaker:
the Revolutionary War memoirs of Governor Blacksnake
as told to Benjamin Williams/
edited and with an introduction and notes
by Thomas S. Abler.
p.   cm. — (American Indian Lives)
Bibliography: p. Includes index.
ISBN 0-8032-1446-4 (alk. paper)
1. Blacksnake, Governor, ca. 1753–1859.
2. Seneca Indians—Biography.
3. Seneca Indians—History.
4. Indians of North America—New York (State)—Biography.
5. Indians of North America—History—Revolution,
1775–1783—Personal narratives.
I. Williams, Benjamin, 1803–1861.
II. Abler, Thomas S., 1941–   . III. Title. IV. Series.
E99. S3 B533 1989   974.7′00497—dc19 [B]   88-28085   CIP

To the memory of
Merle H. Deardorff

Contents

Illustrations

MAPS

Preface

In June 1965, as a recently enrolled Ph.D. student at the University of Toronto, I set off to the Allegany Reservation in New York State. I had the encouragement of the informal dean of Iroquoian studies, William N. Fenton, and the support of grants from the Phillips Fund of the American Philosophical Society and from the New York State Museum and Science Service. I had been on the Allegany Reservation for little more than a week when reservation residents suggested I get in touch with a white man in Warren, Pennsylvania, by the name of Merle Deardorff. "He knows a lot about Indian history," I was told. A phone call confirmed that I would be welcome, so off I drove to nearby Warren. The evening proved delightful, as Deardorff provided me with story after story of his own experiences among the Senecas and the results of a lifetime of delving into their history. It was that evening that I first heard of the Blacksnake manuscript in the Draper Manuscripts of the State Historical Society of Wisconsin. Although it had no bearing on my Ph.D. research, which was on the post-1848 history of politics of the Seneca Nation, from that evening I had a desire to read the manuscript. This book (or rather, my part in this book), then, had its beginnings in the living room of Merle Deardorff that June evening in 1965.

I later discovered I was not the first young anthropologist to arrive on Deardorff's doorstep. I have been told that his home was a usual stopping place on the route from the university to the Allegany Reservation. Deardorff was an amateur scholar and part-time fieldworker and historian, but his rapport with the Senecas and his familiarity with archival resources were matched by few professionals. He also had the ability to communicate his experience. He filled the dual role of gentleman and scholar far better than many earning their salaries as academics. I count myself fortunate that I entered the field of Iroquoian studies before his passing.

Although Merle Deardorff pointed me toward the Blacksnake manuscript in 1965, it was another half-dozen years before I got to Madison to look at it. After reading it I was determined to get it into print, and I have been working on that task, off and on, ever since. Over the years I have incurred many debts while pursuing this end, and it is likely that I will fail to acknowledge some of them here. I extend my apologies if I forget to mention by name someone who has contributed to this project.

The staff of the State Historical Society of Wisconsin, particularly those in the Manuscripts Division, then under the direction of archivist Josephine Harper, were kind and helpful over several periods of work in that institution. I also made considerable use of the State Historical Society's monograph collection. The University of Wisconsin Library also treated me well while I was in Madison. Among other libraries I have used in working on this book are those of the University of Waterloo, the University of Toronto, Dalhousie University, Saint Francis Xavier University, the London School of Economics, and the Buffalo and Erie County Historical Society. Although none of their documents are cited directly in this book, I also benefited from the sources available and the kind treatment I received in the Public Records Office and the British Library in London.

Grants from various agencies have contributed to the project, including a University of Waterloo Faculty Grant, a Sabbatical Leave Fellowship from the Canada Council (now the Social Sciences and Humanities Research Council of Canada), and a Small Grant from the University of Waterloo, Social Sciences and Humanities Research Council. Word processing has been supported, when grant funding was lacking, by the Faculty of Arts at the University of Waterloo.

The generation of this book has been long, and several readers, most anonymous, have strengthened it. Two who have shed their anonymity are William N. Fenton and Elisabeth Tooker. I thank them for their comments on the drafts they read, and also for the numerous times over the past twenty-odd years when we have shared our thoughts on various problems in Iroquois history and culture at conferences and on other occasions.

An initial typescript of the text of the Blacksnake manuscript was produced by Alice Stangret. Later preliminary drafts were typed by Judy Remple, Barbara Faulkner, and Nancy Bannister. Assistance in editing and proofreading was provided by Rita T. Hayes and Linda Arbuthnot-Moroz.

Finally, over the past seven years revision after revision has been patiently and efficiently typed by Mrs. Rosemary Ambrose, secretary of the Department of Anthropology at the University of Waterloo. Mrs. Ambrose helped in other ways too, for over much of that time I was serving as chairman of the department, and her efficient handling of its day-to-day affairs, not to mention such things as the budget, left me free to worry about the problems of Indians and Loyalists in the eighteenth century rather than those of an anthropology department in the twentieth.

A Note on Orthographies

The Iroquoian languages have been transcribed into European alphabets by numerous individuals over the past 450 years (someone on the expedition recorded two Iroquoian languages encountered when Cartier sailed up the St. Lawrence in 1534 and 1535–36 [Lounsbury 1978:335]). I am not certain when the first recording of a Seneca utterance occurred. When Seneca has been written the spelling has been highly varied: persons attempting to write the language have possessed highly varied linguistic backgrounds and skills, and writers familiar with an orthography for another of the Iroquoian languages (for example, Mohawk) might continue to spell words according to the conventions developed for the first Iroquoian language they learned.

I have drawn together materials from a wide variety of historical and anthropological sources. Correcting the spelling in the many sources to a single standard orthography would constitute a monumental (and probably impossible) task, one peripheral to the story being told. In direct quotations containing Seneca words I use the spelling of the original. In my text I have utilized the spelling of Wallace Chafe (1963) if such was available; otherwise I used a spelling common in the published literature or in the documents.

I urge readers interested in the pronunciation of the Seneca words used to consult the writings of Wallace Chafe, whose linguistic research and publications have given us our standard description of Seneca.

It might be useful, though, to present here a brief summary of Chafe's Seneca orthography. For less distortion and greater sophistication, consult Chafe's publications (1963, 1967; see also Abler and Tooker 1978:511).

Chafe notes that Seneca has a small number of phonemes. He recognizes nine consonants plus four combinations of consonants that he feels require special comment (here modified from Chafe 1963:8):

For what sounds like English	Write Seneca
n (not word-final after Seneca ę or ǫ)	*n*
w	*w*
y	*y*
s, z	*s*
ch (before Seneca *i*)	*ts*
k, g, ng (if the *ng* is word-final after Seneca ę or ǫ)	*k*
t, d, n (if the *n* is word-final after Seneca ę or ǫ)	*t*
dz, j (if the *j* is before Seneca *i*)	*j*
glottal stop	*ʔ*
sh-y	*sy*
j (not before Seneca *i*)	*ty*
ch (not before Seneca *i*)	*thy*

Chafe (1963:5) describes the pronunciation of the Seneca vowels *a, e, i,* and *o* as the same sounds associated with those long vowels in German. He uses *æ* as equivalent to the *a* in English *man.* All but *i* are pronounced somewhat differently if unlengthened when followed by *i, j, k, s,* or *t.* Lengthening of vowels is indicated by a raised dot (˙). Nasalized vowels are ę and ǫ. Finally, Chafe recognized as significant "a greater degree of loudness, usually accompanied by a relatively higher pitch" on some vowels, and he marks this with an acute accent (Chafe 1963:4–5).

Readers who wish to delve more deeply into the phonemic structure of Seneca should consult Chafe's work. I hope this brief summary does some justice to his analysis and portrays the sounds uttered by Seneca speakers that were recorded in the sometimes (but not invariably) crude and unsophisticated orthographies used in the past.

Introduction

"pretty Smart for his age"

Blacksnake, Williams, and Draper

In December 1859 the Seneca people of the Coldspring community buried Governor Blacksnake, a respected, even venerated, chief, who had probably reached the age of 106. "Governor Blacksnake" was how whites addressed him; Blacksnake's Seneca name was Thę́ wǫ nya?s, which Benjamin Williams, his young English-speaking Seneca neighbor, translated "Chainbreaker." Blacksnake was born near Seneca Lake, probably in 1753, when the English and French were still contesting dominance in North America. Although his people, the Senecas who formed part of the famous Iroquois Confederacy, had been using European trade goods for almost two centuries, they still maintained a politically autonomous existence remote from the white settlements in Canada, New York, and Pennsylvania. Indeed, colonial and imperial governments sought friendship and alliance with the powerful Iroquois Confederacy. When Blacksnake died, however, his people retained only a few small reservations. Railroads had been built through his Allegany Reservation, and white villages had been established to service these new machines and their steel tracks. In his 106 years Blacksnake had seen much.

Blacksnake's life was active and eventful. He was of the appropriate age and disposition to play an intense and dangerous role in the American Revolution. His Revolutionary War experience brought him into contact with native leaders such as the Mohawk captain Joseph Brant and the venerable Seneca chief Old Smoke, as well as many prominent loyalists including John Butler and the Johnson family. Blacksnake's own uncle was the famous Cornplanter, so conspicuous in that conflict. Cornplanter also played a key role in the Seneca peace negotiations with the Americans after the war, and as Cornplanter's nephew, Blacksnake was also a participant. The Americans Blacksnake met after the Revolution included George Washington. Blacksnake was also a relative of the Seneca orator Red Jacket, who attained considerable fame and influence.

Another of Blacksnake's uncles was the Seneca prophet Handsome Lake, and Blacksnake was among the first to come to his uncle's side when he was believed dead. Blacksnake found a warm spot on the prophet's chest, and later Handsome Lake revived and told the people that angels had come to him and related what they had revealed to him. This experience and later visions form the basis of contemporary Iroquois religion (see Parker 1913).

That Cornplanter and Handsome Lake were brothers of Blacksnake's mother was of considerable importance in the life of the young warrior, for the relationship of mother's brother to sister's son (uncle to nephew) is particularly significant in matrilineal societies such as the Senecas. The Senecas were divided into eight exogamous clans, and children were members of their mothers' clans. Each clan was divided into smaller units, called lineages by anthropologists, which in fact comprised all the descendants, through females, of a single woman or a group of sisters. In matrilineal societies marriage tends to be fragile; the bond between husband and wife is not as strong as that between mother and daughter or between sisters. The relationship of men to their children is limited by the brittleness of the marriage bond and even more by the children's belonging to the mother's clan and lineage rather than the father's.

A child's mother's brother, however, has a lifetime relationship with his sister's children. They belong to the same clan and lineage, and he has a responsibility to see that they are raised properly. His sister's children will inherit his lineage's property, privileges, and obligations. When boys mature, they replace their mothers' brothers rather than their fathers.

It was thus of major importance that Blacksnake had such illustrious mother's brothers. Since the Senecas extended sibling terms to an entire generation within lineage and clan, it is possible that Blacksnake's "uncles"—Cornplanter and Handsome Lake—were not actual brothers of his mother but rather were her cousins (her mother's sister's sons), but that is not necessarily of great significance, for a classificatory mother's brother would play the same role as a biological one.

Blacksnake was therefore in a central position to observe the important historical involvement of the Senecas and other members of the Six Nations Confederacy in the American Revolution and its aftermath. Though his youth precluded his assuming a leadership role in campaign and council, that same youth gave him the vigor to participate in or witness almost every battle or council session where there was significant Seneca presence. Since he could not write, Blacksnake could only relate his vision of these events orally from memory, but as we shall see, his memory proved keen indeed.

When he was in his ninth or tenth decade of life, Blacksnake recited to a neighbor his dramatic and exciting experiences in the Revolutionary War and in the councils that preceded and followed it. This Seneca, Benjamin Williams, had some of the whites' schooling. Blacksnake told the story in Seneca; Williams set it down in his own somewhat individualistic English. Williams appears to have written the story with a view to publication, and it is at least probable that Blacksnake had a similar motivation in dictating the manuscript. We know that Blacksnake's son was eager to see the story in print (see B. Williams to L. C. Draper, 14-i-1860, DM 16-F-247).[1]

Williams was born in 1805 and is said to have witnessed the

A portrait of Governor Blacksnake painted in 1845 by John Phillips (see Rose 1983:8). Once owned by the pioneer student of Iroquois culture and anthropology, Lewis H. Morgan, the portrait is now in the Rochester Museum and Science Center. From the collection of the Rochester Museum and Science Center, Rochester, New York.

execution of a Seneca woman accused of witchcraft when he was three years old (DM 4-S-116). Draper's notes (ibid.) identify him as "a Seneca Chief under the old regime," but I have found no evidence to support this claim. He did serve as a presiding officer in the 1848 election of clerk, treasurer, marshal, and peacemakers of the Seneca (MBPP).

Williams resided near Blacksnake at Coldspring on the Allegany Reservation. Because he was bilingual, he served as an interpreter; he is mentioned by Schoolcraft (1851–57, 4:345) as "an educated Indian" who interpreted an interview with Governor Blacksnake.

Just before America entered World War II, Charles E. Congdon (1967:165–68) inquired about Williams among Indians from the Allegany Reservation who had known Williams when they were young. They reported that physically he was "tall and slender, [with] quite light complexion." One of Congdon's informants, Jonas Crouse, noted that "he lived in big house and store. . . . They used to have fiddle dance in that store." Williams had no children, but his wife had a daughter whose own daughter, Williams's wife's granddaughter, "used to see him writing but does not know what he wrote. He had a big desk, old one, all full of papers. He had a lot of books. . . . They all burned when the house burned." Among the papers lost in the fire there might have been a manuscript relating directly to Cornplanter—we know that Williams prepared such a manuscript (B. Williams to L. Draper, DM 16-F-223).

Fortunately the Blacksnake manuscript was not lost along with the other papers of Benjamin Williams when his house was destroyed, for before this tragedy it had passed into the hands of Lyman C. Draper, who was well into his lifelong project of gathering data on the border wars. Draper somehow learned of the manuscript and obtained it by paying Williams ten dollars with a promise of another fifteen when the manuscript reached print (Hesseltine 1954:57). Though he never published the manuscript, he may have eventually paid the latter sum, since in 1874 he listed twenty-five dollars as the amount paid for the Williams-

Blacksnake manuscript (Hesseltine 1954:303). The manuscript
was the first Draper ever purchased (Hesseltine 1954:267).

Draper, the grandson of a Revolutionary War soldier, was born
in Erie County, New York, on September 4, 1815. At that time
most members of the Seneca Nation resided in Erie County, on
the Buffalo Creek Reservation (where Red Jacket exerted great
influence) and the Cattaraugus Reservation. He spent two years
(1834–36) at Granville College in Granville, Ohio, but withdrew
for financial reasons. He worked as a clerk and a newspaper
editor but, apparently aided by the hospitality and financial support of his cousin, Lydia Remsen, and her husband, Peter Remsen, devoted much time and energy to his historical research.

As Reuben Gold Thwaites reported, "It was in 1838, when
twenty-three years of age, that Draper conceived the idea of
writing a series of biographies of trans-Allegany pioneers. . . . This
at once became his controlling thought, and he entered upon its
execution with an enthusiasm which never lagged through a half
century spent in the assiduous collection of material . . . ; but
unfortunately he only collected and investigated, and the biographies were never written" (Thwaites 1903:xii). It has been estimated that Draper traveled sixty thousand miles (Thwaites 1903:
xiii), and the documents, notes, and papers he amassed constitute
the 484 volumes of the Draper Manuscripts at the State Historical Society of Wisconsin.

Draper journeyed to Blacksnake's home in the Coldspring
community on the Allegany Reservation in southwestern New
York in 1850. He interviewed Blacksnake at some length, with
William Crouse, son of the white captive Peter Crouse, acting as
interpreter. Hesseltine (1954:57) considered this interview "the
prize of the trip" in which Draper had interrogated both Indians
and whites from Pittsburgh to Coldspring. At this time Blacksnake was still, to use a favorite phrase of Benjamin Williams's,
"pretty Smart for his age" (B. Williams to L. C. Draper 12-ix-
1854, DM 16-F-238, plus numerous letters before and after this
one). Draper described Blacksnake as having "the appearance of
men generally from 60 to 65" and being "spare, slim, about 6 feet

in height—with a mild eye & intelligent countenance" (DM 4-s-81).

Draper joined the State Historical Society of Wisconsin in 1852; on January 18, 1854, he became corresponding secretary, and as such the executive officer of the society (Thwaites 1903: xix). He found the society with a library of fifty volumes; in his first year as secretary he added one thousand books and one thousand pamphlets. He continued with the society through 1886. Thwaites (1903:xxvi) notes that "his work for this Society has of itself been sufficient to earn for him the lasting gratitude of the people of Wisconsin, and of all American historical students." Draper died in Madison on August 26, 1891.

Draper once wrote regretfully, "I have wasted my life in puttering, . . . but I see no help for it; I can write nothing so long as I fear there is a fact, no matter how small, as yet ungarnered" (quoted by Thwaites 1903:xviii). It was his ceaseless quest for facts that has preserved for us so much of the life of Governor Blacksnake.

The Manuscript

Blacksnake's story, an important and often-cited manuscript, now forms a small part of the extensive Draper Manuscripts of the State Historical Society of Wisconsin in Madison (see Harper 1983). A fragment of it was published by Thwaites and Kellogg (1908); it continues to play an important scholarly role, demonstrated by its frequent citation in ethnohistorical studies as, for example, in Barbara Graymont's (1972) analysis of the Iroquois role in the American Revolution and in Anthony F. C. Wallace's (1970) study of the revitalization of native religion among the Senecas following that conflict.

Thus the scholarly world owes a debt to these men, of varying generation and background, from the nineteenth century. It was the white man Lyman C. Draper who brought the manuscript to Madison; it was the younger Seneca Benjamin Williams who wrote it down; but most important it was dictated by the Seneca "Chainbreaker" or Governor Blacksnake, two generations older than Draper and Williams and a veteran of both the American Revolution and the War of 1812.

This volume presents the text of Williams's manuscript and discusses in detail those episodes and aspects of Blacksnake's life that he outlined to Williams. It provides a rare Indian view of warfare and of diplomacy in a period when the Six Nations of the Iroquois still played a prominent and significant role in the development of North America.

Although I have been referring to *a* manuscript, in fact there are two manuscripts, filed together in volume 16 of the "Joseph Brant Papers" in the Draper Manuscripts (16-F-107–219). Both versions were written by Williams, and large portions of the two texts are identical. Neither variant is clearly superior to the other in completeness, accuracy, or seeming closeness to what Blacksnake must have dictated. Nor does it appear that one is an initial or early draft and the second a more polished version. Each variant contains episodes the other lacks. It does seem likely that each includes modifications Williams made altering the sense of Blacksnake's testimony either through an inability to reasonably translate Blacksnake's utterances or in an attempt to bring his own ideas of order and literary quality to the finished work.

In addition to these two versions of Blacksnake's story, there is another fragment dealing with a later episode in Blacksnake's life. An account of the revelation of the prophet Handsome Lake is found in this same volume of the "Joseph Brant Papers" (16-F-226–266), set down by Williams possibly on Blacksnake's dictation. This is included here as chapter 6. Williams also set down the Iroquois creation myth (22-F-23–44). Although it seems highly probable that Blacksnake also contributed to this final manuscript, it has been published elsewhere (Abler 1982) and is not included in this volume.

Blacksnake's Story as Life History

In North America there is a long tradition involving the publication of materials purporting to be autobiographies of native persons (Krupat 1985; Brumble 1981). The vast majority of first-person accounts of the lives of Native North Americans involve collaboration with someone else who is not a native. Watson and Watson-Franke (1985:2) have made a useful distinction between a life history, "*elicited or prompted by another person,*" and an autobiography, "a person's *self-initiated* retrospective account of his life." Clearly life history and autobiography as so defined are ideal types, since few autobiographies reach publication without some sort of collaboration. Although Krupat (1985:7) overstates the case when he argues that "Indian texts are always the consequence of a collaboration," it is certainly true as he states that "no matter what we wish to say about them, it is useful to know, as far as we can, just how they were made."

Many life histories of Native North Americans have involved collaboration with anthropologists, and such documents have been used by social scientists investigating in a variety of cultural settings (Langness 1965; Langness and Frank 1981; Watson and Watson-Franke 1985; Plummer 1983). Even social scientists intrude on the product of life histories and are at times not candid about the degree of intrusion (see Krupat's [1985:75–106] critique of Radin's Crashing Thunder as well as numerous annotations in Brumble's [1981] bibliography). Nonacademics are similarly guilty. It is clearly desirable to know the motives behind the collaboration so that one can judge the final document for what it does and does not say.

The narrative presented here is unusual among life histories of Native North Americans in that the collaborator was also a native person and in fact a member of the same community. One might ask what led Blacksnake and Williams to collaborate in the production of the manuscript. Williams of course could read and write, and I think it highly probable that an item or items in the published record motivated his collaboration with Blacksnake.

The tradition of published Indian autobiography had its beginnings sometime before the production of the Williams-Blacksnake manuscript. At least four autobiographical works proclaiming the native ancestry of their subjects were published before 1840 (Anderson 1825; Apes 1829; Black Hawk 1955 [1833]; and Cuffe 1839), and three more such works appeared before 1850 (Copway 1847; Tubbee 1848a, 1848b).

It is possible that one or more of these early autobiographical works had some impact on the Williams-Blacksnake collaboration, and it seems likely that other works being published in the same period influenced them. Several white authors were publishing biographies of Indians. Collections of Indian biographies are found in Drake (1832), Thatcher (1832), and McKenney and Hall (1933–34 [1836–44]). Stone's study of Joseph Brant appeared in 1838, to be followed in 1841 by his biography of Red Jacket. It also has been suggested that autobiographies of frontiersmen, such as Boone and Crockett, may have influenced Indian life histories (Krupat 1985:41–44).

The interest neighboring whites showed in Blacksnake's recollections may also have had an influence. The old chief was something of a local celebrity. Morgan (1851:74) mentions him, and interviews are recounted in the works of Schoolcraft (1847: 261, 457; 1851–57, 4:345–46) and Parkman (1851:376n). At this time Americans were constructing their national myth, so questions about the Revolutionary War (as well as other frontier conflicts) were pervasive in these encounters with Blacksnake.

Two other published works very likely, in my view, had an impact on the Williams-Blacksnake collaboration. The first is a strange book published by the Tuscarora David Cusick in 1825 (Beauchamp 1892). Cusick certainly provided a model for the publication by a native person of a text internally rather than externally generated. I do not suggest that Cusick's text was not influenced by the products of the Euro-American civilization that surrounded the Iroquois reservations in New York. However, the book appears to reflect Cusick's view of a properly written text about his people rather than that of a white editor or amanuensis. Cusick's work deserves evaluation as a product of cultural fusion; he appears to have consciously imitated the style of pretentious white publications of that era. Williams seems to have done likewise in the manuscript being discussed here, but we cannot be certain whether Williams imitates Cusick or simply the same literature Cusick imitates. In another manuscript that may be the product of a Williams-Blacksnake collaboration (Abler 1982), Williams put the Seneca creation myth into a format resembling the English Bible, complete with numbers for chapter and verse. It of course is not surprising that members of a formerly nonliterate community adopting the literate traditions of a neighboring community would, when writing internally generated texts, ape the format of their neighbors' written literature. Parallels between Cusick's work and the literary production of Benjamin Williams, then, may be the result of either direct or parallel influences.

A second book that may have influenced the Williams-Blacksnake collaboration has been ignored by students writing about Native North American life histories. I argue that it is such a life history and indeed could be considered the first Indian autobiography to reach publication. I refer to the story of Mary Jemison (Seaver 1824; ten more editions were printed before 1850 [Newberry Library 1912:84–87]). Jemison's story is invariably considered in the captivity narrative genre (Vail 1949; Vaughan 1983), but I feel it can with equal justification be considered an Indian autobiography. At the time her story was published, Mary Jemison had been living among the Senecas as a Seneca for over sixty years. The story is not the typical captivity genre ("the redeemed captive returned from . . .") but rather is the story of the adult life of a Seneca female whose interaction with white settlers was neither more nor less than that of her Seneca sisters. Clearly her white birth contributed to the fact that her story was recorded and published, but it still remains the story of a Seneca woman. It also is a story that covers the period, and some of the same events, found in the Williams-Blacksnake manuscript.

Jemison was not an Allegany Seneca; her home was on the Genesee River. When the small reservation there was sold she moved to Buffalo Creek, where she died in 1833. There is no evidence that either Williams or Blacksnake knew Jemison, but I think it very likely that Williams was aware of Seaver's publication of her story (Congdon's informants spoke of Williams's library).

There is no way of knowing if Williams read any of the works that have been mentioned, but it does seem likely that he would have been aware of the popularity of using biography to deal with frontier war and diplomacy during the American Revolution. Blacksnake also may well have known of this literature through conversations with educated Indians and whites. I strongly suspect that it was this volume of literature, so much of which dealt with Iroquois subjects, that led Williams and Blacksnake to attempt to add yet another life story to it.

Blacksnake's Narrative and Problems of Transcription

Readers must be forewarned that Blacksnake's narrative is not elegant or lucid prose. Williams's writing has been described as "very bad reservation English" (Wallace 1970:345). In some respects it is even worse than the "reservation English" encountered over the years by ethnographers,[2] since one must add confusion about spelling and punctuation to the other nonstandard aspects of English as spoken by Indians for whom it was neither a first language nor even one used in everyday communication.

Some of the written errors probably reflect oral reservation English. Seneca does not distinguish between *t* and *d* as English does. In reading Williams's text one is immediately struck by how often a *d* replaces a *t* in his spelling of a word (or the reverse). Similar problems surround the use of *l* and *r* and *f* and *v*. Thus "breakfast" becomes "blackvest" in Williams's orthography. Once one is aware of these problems, one can attack the reading of the text as an interesting and challenging puzzle, but I must confess that even with the most positive of attitudes, coping with the text is at times a formidable task.

Since there is no *r* in Seneca (see "A Note on Orthographies," above), readers may be puzzled by the fact Williams frequently uses *r* in spelling Seneca words. It is likely meant as a vowel.

Horatio Hale (1883:166) noted his informants used *r* for a vowel, as the *a* in *father.*

In approaching the original manuscript, one also faces the problems inevitable in dealing with handwritten documents. That is, bumps and squiggles can represent a variety of letters in the alphabet. As an example of the type of error the contemporary scholar can introduce when transcribing this material, one can contrast my interpretation of a line in the manuscript with that of a distinguished ethnohistorian, Anthony F. C. Wallace. Wallace quotes Blacksnake's recollection of a British speech: "here is the Buckenknife and Bowisknife that you will also take for to take the American lock and scalps" (Wallace 1970:132). My own interpretation of the line in the manuscript is: "here is the Butcherknife and Bowieknife that you will also take for to take the American luck and sculps" (DM 16-F-125). I feel it is clear that this is a reference to butcher knives (which in fact is what "scalping" knives were) as well as an anachronistic reference to Bowie knives. I disagree also with Wallace's transcription of the final three words, although it is clear that "lock and scalps" are the English words Williams had in mind when he wrote the manuscript.

The text presented is as close to the written manuscript as I can make it. I have not introduced changes except that double commas have been replaced by dashes for ease in reading. Material enclosed in square brackets is not in the original and may be either the page number of the manuscript or an editorial correction or explanation. Hence, sometimes this might be a correct date or my best guess as to a correct date; in other places it might be my best guess as to the interpretation of a word or phrase that I felt readers might find obscure. Any parentheses or braces in the text are found in the original manuscript.

There was also the problem of how best to present the two texts Williams had set down. The two variants of the story found in the Draper Manuscripts are for the most part identical or nearly so. There seemed little point in publishing both. Yet each does contain material the other lacks. My solution has been to look at the manuscripts as series of episodes. If for a given episode the content in the two variants was similar or identical, I used the text from the first variant in the Draper Manuscripts; if one variant had an episode that was in my judgment clearly superior (usually longer with more detail), only the text of the superior variant is presented here. Obviously, where an episode is unique to one variant the text of the episode has been used.

After deciding for each episode which variant constituted the better text, I combined the episodes from the two variants in what I feel is proper chronological order. Page references (from volume 16-F in the Draper Manuscripts) are given in square brackets preceding the text found on that page, and a line of ellipsis dots signals a shift from one variant to the other, so it will be readily apparent where (and indeed, how infrequently) I have altered the ordering of Williams's text or had to utilize material found in the second variant of his presentation of Blacksnake's memoirs.

I then divided the combined text into six major sections, each of which constitutes a major phase in the story Blacksnake has told. I have provided a long introduction to each section to equip readers with enough background to read and appreciate the significance of the story. These introductions include critical commentary and notes, offer alternative interpretations of the textual materials, and present tangential issues raised by the text. References will also lead serious students elsewhere in the literature. Since these introductory sections might interfere with the narrative line of Blacksnake's story, some readers may choose to ignore them; others may share my feeling that dealing with the ambiguities and puzzles posed by historical documents contributes to the challenge and enjoyment of historical research and may well find the critical commentaries intriguing and valuable.

I hope what is offered here will be appreciated as an exciting opportunity to sample recollections from the life of an Indian veteran of the American Revolution as written down by another Indian a half-century after the events took place. The text deals with a time when both the Senecas and their white neighbors were undergoing substantial political and cultural transition. It presents an Indian view of violence and war, but even more, it presents an Indian view of council and diplomacy.

In evaluating what Blacksnake has to say, it is too easy to give undue importance to the lurid and violent sections. Blacksnake was of an age and a disposition to take part in combat; he was a killer of men. However, in this memoir he devotes more space to describing the council fire and diplomatic process than to portraying the violence and gore of the battlefield. One could accrue prestige in battle among the eighteenth-century Senecas, but the really predominant men in Seneca society were those who could acquit themselves well in council. Blacksnake did distinguish himself in combat, but he was too young to take a leading role in council. Men who aspired to leadership roles, however, learned by observing such events. Blacksnake proved a keen and careful observer of his elders' famous oratorical and diplomatic skills.

Blacksnake's story, then, is one of violence and war, of cementing military alliances, and of building a peace at the conclusion of the war. There are victories and defeats, triumphs and humiliations. Yet it is very much a personal story of an ambitious and able young man caught up in dangerous and tumultuous times.

Chapter One

Prelude to Conflict

"where is the covenant chain of Peace"

INTRODUCTION

Blacksnake's earliest memories were of a society in the midst of
war—not a distant war, but one close to home. He saw his
relatives and neighbors leave home to return, often within days,
with tales of terror and heroism, in the exaltation of victory or
the dejection of defeat, but in either case to tell of death and the
horrible wounds men inflict on each other when using weapons
is viewed as expedient in the pursuit of political or economic
goals. This must have had a profound effect on the young boy in
the first decade of his life. It prepared him well for the violent
scenes he was to witness after he reached his twenties and for the
bloody role he himself was to play.

But it is incorrect to view Blacksnake's socialization as valu-
ing military skills above all others. He was raised in a society
that, with considerable validity, viewed itself as the diplomatic
hub of the North American frontier. It honored those with the
skills to sway councils and manipulate men not by raw power
but by the force and eloquence of argument. It was a society
where diplomacy was a spectator sport and attendance at diplomatic conferences was not limited to a small elite but rather was
a privilege enjoyed by the community at large. Blacksnake in his
youth undoubtedly learned the importance of the council fire
and the central role his people played in frontier diplomacy.

In his formative years, then, Blacksnake was educated to the importance both of the war trail and of the council fire, preparing him for the early years of his adult life when he was a keen participant in each of these.

Birth and Boyhood

In the initial section of Blacksnake's memoirs, Williams refers briefly to Blacksnake's birth and boyhood. Regrettably, he gives us no details, for it would have been fascinating to have Blacksnake's memories of his childhood and adolescence. We do know, from Lyman Draper's interview, that Blacksnake grew up in an atmosphere of conflict and was well acquainted with prime actors in that conflict.

Unfortunately the narrative is preceded by a lengthy, confused introduction not closely related to the story that follows and possibly more difficult to read than any other section of the text. For that reason I have relegated it to appendix 1. Here it seems best to begin the narrative with Blacksnake's birth and boyhood, which Williams has written in the third person. After this short paragraph the narrative shifts to the first person (for Blacksnake), giving us some confidence that the remainder of the text constitutes a reasonably direct translation of the story the old chief dictated to Williams.

Blacksnake was born in the mid-eighteenth century in the hamlet of Kendaia on Seneca Lake (see map 1). Williams has written the name as "gan,dr,a." There is no way to be certain of his birthdate. Williams has given the year as 1749, certainly one of the more credible of the many dates appearing in the document. This date is supported by a commentator who gave Blacksnake's age as 107 when he testified in court in the Oil Spring suit in 1856 (Donaldson 1892:28).[1] An even earlier date for Blacksnake's birth has been suggested by Paul A. W. Wallace (1945: 195), who thought Blacksnake might have been born before 1744. Draper reports, though, that Blacksnake said he was two years old in 1755, when William Johnson defeated the French on Lake George, and twenty-two at the time of the Battle of Bunker Hill (1775), pointing to a birthdate of 1753 (DM 4-s-13).

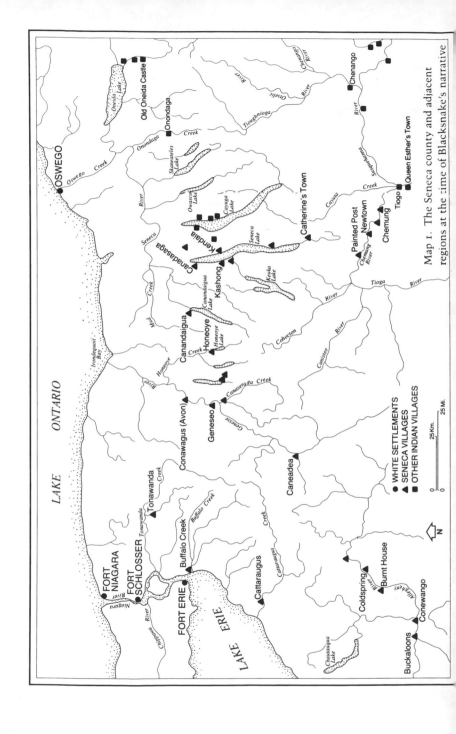

Map 1. The Seneca county and adjacent regions at the time of Blacksnake's narrative

Evidence concerning Blacksnake's parents is sketchy. His mother seems to have been a sister (or half-sister) to both Cornplanter and Handsome Lake. Cornplanter's father was a Dutch trader, John Abeel (or O'Bail), but it seems most unlikely that Abeel also fathered Blacksnake's mother. Both Cornplanter and Handsome Lake were members of the Wolf Clan of the Senecas, as was Blacksnake's mother. The Senecas being a matrilineal society, Blacksnake, like his two illustrious uncles, was a member of the Wolf Clan.

Draper reports that Blacksnake identified his paternal grandfather as a French officer at Niagara and his paternal grandmother as a Seneca woman of the Wolf Clan (DM 4-S-13). If this is true it would mean that both of Blacksnake's parents were members of the Wolf Clan. It is usual to speak of Seneca matriclans as being exogamous, but it is known that this "rule" of clan exogamy was breached in the early nineteenth century (see Abler 1971). Hence the attribution of Wolf Clan membership to Blacksnake's father is curious but not necessarily invalid.

Draper transcribes the name of Blacksnake's father as "*De-ne-o-ah-te* or *The Light.*" After fathering Blacksnake, he had two sons by a Cayuga woman of the Snipe Clan who possibly lived in Canada, later returning to Blacksnake's mother to father a daughter (DM 4-S-13). It seems likely that Blacksnake's half-brothers remained with their mother. Like their mother they were Cayugas, and like most Cayugas they settled on the Grand River in Canada after the American Revolution.

Blacksnake bore at least two Seneca names during his life, as was the usual practice. Each Seneca was given a "baby name" at birth, replaced by a second name upon assuming adult status. Blacksnake's names, like every other Seneca name, came from two sets, juvenile names and adult names, belonging to the individual's clan. At any point in time only a portion of the list of names is in use, so a newborn infant can be assigned a child's name from the roster of unused names. The burden of remembering the list of clan names falls upon the clan matron, the most capable senior female in the matrilineage. New Seneca names

are publicly announced during the two most important ceremonies in the Seneca religious calendar—the midwinter ceremony in late January or February and the green corn ceremony
in August. The speaker (a male) who announces the names is
prompted by the clan matron seated beside him.

Williams states that Blacksnake utilized his juvenile or boyhood name through the American Revolution. Williams writes
this as Dahgr,ya,Doh, and he indicates that its meaning has
something to do with gambling and betting (DM 16-F-107). Draper, in his notes on his interview with Blacksnake, presents the
simple translation "Boys Betting" (DM-S-80). Kent and Deardorff
(1960:454) transcribe the name as Tekayē:tũʔ and render its
meaning as "two (betting) games going on at the same time."
Some Seneca names do have meaning in Seneca and hence can be
"translated," just as some English surnames have meaning or
meaningful elements (e.g., Curtin, Hunt, Schoolcraft, Speck).
Many Seneca names, however, like many English surnames, are
in fact untranslatable—they are simply names.

It seems that Blacksnake bore the name Tekayē:tũʔ throughout the American Revolution. It is not clear, however, when this
name was replaced by the title that Williams has written as
"Tan,wr,nyrs" and that both he and Draper have translated as
"Chainbreaker." Morgan (1851:74) who wrote the name "Ta-
wan'-ne-ars," translates it less dramatically as "needle breaker,"
while the modern authority on the Seneca language, Wallace
Chafe, renders the name "he breaks wire, nails." In Chafe's orthography the name is written Thệ·wǫnyaʔs (Chafe 1963:57,
modified as noted in Abler and Tooker 1978:511n).

After interviewing Blacksnake, Draper asserted that "about
1787 or 1788, . . . at a grand council at Buffalo Reservation . . .
[Blacksnake] was there invested with the new official name of
Tah-won-ne-ahs." Draper states that "under this new name,
Blacksnake signed the treaty of Fort Harmar" (DM 4-S-80).

Kent and Deardorff (1960:455) argue that Blacksnake continued to be known as Tekayē:tũʔ (Tekianindau) as late as 1802.
There is a name on the 1789 Fort Harmar treaty that does resem-

ble the name Blacksnake bore in the nineteenth century—"Tewanias or Broken Twig" (Kappler 1901–41, 2:25). But Kent and Deardorff believe this signatory of the Fort Harmar treaty was neither Blacksnake nor even his predecessor holding the title or name of Thę́ wǫ nya?s. They assert the treaty at Fort Harmar was signed by a Seneca named Tewa?'enya?s. "Broken Twig," they argue, is the correct translation of this name.

When Blacksnake took the name Chainbreaker probably can never be firmly resolved, given the nature of the evidence. I do not find the argument of Kent and Deardorff completely convincing, but the information found in Draper's notes from his interview with the chief is also suspect. It is possible that the old chief's memory failed him. It also is seldom clear in Draper's notes from the interview what constitutes a translation of the chief's response to a question and what constitutes a conclusion Draper reached based, often quite tenuously, on something said by the chief or his translator.

Blacksnake also bore two English names in his lifetime. Initially, because of his relationship to Cornplanter, he was known simply as "the Nephew." The name Nephew continues to be a common surname among the Seneca Indians on the Allegany and Cattaraugus reservations in New York State today. It is not clear when or why he assumed the name Governor Blacksnake. Draper states in the notes of his interview with Blacksnake that the name was given to him by Cornplanter's son Henry O'Bail sometime before the War of 1812 (DM 4-s-81). Others have suggested that it was George Washington himself who suggested that the young chief growing in influence be called Governor Blacksnake (Donaldson 1892:28).

The Seneca World about 1750–70

Blacksnake was born in Kendaia, a hamlet of probably no more than twenty houses on the east side of Seneca Lake, about ten miles from its foot. Blacksnake later recalled the extensive orchards surrounding the town (DM 4-s-14). Early in his youth his family moved to the town of Conawagus (see map 1). This Seneca town was near the site of the later white town of Avon, New York; hence throughout the manuscript Williams has chosen to write the name of the Indian town as "avone." Blacksnake continued to live in Conawagus until 1779 (DM 4-s-82).

The domain of the Senecas at the time of Blacksnake's birth was extensive. It spread from a line between Cayuga Lake and Seneca Lake westward and southward to include all of western New York as well as portions of Ohio, Pennsylvania, and perhaps southwestern Ontario. In this territory the Seneca men hunted, traded, and trapped. The Senecas lived in about twenty small villages in the river valleys, averaging twenty to twenty-five cabins each, for the most part single-family dwellings. This settlement pattern was markedly changed from that of the Senecas and other Iroquoians when they were first encountered by Europeans (Abler 1970). Gone were the communal longhouses and the large, densely populated hilltop palisaded villages of the previous century. The newer single-family houses might be of traditional pole and elm-bark construction like the longhouses they replaced, but log cabins were found with increasing frequency through the eighteenth century. Seneca log houses dating to the eighteenth century are still preserved at Letchworth State Park in the Genesee Valley of New York.

Around the cabins were the Seneca fields, hacked from the forest by slashing and burning, growing the traditional Seneca foods, the life supporters—maize, beans, and squash. Added to these as a result of contact with their white neighbors were more exotic foods such as peas, watermelons, potatoes, turnips, and carrots. Surrounding the villages were orchards, often with hundreds of apple and peach trees. Cattle, pigs, and chickens were raised for food (Cook 1887).

These small villages had distinct advantages over the large palisaded towns of the early historic period. Their smaller populations did not exhaust firewood or soil fertility so rapidly, nor were there the problems of hygiene found in the earlier towns with populations in the thousands. The large towns of the previous century had had defensive advantages, but Iroquois victories on battlefields in the late seventeenth century made Iroquoia safe from the raiding parties that had proved such a danger in the early 1600s.

Although the products of the chase were still used, almost all Seneca clothing and household effects came from the trading posts of Albany, Montreal, or Niagara. The Senecas had given up making pottery seventy-five years before Blacksnake's birth (Wray and Schoff 1953:59). Archaeological investigations of late eighteenth-century Seneca sites yield no native-made potsherds, effigy pipes, or chert projectile points; instead there are imported ceramics, clay pipes (from Scotland), and lead musket balls (Hayes 1965).

Although the Senecas cut and tailored the materials to their own styles, they preferred the whites' cloth and blankets to leather and fur. A notable exception was the continued importance of deer hides for footwear. Most Senecas, male and female, wore deer-hide moccasins, though it was not remarkable for a Seneca to appear wearing shoes complete with brass buckles (as well as dressed in a gold-laced coat and hat and carrying a silk handkerchief).[2]

Since deer hides were important for the manufacture of moccasins, hunting skills retained considerable value in Blacksnake's time. Draper reports, "*Blacksnake* was early taught to hunt, & the use of the gun—& being naturally smart, gave promise of distinction among his people" (DM 4-S-15). As a youth Blacksnake hunted in the vicinity of Conawagus (DM 4-S-82–83).

The Senecas continued in the religion of their ancestors. Medicine societies, such as the Society of Faces and the Little Water Society (see Parker 1909; Fenton 1941a), cured illness. Most religious activity, however, was geared to the agricultural and food-gathering year. The importance of wild foods is indicated by the strawberry and maple festivals that took place every spring, while such events as the corn sprouting, green corn, and midwinter ceremonies reflect a people dependent upon domesticated plants. These last two continue as the most important ceremonies in the Seneca religious calendar.[3]

The retention of ancestral religious practices was not due to ignorance of Christianity. Christian Hurons were incorporated into the Senecas in 1650, and the Senecas received their first missionary in 1656 (Abler and Tooker 1978:505–6). One can contrast the reception of Christianity among the Senecas with the reaction of their Mohawk brethren. In the seventeenth century a large number of Mohawks converted to Catholicism and removed to the St. Lawrence (Fenton and Tooker 1978:469). Those who rejected Catholicism received Anglican missionaries, and "most of the Mohawks were reported to be at least nominal Christians" in 1743 (Fenton and Tooker 1978:475). One can also note that large numbers of the Oneidas joined the flock of the Presbyterian minister Samuel Kirkland in the 1770s (Campisi 1978:483). Kirkland went to the Oneidas only after he and his teachings had been rejected by the Senecas (Graymont 1972:34).

The Senecas of 1750 were of mixed ancestry. Population losses caused by warfare and disease had been compensated, at least partially, by captives and refugees who settled in Seneca villages. A Seneca of 1750 could perhaps count Hurons, Eries, Neutrals, Petuns, Ottawas, Algonkins, Foxes, French, Dutch, English, and even others among his ancestors and kinsmen. Blacksnake's uncle Cornplanter was fathered by the Dutch trader John Abeel (or O'Bail), while Blacksnake himself thought he had French ancestry.

Blacksnake's story is a tale of war, but it is also a tale of politics and diplomacy. Hence, for a proper understanding of the history Blacksnake presents it is necessary to discuss in some detail the political milieu of the northern frontier in the eighteenth century. The political environment was complex, in part because of the large number of political units involved in the forest diplomacy. It is also necessary to understand the nature of tribal political systems and the degree of control native "chiefs" enjoyed over their populations. One might also add that in the turbulence of the era and of the area, white officials of whatever nationality or political stripe had only limited control over their own supporters.

The Senecas were allied to the five other Indian nations in the famous Iroquois Confederacy—the Cayugas, the Onondagas, the Tuscaroras, the Oneidas, and the Mohawks. The confederacy council consisted of fifty "sachems" who were installed in office at the council fire at Onondaga, the capital of the confederacy.[4] Here too foreign policy would be debated and decisions reached.

Although larger in population than any of the other Iroquois nations, with eight positions the Senecas had the fewest sachems on the league council. The Onondagas had fourteen, the Cayugas ten, and the Mohawks and Oneidas nine each. Since the Tuscaroras were not founding members of the confederacy they had no sachems on the league council. Since the council required unanimity in its decisions, and since implementation of those decisions was dependent upon broad support within the general population, the disparity of representation was of no real importance.

The political structure of the league was tied to the lineage and clan structure of native society. The Senecas were and are divided into eight matrilineal clans grouped into moieties of four clans each. The other Iroquois nations have a similar, but not identical, clan and moiety structure. The names of the clans are associated with animals or birds, although there is no feeling of kinship toward the clan eponym. Among the Senecas, one moiety consists of the Wolf, Bear, Turtle, and Beaver clans; the other moiety consists of the Deer, Snipe, Hawk, and Heron clans. These clans, but not the moieties, were exogamous. The moieties performed ritual obligations toward each other.

The clan was in turn divided into a number of matrilineages, each a body of people who through female links could trace their descent from a single woman. The matrilineage controlled the land, and political office resided in the matrilineage. Each of the eight Seneca sachem titles, the titles of the men who sat on the fifty-member council of the Iroquois confederacy, belonged to a matrilineage, and its ranking female—its matron—played the leading role in determining which of the males in the matrilineage would attain the status. The office usually passed from a man to his sister's son.

Although the number of Seneca sachems corresponds to the number of Seneca clans, in fact several seem not to have been represented by sachems—the Deer, Heron, and Beaver clans. The Snipe clan has three sachems, and the Turtle clan has two. The remaining clans (Hawk, Bear, and Wolf) have one sachem each. Examination of this distribution reveals that while there is unequal distribution among the Seneca clans, each Seneca moiety has four sachems, each paired with a sachem of the opposite moiety, with whom he meets to "come of one mind" as the first step in the decision making of the league council. There is a similar, but more complex, division of sachems into classes, or "committees" as they are sometimes called, among the other four nations represented on the league council (Morgan 1851:64–65; Fenton 1950, 1986a; Shimony 1961:101–17).

A note of caution is in order here. The council of the Iroquois League was not described in detail until almost a century after Blacksnake's birth, in Lewis Henry Morgan's classic (1851) description of Iroquois culture. For the eighteenth, and indeed the seventeenth, century there are abundant records of the politics of the league from the viewpoint of white colonial officialdom. These documents describe in some detail portions of the political ritual, the condolence council, that surrounded the appointment of sachems, which have been well documented by later ethnographic description (as Hale 1883; Hewitt and Fenton 1944; Fenton 1949, 1950). Not to be found, however, is a description of the Council of Fifty, nor are names from that council frequently recognizable among prominent representatives of the Iroquois' Confederacy.

Of course the names that do figure most prominently in the historical record are the names of the orators the Iroquois nation produced in such abundance. It was individuals skilled in oratory

or diplomacy who came into most intense contact with the
white world. It is possible that the league council was deliberating quietly in the background. Even if it was, however, we must
remember that the Six Nations was an egalitarian rather than a
stratified society. Those holding political office had influence,
but little authority, over their populace. The Iroquois Confederacy must not be thought of as a modern federal system, for the
league council had no police powers to prevent member nations,
or even individuals, from pursuing private policy and goals, even
when these were antithetical to the wisdom of the league sachems.

Because of this a great deal of diplomatic activity involved
public meetings attended by a large segment of the population.
As Jones (1982:29) has noted, since "policy decisions among the
Iroquois had to rest on a broad consensus . . . the more individual
Iroquois who were present and involved in negotiations, the
greater the likelihood of reaching an agreement that would be
binding on the League." This aspect of the Iroquois political
process allowed Blacksnake, still a very young man, to participate in the important councils that led to Seneca involvement in
the American Revolution.

Whatever the form and power of the council of the Iroquois
Confederacy, at the time of Blacksnake's birth that confederacy
was universally viewed as the most powerful native political and
military body in the Northeast, if not in North America as a
whole. Some later historians and anthropologists have perpetu-
ated this view with references to an Iroquois "empire" and assertions that the confederacy controlled northern North America
from the Mississippi eastward. These views of Iroquois power
and empire are overdrawn, as Jones has effectively asserted in her
critique of the "Iroquois mystique" (Jones 1982:21–35). Jennings
(1984) has assembled further evidence in support of this view.

Several factors led to the view of the power of the Iroquois
current in the eighteenth century. Part of this was real military
victories won by armies of the Iroquois nations acting individually or collectively, which led to the dispersal of several of their

populous and powerful neighbors (see Trigger 1978). These wars resulted in an expansion of the territory the Iroquois controlled and placed some neighbors in a tributary status relative to the league. These "conquered" peoples who were "tributary" to the Iroquois in fact were not vassals; rather, their position was more like that of less powerful allies or even junior members of the league.

The seventeenth and early eighteenth centuries also saw the dispersal of many native societies by the expansion of white settlements on the continent. Many of these peoples responded to the growing myth of Iroquois power by moving close to the Iroquois to live under the protection of the fabled league. The Iroquois actively encouraged this, for they were beset with tragic losses in population, largely because of the ravages of the whites' diseases, although losses in war also reduced the population of Iroquois fighting men.

Jones (1982) has also pointed out the advantages to the British Indian Department of perpetuating the view that the Iroquois were the predominant political and military power in the area. The Indian Department in the north was under the control of Sir William Johnson, who had strong ties to the Iroquois Confederacy. Johnson knew the language and customs of the league and resided with Molly Brant, daughter of a prominent Mohawk family. Exaggeration of the Iroquois "empire" was also useful in British claims relative to French expansion, and it was not unknown for Iroquois and British officials to cooperate contrary to the welfare and interests of the tributary nations under Iroquois "protection." In turn these so-called tributary nations usually acted in concert with policies advocated by the league council at Onondaga only when these policies served their interests.

Nor was it unknown for members of the league itself to follow an independent policy contrary to the wishes of the rest of the confederacy. At the time of Blacksnake's birth his people, the western Senecas, took a pro-French stance to the point of actually fighting on the French side at the defeat of Braddock when in

1755 he attempted to drive the French from Fort Duquesne at the forks of the Ohio.

The Aftermath of the British Conquest of North America

French military power on the continent was soon to ebb, however. Fort Duquesne fell in 1758, and in 1759 Sir William Johnson besieged the French stone fortress and trading post at Niagara that had been so important in French influence over the Senecas. Draper found that Blacksnake "well recollects" the siege of Niagara, although he was but "a small boy" at that time. The Senecas had joined the large contingent of Iroquois in the British force. Among the Senecas present, according to Blacksnake, was Kayę?kwæ̃htǫh or Old Smoke, who had been among the large body of Iroquois who formed the left flank as they and two companies of British regulars from the Forty-fourth and Forty-sixth regiments of foot defeated a French force from the western posts that was attempting to raise the siege (DM 4-S-58–59; Hamilton 1976:255–57). Niagara surrendered to the amateur general Sir William Johnson.[5]

Later that same year Quebec fell, but the triumph of the English spelled economic disaster for the Indians on the frontier, whether they had fought on one side or the other or neither or both. The British commander, Amherst, instituted economy measures in the Indian Department, discontinuing the practice of cementing alliances between the Indians and the Crown with gifts that had become essential to native survival. Combined with other elements of friction between the red-coated soldiers now occupying the western posts and the native population surrounding them, this led to widespread agitation among the Indians to take up the hatchet again. As early as 1761 the Senecas were circulating war belts.

Native frustration and fears finally broke into open hostilities in 1763. This war has been given the name of an Ottawa chief, being dubbed "Pontiac's Conspiracy." It was a general uprising rather than a conspiracy, but most of the Indians of the northern frontier participated. The eastern Senecas and the other five members of the famed confederacy were exceptions, being kept at peace through the skill and influence of Sir William Johnson. But Blacksnake's people took up the hatchet and inflicted severe damage on their British enemies.

The western Senecas participated fully in Pontiac's Rebellion and perhaps helped to instigate the conflict (see Jacobs 1950; Wallace 1970:114–21). Blacksnake heard stories of victory from the war. He described the taking of Fort Venango (now Franklin, Pennsylvania).

> Forty Senecas under *Hod-own-da-o-go,* —*Gi-yo-so-do* [*Kayáh-sotha?*]—& *Goh-no-dunk,* started on an expedition against the Cherokees: Encamped at the mouth of French Creek, & there concluded they would first attack the English fort there. They easily gained admittance under the guise of friendship, with their tomahawks & knives concealed, relying upon these to effect their purpose. Then suddenly & unexpectedly fell upon the unsuspecting inmates & killed 30 persons, some below & others in the Chambers. One prisoner only was taken—a woman, who was carried to Cattaraugus, where she lived some time & finally went to Canada . . . this party then continued on their expedition against the Cherokees. (DM 4-S-61)

Blacksnake's son-in-law, William Patterson, reported to Draper that he was told by a member of this party that the Senecas went on to find a Cherokee hunting camp in Kentucky and there killed eight Cherokees. The party was pursued as it retreated, but from a strong defensive position the Senecas killed two more Cherokees. Although some were wounded ("none dangerously"), the party returned home in time to fight at Devil's Hole (DM 4-S-61–63).

Within days of the fall of Fort Venango, Fort La Boeuf (Waterford, Pennsylvania) and Fort Preque Isle (Erie, Pennsylvania) were in flames, both apparently attacked by Senecas, although two hundred Ottawas, Hurons, and Ojibwas aided in the attack of the latter. It has been suggested (Peckham 1947:168) that the same Senecas destroyed all three posts. The testimonies of Blacksnake and his son-in-law indicate that this was not the case. Indeed, Blacksnake claimed to know nothing of the capture and destruction of La Boeuf and Presque Isle (DM 4-S-61).[6]

Niagara Falls prevented direct communication by ship between Fort Niagara below the falls and the posts on the upper Great Lakes. A road along the edge of the chasm served to transport men and material to and from Fort Niagara. Here on September 14, 1763, a body of Senecas lay in wait. Their action has been described as "a bloody piece of work" (Wallace 1970:116) and "the worst drubbing of the war to British arms" (Peckham 1947:226).

Initially the Senecas ambushed a convoy of packhorses and wagons guarded by some twenty-five men. Men and animals were driven over the precipice. Parkman relates the tradition of the drummer boy who was saved when his drumstrap caught in the branches of a tree and of "Stedman, the conductor of the convoy; who, being well mounted, . . . resolutely spurred through the crowd of Indians" (Parkman 1851:375). He suggests that there was one other wounded British survivor of this action. Two companies of light infantry, some eighty men, rushed to the sound of this action and were caught in a second ambush. All their officers fell in the initial volleys. In total the British suffered five officers and sixty-seven men killed (Peckham 1947:224–25; Parkman 1851:374–76). Blacksnake reported that he "Never heard of any Indians being killed in that affair—& only one, *Hod-own-da-o go*, wounded, & he recovered" (DM 4-S-60).

Because of his age (probably ten years old) it is doubtful that Blacksnake was present at the battle. Francis Parkman has given us a footnote, however, that is worth quoting for what it reveals to us about Parkman's attitude toward Indians.

> One of the actors in the tragedy, a Seneca warrior, named Blacksnake, was living a few years since at a very advanced age. He described the scene with great animation to a friend of the writer; and, as he related how the English were forced over the precipice,

his small eyes glittered like those of the serpent whose name he bore.[7] (Parkman 1851:376n)

Blacksnake did provide Draper with some information about the battle (Draper does not comment on whether Blacksnake's eyes glittered).

> One English officer on horseback got off—his horse jumping over one corner of the Devil's Hole. Understood that 3 were saved by falling into the tops of standing trees beneath: Took a few prisoners—thinks about 30, but does not know whether any of these were wounded or not: thinks those who were wounded & fell helpless on the battle-ground, were killed after the affair was over: The (30) prisoners were taken to Genesee, & kept till Sir Wm. Johnson sent word to have them given up, when they were sent to their friends. The prisoners were kept sometime, when the breach was made up with Sir Wm. Johnson, & they surrendered. (DM 4-S-60)

Blacksnake grew up in an era of conflict. It is easy, though, to overstate the "warlike" nature of Iroquois society. Paul A. W. Wallace (1945:19) cautions us about blind acceptance of the stereotype:

> We have known it from childhood: war whoops, scalps, dripping tomahawks and all; naked bodies gliding through the woods on noiseless moccasins; not a twig snaps and only the melancholy call of the loon breaks the unearthly stillness. Forget the melodrama. The Iroquois were human, man for man neither more brave nor more cunning, and indeed no more cruel, than their white brothers. They had much the same aptitudes, the same fears, the same hopes, even some of the same vices.

Although it is impossible to prove this assertion, my reading of Iroquois culture history and of the anthropological literature leads me to look favorably upon Wallace's viewpoint. The ethnohistorian examining the behavior of members of another culture must take considerable care to recognize both the uniqueness of the subjects' culture and the common humanity we all share.[8]

The military successes of the Senecas and the native population throughout the upper lakes did not drive the British from the Great Lakes. Detroit and Pittsburgh, though besieged, did not fall. Moreover, the Indians were trying to wage war while having no one other than their enemy to serve as a source of powder and arms. Such a war had to be short-lived. By July 1764 the Senecas sued Sir William Johnson for peace. A strip of land the entire length of the Niagara River was the price they paid for their victory (Wallace 1970:116). This land was surrendered to the Crown.

Neither Draper's notes from his interview with Blacksnake nor the Williams manuscript give us a clue to the impact of the next decade on Blacksnake as he moved from boyhood to adult status. It was a decade of unrest and open conflict as well as of declining Iroquois influence. The principal difficulties lay in lands to the south and west of the Senecas. The Iroquois League was at least in part responsible for the unsettled state of Indian-white relations in that region.

The lands to the south of the Ohio River were coveted by whites. Sir William Johnson, for a variety of reasons (see Marshall 1967), negotiated at Fort Stanwix (which controlled the carrying place or portage between Oneida Lake and the Mohawk River) the cession of all lands south of the Ohio to the mouth of the Cherokee River, just a few miles from the Mississippi. The treaty signing was attended by over three thousand Indians as well as by representatives of Virginia, Pennsylvania, and New Jersey. Indians with a direct interest in the lands ceded, principally Shawnees and Delawares, were present, but the treaty was signed by only five Indians, one chief from each of the founding nations in the Iroquois League (NYCD, 8:137). Johnson and the Six Nations maintained that the Iroquois held title to the lands in question and thus had the right to relinquish them. Those Indians who in fact lived or hunted there thought otherwise.

Their sale at Fort Stanwix left the Iroquois, as has been noted by Wallace (1970:122), with "an impossible task to perform: to please, and retain the friendship and alliance of, both the Shawnee and the British." A key figure in this attempt to perform the impossible was an elder clansman of Blacksnake's. This member of the Wolf Clan, Kayáhsotha?, may even have been his great-uncle, his mother's mother's brother. The murder of several Indians by white settlers provoked the Shawnees and Mingoes (Iroquois who had left their homeland and settled in the Ohio Valley) to go to war. Kayáhsotha? tried to convince the Shawnees to remain at peace and the Mingoes to return to the villages of their kinsmen (Downes 1940:171–72; Abler 1979). He was successful in neither enterprise, but the defeat of the Shawnees by an army of Virginians at Point Pleasure in October 1774 brought an end to Lord Dunmore's War. The conflict has been aptly described as "that brief orgy of irresponsibility, cruelty and despair" (Wallace 1970:123).

Sir William Johnson had died that summer while cementing the alliance—or to use the common metaphor, "brightening the covenant chain"—between the Six Nations and the Crown. He left as his successor as superintendent of Indian affairs for the Northern Department his son-in-law and nephew, Guy Johnson. A white son, John Johnson, was heir to his title and much of his wealth. Another son-in-law, Daniel Claus, also served in the Indian Department. Sir William also left an Indian widow, Molly (or Mary) Brant, who had managed his household and borne him several Mohawk children over two decades. And Molly Brant had a brother, the bilingual, literate, and able Joseph Brant or Thayendanegea. Sir William's family stepped into the gap created by his death.

Elsewhere the British government was having increasing difficulties managing dissident elements in the American colonies. Open hostilities broke out in the spring of 1775. Both sides looked to the frontier and its native population, fearing that Indians might be drawn into the conflict on the side of the enemy. Agents from both sides sought the ears of Indian chiefs and warriors. Blacksnake, a young man who had recently passed his twentieth year, was a keen observer of this diplomatic activity, and it is with a detailed description of this activity that his memoir dictated to Benjamin Williams begins.

The Outbreak of the American Revolution

The outbreak of hostilities between the Crown and rebels in the American colonies led both sides to cultivate the body of experienced fighting men residing in the Indian towns on the frontier. Each side extended intensive diplomatic efforts to enlist these warriors in its cause or at least to ensure that they did not take the field for the enemy. The Crown had several advantages in this diplomatic contest. Of prime importance, experienced members of the Indian Service remained loyal, and their skills and contacts gave them considerable sway in Indian councils.

Indian affairs in New York had long been handled out of Johnson Hall, under the guidance of Sir William Johnson. His entire household and most of his department remained loyal to the Crown. This included his widow, Molly Brant, who was most influential with the Mohawks in her own right; Sir William's successor as Indian commissioner for the Northern Department, Colonel Guy Johnson; Sir William's son Sir John Johnson; and such Indian Department notables as John Butler and Daniel Claus, all with considerable expertise in dealing with the native populations, even if they often experienced difficulties in dealing with each other. Closely allied with the Indian Department, and perhaps almost as much a white as an Indian, was the Mohawk Joseph Brant, who exerted considerable influence on behalf of the Crown.

An additional factor aiding the Crown was the greater resources the British commanded. Indian diplomacy in times of warfare required a heavy flow of presents into Indian country, and the British treasury had far more wealth to devote to this than did the rebellious American colonies. Also, that the rebels more or less openly coveted Indian lands lent considerable support to the arguments of representatives of the Crown.

The rebels did have a short-lived initial advantage. Their invasion of Canada in 1775, although it failed to achieve its goals, cut British communications up the St. Lawrence. Supplies needed to win the Indians to the British-Loyalist cause and to support any intensive Indian military activity could not reach the British posts at Niagara, Detroit, and other points in the interior.

At first both sides seemed to desire Indian neutrality—at least belligerent neutrality favoring themselves. The British met with a portion of the Six Nations at Oswego in July 1775, and Guy Johnson, according to the Mohawk chief Abraham, asked the Six Nations "to sit still and maintain peace" (Stone 1838, 1:102). Blacksnake told Draper (DM 4-S-15) that "few or no Senecas attended" this council. In August representatives of all the Six Nations and the Stockbridges (a remnant of the Mahicans, who in the previous century were eastern neighbors of the Mohawks) met with officials of the rebelling colonies in Albany and assured them that they would follow this policy (Graymont 1972:71–74). Seneca participation in this conference was also slight; those present were mainly eastern members of the Six Nations.

In September and October of 1775 the Americans held yet another conference with the Indians, this time inviting the western nations more or less under the domination of the Six Nations. Also at this conference were Allegheny Senecas and Mingoes, although it is often difficult to distinguish between the two. Prominent Senecas present included Kayáhsotha?. Although "a firm commitment to neutrality" (Wallace 1970:129) was a goal of this conference, as much energy seems to have been devoted to grievances still outstanding from Lord Dunmore's War, such as the failure of the Indians to return "our flesh and blood and all our Negroes and Horses" as to anything else (see Thwaites and Kellogg 1908:70–124).

The conference was primarily between the Americans and the Delaware, Shawnee, Ottawa, Wyandot, and Mingo Indians, with the Six Nations as interested spectators. The Delawares used this occasion to demonstrate their independence of the Six Nations. Half a century earlier they had been "made women" and denied the right to go to war or engage in diplomacy without the

Six Nations' sanction. They openly declared that their sex had now changed. A Delaware chief boasted: "Look ... at my legs![9] if, as you say, you had cut them off, they have grown again to their proper size! —the petticoat I have thrown away, and have put on my proper dress! —the corn hoe and pounder I have exchanged for these fire arms, and I declare that I am a man!" (Heckewelder 1820:141).

Wallace (1970:129) feels that the Pittsburgh meeting Blacksnake describes in his narrative refers to this autumn 1774 council. Others (Thwaites and Kellogg 1908:15) have felt that the Blacksnake narrative describes a meeting at Fort Pitt in the summer of 1776. Evidence from the narrative supports this latter view.

One must remember that Blacksnake was discussing his experiences in 1845, a full seventy years after the events described here, so he may have become confused. That he remembered as much as he did is remarkable. I do feel, though, that here, as at most places in the document, his memory is faithful to the facts.

Conferences were held at Fort Pitt through the summer of 1776. It is likely that the narrative describes one of these, perhaps the meeting that again included Kayáhsotha? on July 6, 1776 (Thwaites and Kellogg 1908:171).

Blacksnake indicates a spring meeting, however. In any case the narrative describes a meeting with the Indian commissioners representing the Continental Congress at Pittsburgh or Fort Pitt, sometime before a council, also attended by Blacksnake, at German Flats in the Mohawk Valley in August 1776.

Meeting American Rebels at Pittsburgh

When Blacksnake was twenty-two (not fourteen) in the fall of 1775, a messenger came to his home village of Conawagus ("avone" or Avon, New York) announcing a conference to be held at Pittsburgh. This was the customary manner of convening a council—runners traveled from village to village carrying tally sticks indicating the day of the council and strings of wampum (cylindrical white or purple shell beads) as proof of the sincerity and authenticity of the call. The messenger indicated that the council was being held so representatives of the rebellious Americans could explain the nature of the troubles between them and the Crown.

Blacksnake suggests that both Cornplanter and Red Jacket, as "head men among the Seneca chiefs" and with "considerable influence amongst all others tribes," played major roles in assembling the delegation and later at the conference itself. This is an overstatement. At the time of the messenger's arrival Blacksnake's uncle, ten years his nephew's senior, was a rapidly rising young man who was really to come to prominence because of his military role in the Revolutionary War. Undoubtedly he already had influence, but not to the extent that he could be ranked higher than other chiefs. Red Jacket, only twenty-five years old, might have already gained some influence because of his ability as a speaker, and it has been asserted that he did speak publicly in councils against Seneca entry into the Revolutionary struggle (Hubbard 1886:45–46). However, I consider it doubtful that Red Jacket played the prominent role in councils before the Six Nations entered the Revolutionary War that Blacksnake has ascribed to him.

In their journey from Conawagus to Pittsburgh, Blacksnake and the rest of the delegation encountered the advance guard of the frontier. The Senecas passed through small white settlements at both Erie and Franklin at the junction of French Creek and the Allegheny River.

At Pittsburgh the Indians met with the commissioners from the Continental Congress. One of the commissioners explained the justice of the American cause and appealed to "our Red Brethren the Six Nations and others to not Join Either Party." Blacksnake reports that Red Jacket replied that the delegation supported this stance but would have to take the matter home to be discussed by the entire population.

Blacksnake's account of the Pittsburgh council shows it to be typical of Iroquois political meetings. Cornplanter urged unanimity (using the Iroquoian phrase "to hold one mind") among the delegation before the meeting with the American commissioner. The use of metaphor in the speeches and Red Jacket's noncommittal response are both typical of Indian councils.

Speeches at the council contain references to the mythology of the Iroquois, who viewed the world, or at least the American continent, as an island sitting on the back of a great turtle. Speeches also include references to the tree of peace. When Deganawida founded the great Confederacy of the Iroquois, he cast the weapons of war into a pit, and over these he planted the tree of peace. The nations of the confederacy and its allies sat in the shade of the tree. It is to this that the American commissioner alluded with the declaration: "the Same Island is our common birthplace we Desire to sit Down under the Same tree of peace with you."

The commissioners were aware of the expensive nature of Indian affairs in the eighteenth century. Traditions of native diplomacy dictated that delegations to councils be fed. Blacksnake reports their receiving "Blackvest" (breakfast) each morning and also their going for provisions. Delegations also expected to return home laden with presents. In addition, alcohol was used by diplomats in Indian councils then as it is used in embassies in world capitals today. A line added to the second variant of the Blacksnake manuscript notes at that the conclusion of the conference "we have some wine to Drink for Better friendship & Exsess &c" (DM 16-F-177).

Deliberating the Message of the Pittsburgh Conference

Blacksnake reports that the returning delegates from Pittsburgh called a conference in the summer of 1776 at Conawagus ("avone"). Red Jacket and Joseph Brant are said to have clashed here over participation in the war. Conflict between the two personalities over this issue (Brant was as enthusiastic as any other agent of the king about drawing the Iroquois into the war on the British-Loyalist side) has been reported elsewhere (Hub-

bard 1886:45–46), but it could not have taken place at Con-
awagus in the summer of 1776, for Brant was in England with
Guy Johnson to press Indian claims to land around Albany. He
left North America in November 1775 and did not return until
July 29, 1776. He landed at New York City, having fought off
American privateers en route from England (Smith 1946:22; Kel-
say 1984:175). He remained at New York City to fight in the
Battle of Long Island and was not back in the Indian country until
November or later (Graymont 1972:81,105–09; Kelsay 1984:
182–85).

After reaching Niagara and being "coolly" received by John
Butler, commander of that post, Brant had a wampum belt made
and carried it through the villages of the Six Nations urging the
Iroquois to take up arms in the cause of the king (Graymont
1972:110–11). This is perhaps where the debate between the
young Red Jacket and Brant, approaching the peak of his influence, took place. Even though the encounter did not happen as
described in the narrative, this description reflects the feelings of
these two strong and able Iroquois men.

Meeting Schuyler at German Flats

The American rebels attempted to manage Indian affairs through
three departments—Southern, Middle, and Northern. The Senecas resided on the borderline between the Middle and the Northern departments. Hence sometime after meeting Middle Department officials at the Pittsburgh conference described by Blacksnake, they were invited to a council in the Mohawk Valley. Philip
Schuyler, appointed an Indian commissioner for the Northern
Department by the Continental Congress, had hoped to convene
a council at German Flats, in the Mohawk Valley, on July 16. As
late as August 3, however, Schuyler reported that the Senecas had
not yet arrived. The council finally began on August 6. Schuyler
reported, "The Consumption of provision and Rum is incredible.
It equals that of an army of three thousand Men; altho' the Indians
here are not above twelve hundred, including Men, Women and
Children" (Graymont 1972:106).

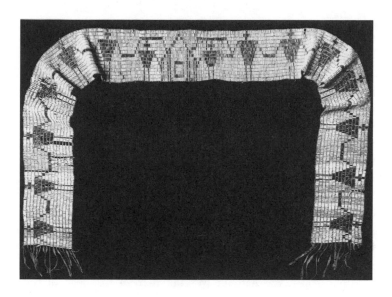

The Washington covenant belt. Wampum belts were exchanged at councils and later served as records of agreements or alliances formed at those councils. The belt illustrated here contains some 10,000 shell beads and is the longest Iroquois belt known—1.92 meters long and 13.3 centimeters wide (Fenton 1971:443). Traditionally the two central figures on each side of the house are said to represent the doorkeepers of the Iroquois Confederacy while the thirteen other figures represent the thirteen rebellious colonies or states. Attempts have been made to associate it with the council at Albany in 1775 or the treaty at Fort Harmar in 1789 (Tooker 1978c:423), but the council at German Flats in 1776 appears to be another possibility. The belt is in the New York State Museum (Catalog no. 37310). Photograph courtesy of The New York State Museum, The University of the State of New York.

Schuyler wanted to prevent the Iroquois from taking up the hatchet on the side of the British. He was fearful of the rumors he had heard about the pressure John Butler was exerting on the Six Nations from Niagara. The council opened on a note of tension, however, for some of the chiefs thought a condolence council was necessary. It was normal in northeastern Indian diplomacy for one side to "condole" the other for the losses of those chiefs who had died since the two groups last met. The rub in this situation was that the chief for whom the condolence council was to be conducted had been killed while fighting Americans at the battle of the Cedars. Schuyler and his associates refused to conduct the ceremony.

Events brightened for the Americans after that, however. The Iroquois apologized for the impolite activities of hotheaded warriors and promised these men would be restrained in the future. Metaphorically, the hatchet was taken from the head of the Americans and buried so deep that no one could henceforth find it (Graymont 1972:106–8).

I believe that Blacksnake was among the Senecas at German Flats to hear Schuyler's speech and that he records the conference in his narrative, but we again encounter a dating problem with this segment of the Blacksnake manuscript. Wallace (1970: 347) identifies this segment with the Albany conference a year earlier. It certainly seems strange that Blacksnake, who should have been familiar with the Mohawk Valley through his raiding activities later in the war, should confuse German Flats and Albany, particularly in view of the knowledge of geography displayed in the previous section. The fault, of course, may well lie with his translator, who was much more familiar with the Allegheny-Ohio Valley than with the Mohawk Valley.

The narrative does clearly indicate that this council followed one at Pittsburgh (Fort Pitt). No such conference preceded the 1775 Albany conference. One should also note that Blacksnake recalls the American speaker as stating, "we the americans Determined to Depart from the great Britain government and made our own Rules and laws and united with Several States of this amcrica." Not only does this suggest a speech made after the signing of the Declaration of Independence on July 4, 1776, it is indeed remarkably parallel to our records of Schuyler's words at German Flats on August 6, 1776. He stated that because of grievances against the king the Americans

> have unanimously left his House, and now no longer consider him as their Father and King, and have accordingly proclaimed to all the World that they will never acknowledge him or any of his Family to be their King, but that they will always be and remain a free and independent people, and therefore have called themselves the independent States of America, and solemnly agreed to remain firmly united. (Lossing 1872–73, 2:107–8; see appendix 2 for the complete text of Schulyer's speech)

Because of this I think it likely that the Mohawk Valley council Blacksnake describes here is the one Philip Schuyler conducted in August at German Flats.

The manuscript suggests that before starting east the Senecas themselves conducted a condolence council. The phrases recorded—clearing the eyes, unstopping the ears, raising the head—are all part of the ritual of the condolence council in which one side (in this case it would be one of the Seneca moieties) clears the grieving mind of the other so that proper decisions can be made in council. One can compare Blacksnake's phrases with the phrases in a condoling speech delivered in 1742 to Sir William Johnson: "We now . . . wipe away the tears from your eyes, that you may look pleasant at us. We likewise remove all obstructions and clear your throat, so that you may speak clear and friendly to us. . . . With this belt [a wampum belt] we cover his face, that the sight of it may no longer give you or us concern. . . . With these strings [of wampum] we raise up your head, now hanging down with concern for the loss of one of our brethren, and beg you will no longer keep sorrow in your mind" (quoted in Stone 1838, 1:14–15; for further documentation of the condolence ceremony see Hale 1883; Fenton 1950).

Blacksnake describes the events of the council. The commissioner outlined the rebel goals and asked that the Indians stay out of the "family quarrel." The council then adjourned for the evening, and the Indians met and unanimously agreed to take a neutral course. Iroquois political officials often took a troublesome question "to use as a pillow for the night," but in this case Blacksnake reports it was good feelings that served as a pillow.

The reply Red Jacket is reported to have made the next day is garbled and open to at least two interpretations. It makes reference to a "covenant chain," which usually is a metaphor for the alliance between the Iroquois and the Crown. In the past councils had frequently been held to "brighten" that chain. Red Jacket may have implied grievances the Six Nations felt toward Albany, mainly over land issues, when he claims "the chain got Rusted." His complaint that no shop was available to sell pincers to fix the chain may be a reference to the conflict's interference with the all-important trade.

As presented in the document, however, the speech appears to be an Indian view (and an ethnocentric one) of the relationship between the rebellious colonies and Great Britain. If this is correct, Red Jacket saw trade as the key issue or cause of conflict between the colonies and the mother country. It is not unusual to see modern historians criticized for imputing economic motives to actions of Indians in the past; it is interesting that an Indian saw economic motives as the prime cause of conflict among his white neighbors.

Red Jacket, speaking for the Six Nations, promised neutrality, and the commissioner thanked them and adjourned the council. Blacksnake and the rest of the delegation returned home.

The Return to Conawagus

The Onondagas played host to the returning delegation for some time, with Blacksnake praising "a great deal of fine times with good Dances." Visiting other communities and playing host to visitors has always been an important aspect of traditional Iroquois culture.

Blacksnake reports considerable luck in hunting on their return to Conawagus. This recalls Morgan's (1851:108) observation: "It may be said that the life of the Iroquois [male] was either spent in the chase, on the warpath, or at the council-fire. They formed the three leading objects of his existence; and it would be difficult to determine for which he possessed the strongest predilection."

Blacksnake seems to have been skilled in the first of these occupations, that of hunter; he was an attentive listener at the council fire; he was soon to have the opportunity to prove his ability as a fighting man.

[108][10] [Governor Blacksnake] . . . that who was born near Cayuga lake in the year 1749 [1753?] what called by the Seneca Language, gan,dr,a [Kendaia] immediately move from there to avone [Avon, New York—the Seneca town of Conawagus] on genesee River in consequence of having more conexion [relatives] there on father side & mother with which the friends full Desirious to have his father and mother and all family should move to [Conawagus] So they did in the year 1750 [1754?], when he was Rase and Brough him up to be young man—and the people much like it him— more so with his companion agreable with all menkind and the people place him convidantual and with trust—when he was about fourteen [possibly twenty-two] years of his age, at that time [109] began to hear Something wrong between great Britain and America great Dail Disturbances Between them for what Reason he Did not know, in fact he Did not pretend to know much any Such things, until his uncle cornplanter, was called and others by america—from Albany given out Notice to be hold a council or convend at Pittsburgh, that he supposed it must be Something Concerning of the Disturbances according to tiding Sirculation among them with which Notice ready given

In During the America Revolutionary

I Governor Blacksnake

When I was about fourteen years of my age I have than taken Notice of our chiefs councils affairs, at that times my Recollection than was good—Especially the importand Subject and views of the many Difference Nations and tribes of Indians, Residence of one Body,

In the month of April (1763) [1775?] the messenger from Albany arrived at avone [Conawagus], to Notify to our chiefs to attendans to a convention to be held at Pittsburgh, for the purpose of communicating, with the Six Nations of Indians, concerning of the Difficulties Existed Between their own Brother, Great Britain and America, Suppose in order to understanding between Americans and the Indians &c

Cornplanter and Redjackett

was the head men among the Seneca chiefs and other nations of Indians connected with the Iroquois, they again called the Second time to be held a council for to appoint Delegation to attend the convention at Pittsburgh and to Reconsideration on the important Subject all the Six Nations and others Nations which is not included as to be belonging to the six Nations [110] all met at avone a long house Redjackett & Cornplanter Both had considerable influence amongst all others tribes and they concluded themselves it would be Necessary for them to attend the Pittsburgh convention according to invitation So all consented of the Different Nations to Each one make their own appointments to Delegations to the convention to be held at Pittsburgh Chiefs and warriors, and I was particularly invited to go along with them, this is the Early part of the Spring the year, (1763) [1775] So we went to work to make preparations to Start and provides that who is to stay at home, within a few Days was already and Several chiefs and warriors Started from avone, and take westerly course to strik and came into about Eight miles above the mouth of the Buffalo creek into lake Erie and we travellered on the lake Shore and went on up as fars Erie village in Pennsylvania was than But a few houses this village one or two Stores and an tavern and provision stores and thence from this place South and we came into a stream above now called midville and thence on down frinck creek [French Creek] empdies to Allegany River, So on Down this stream Several days travel before we came out to the mouth of this creek, —there was But three or four log cabins of white people first settlers at the mouth of this creek in there we made a stop and camp out Near this Neighborhood [Franklin, Pennsylvania] for Several Days—for Builting Bark canoes to go Down the River with them as far as Pittsburgh while we Stayed at this white Neighborhood, the oldest man use to visit us and Bring Bread timber for us to Eat and we use to give him Every time fresh vension we get Some time five or Six Deer Every Day, while we Stayed at this place, untill we got our Bark canoes was Built Sufficient to carry our Number Down [111] Stream So we Sailed on Down stream on the Allegany River, this was got to be about the fall the year 1763 [1775]   So made Stop 7 miles from franklin over winter at now called big Sandy Creek in the Spring 1764 [1776]   on the thirt day on Journey from Big Sandy, we arrived at Pittsburgh Several white man came to See us, on the Same afternoon the News went to the commissioner Ears that we are come, and he visit it us that Evening and he made induced himself to us, for acquaintance Cornplanter and Redjackett Several other chiefs of the Several Different Nations of Indians proper Delegates, and we conversed with the commissioner and he told us the object of holding a meeting and he wishes to have it opened meeting on the next morning immediately after Blackvest [breakfast] and made appointment a certain ground to meet, and he Set several men to work at it for the Seats in open field. the Next morning after Blackvest and called together— uncle cornplanter give the company advise to hold one mind and appoint Redjackett for Speaker in the meeting and made all prepared on our part and we went on the ground, there was a large number asambled, and one of the officers gives us a seat in the mid of it—the Commissioner appeared and called to order { he first Said the Commissioner we the white people has been long Desirous to have you to meet with us, for the purpose of to make known to you, Brothers, we considered necessary for us to let you Know and to make you acquanted our circumstances and the Difficulties Existed Between America and the King of great britain   the great Britain government use us bad and the American people endeavours to have freedom to Built up our own government   the King ordered his armies and warriorers to fight us, we are therefore would use my utmost Endeavours to great a Number of our Red Brethern the Six Nations, and others to not Join Either Party for we Determint that we Shall have freedom and independent Nation from [112] the British government if posibly can let us fight it out our liberty for we will laid Down our lifes for our independence and freedom and we feel interst and Desirous in your welfairs that you would continue hold on as independent Nations of your people and not to lift it your hands against America or great Britain because he and me alone got into Difficulty and wishes you to Stand notual [neutral] and be Peace to all your White Brethern and if we should lost our liberty, than we always be under the great Britain government we are poor the King is Rich But God look upon us if we are a Right he would help us to again our liberty and we are auth to look to him for our favours, this we Shall Endeavour to Do and would be glad if your advice and assistance to communicate it, the Same with your people at home, and in Broad among your Red Brethern, this object a most importand to have all understand before hand &c—

this is only the Substance of the commissioner Said in this convention, and about intermission at noon, in the afternoon gotother again and there was more people assembled as it was forenoon, before this we had consulted the manners the commissioner had use to his advise, than the commissioner called to order and Ready to Receive the answer

Redjackett given answer

Brothers we are suppose you are Ready to hear the answer we will make of you We are an Indians and citizens of this Island God made us here to habited and grewed large a Number and give us all we Need it, to enjoyed, and we have Several large a Numbers of our Red Brethren and Never have yet wars Difficulties, to any worth while to mentioned [113] our make protect it us through lives our provides us all collors of his children are under heavens, we all Now give thank to God who guard us gather together this Day, and had clean Ears to hear you speaken to us and understand it which we acknowledge it is important to hear to we therefore would take your a word and advice with us to our people and laid the subject before them, Because we are not authorized or power to completed the object, therefore would leaved it to our people,

the Business Shall be Done By majority of them Before we Should
make our Determintion to upon any important Business, Althought all in our Number that are here agreed to us all the
influence over our people at home to go into this affect and we
Should endeavour to Do all can and we shall Send you a Delegation to carried the answer which our people will make, Soon after
passed their opinion on the Subject

Commissioners Repeated

"Brothers and friends we Desire you will hear and Receive
what we have now told you, and that will open open a good Ear
and listen to what are now been Said to you this is a family
quarrel Between us and old England, you Indians, are not concerned in it, we Don't wish you to take up the hatchet the King's
troops, we Desire you to Remain at home, and not Join Either
Side; But keep the hatchet buried Deep, in the name and behalf of
all our people, we ask and Desire you to love peace and maintain
it and love and Sympathize with us in our troubles that the path
may be Kept open with all our people and yours, to pass and
Repass without molestation,

"Brothers we live on the same ground with you, the Same
Island is our common birthplace we Desire to sit Down under the
Same tree of peace with you; &c &c this is all I have [114] to Say,
to amanted what I have said before noon and I feel satisfied what
you have Said in answer you made, &c and wish you this afternoon to take a walk with me and visited to a new garrison—

So we all went with him, there was only a few Regular warriors in garrison and a few pieces of cannons and Balls for them
the United Commissioner ordered us to go to provision Store to
get what we wanted while Stayed in the place, Near at Night
Returned to our camp at the mouth of monangahella, and the
Next morning we made preparation to Start for home about at
noon we got Ready to Start, some of our Bark canoes we away—3
canoes we Kept for to Keep with our provisions in as we came up
the River and Some of us came on foot and Some pushing up our

canoes up stream, we came on about 10 miles that Day, and we Kept agoing Every Day and came Back the same away we went and we got home in the month of June 1764 [1776] at avone on Genesee River, as Soon as we are a Rested and Called to open council to be held at avone and give invitation all the Indians Nations not only the Six Nations But all, that who had interested in it on Subject—

Notice given to several Braves and messengers Sent to East and South and west and north So we held a great Council fire, to Spit what we hear from Pittsburgh, from Several Nations not only the Six Nations But all others Nations Sent Delegations to attendance this great council Joseph Brant was Present this time

RedJackett again took a Stand

and went an told all the words over what we hear from the commissioner at Pittsburgh, Joseph Brant made considerable contraverses for while among people [115] Because that he feels Rather Prejudice against us and the accounts that we feel Desire to Recieve the advice from the commissioner that who has made the council fire at Pittsburgh, although Brant Did not succeeded, that and he agreed with us after while Reconcile with us this great council was one Nation of Indians lackin is not presents that was Delaware from Susquahannah, they therefore postponed to 60 days { } But in the within arrived messenger from East Bringing Notice to given to us for a another to be held a great council at albany this Notice was given to the Six Nations to their attendance this great Council Created by commissioner from Washington, this is in the month of August 1764 [1776] and also we had larnt the object of holding on another council, on the Same Business heretofore held convened at Pittsburgh—&c&c

So our chiefs got together consulted on the subject and they concluded they would pay attention, So again give out and Send out messengers Every adjacents Settlement of Differance tribes of Indians I was one of the messengers Sent to Notified the other tribes Distance about 20 miles East from avone to other Settlements for 10 Days Notice to be convened at avone long house[11] for the purpose of appointing Delegation from Every Nation to Albany to attendance the Council fire, when council Day up and met together according to the Notice Every chiefs of Every Nation and taken the consideration on the Subject which it lays before them whither the question would be Needit to have some the warriors may go with the Chiefs and the question was throw into the warriors[12] to passed their own opinions and we consulted together alone and we concluded that whosoever wish to go he may go and quite a large number Elected [116] to go with chiefs, this Notice particularly given to the Six Nations, we all come together Chiefs and warriors to consulted together and made appoint time to Start for albany it was a Short time for preparation and also appointment was made where we Shall all together meet on the away, and the Same Day Start from home, Day came to hand to Start it, all Senecas from avone went chiefs and warriors, and went on to appointment place, in the Evening there was all met together and we all Retire for night

During the Night we have talked on the subject we are going for, to the opened council fire, concerning the quarrels his father and the Son, considered important for to see clear with the Naked eyes and open our ears to hear truth and to see where we are going, and it appeared this company the opinion of majority wants to be some Body, and heads up and see what going on they Did not want to hold their heads Down and See nothing, this is the consultation of the Six Nations During that Night

the Next morning took every man Backages and went on trail toward Albany, and we traveled one Day together and stayed together on the second Night and the Next Day we Divided a companies on the fifth Days travel we arrived to albany there was large a number already assembled with white people and officers, in the moment we got all together, immediately the officers Came to us, and told us that the assembly Expected we be on the place Every hour and waiting for us to Succeed the Business what to Do with us and with them—

the officer made Requirer that who is the head man of the Seneca Nation

Cornplanter Said I am he Said he, very [117] well said the officer how many Different Indians Nations are you here, Six Said the Cornplanter, who is the head man of Each Nation said the officer. So everyone Nation they have to give answer their own head, and appeared before officer, he than told the chiefs that they got to support us while we Remained in council and the Expenses going home and he also told the chifs to go acertain office to get orders on Some provision stores to get provisions for Each Nation or tribes of Indians that who are come with the Companies, the cornplanter went himself and all the Rest went and got the orders uncle cornplanter gave me the order on the part of the Senecas to get provisions and Serval others went with me and all the Rest went, after their shares of Each Nation So we got our provisions Enouth that Night and we all went to the adge of the woods for to Built our tents So we could be by ourselve all the other tribes Done the same, there all we laid Down By fireside confortable that Night, and Sleep well I supposing the Next morning I should hear something New to me and I feel engaged to hear the subject or whatever will be laid before us and to considered the Next morning after Blackvest immediately the white people begans together at the ground of Council fire, and soon after, one of the officer came to us and called upon us to come on the ground and he took us long into it, where it was Reserve made for us to sited, immediately after Set the commissioner appeared in the mides of it—in congregation, his moral face toward us, and Says to us, this Day we all met together upon this ground, we are the white people Decendence from old countries cross the big waters, and you are the Citizens of this country you are the Indians of Different Nations of Serval Large a number [118] of people of Each Nation, and we therefore Called upon you to meet with us and consulted with us in particular important subject as a friendship, Serve all like mankind Last Spring your the six nations permit you to meet with us at Pittsburgh for the object is the communication to have the understanding Between us and you in Relation to the Difficulty existed among King family and quarrel his children that you Did not know the cause of it, it is our own Business and we the americans Determined to Depart from the great Britain government and made our own rules and laws and united with Several States of this america and we Shall stand against the British in the hour of need Either to conquer or to fall

for our liberty this is the object wish you to understand that you have nothing to Do with our father children quarals and we are therefore wish you to live in peace and we also Desire to get along without put you to any truble in your minds for our trubles as we have said to you before to keep your tomahawk and knifes Down under ground and take up no Either side and keep yourselves quiet and your families at home and at large

again I Repeated

we says unto you Nor put yourselves into truble about our quarals and Difficulties Existed between great Britain and america for which our head men considered it is the Best for us to stand our Right and protected By god against them if possible could consistantly to obtained our independence from the King Laws, and we also feeld Desire that you Should hold perfect independent [119] Nations by yourselves and governed your own Rules and laws

with which our communication will be understood between you and us, all matter may be made, &c.&c. adjourn for Evening

after Supper invitation

all the Six Nations together in the Evening for the purpose of consulting on the subject Now lies before them, for their consideration at this time I was Nothing but passengers among the warriors and to hear all the business going on, and it seem to me very in Deed important Business to be understood on the most impordant part, and put myself to feel intrest in our welfare &c

immcdiatcly thc chicfs got togcthcr at onc of thc Largcst a firc-side this Evening and the chiefs talked over on what the commissioner had Said to us and advise, and they was no truble what unamimously agreed that they would take up the advice was given to us, and the warriors also well Satisfied for the Decisions it was made by the chiefs and warriors, together with all good feeling in Relation to it, which was considered impordant object—So we Retire with good feelling for our pillow through Night and Next morning after Blackvest immediately to be on the ground at meeting, and we went on the same seat when we was seated yesterday, the commissioner then was called to order and asken us whither on the part of the Chiefs was Ready to give answered Cornplanter Replied was Ready, last Night was made choice Redjackett to give answered So he was called to Speaked for a behalf of the Six Nation

Redjackett given answered

to the Americans.

Brothers Now attest—when your fathers Crossed the great waters and came over to [120] this land, the King of England gave them a talk, assuring them that they and their children Should be his children, and that if they wanted leave their Native Country and make Settlements, and live here, and buy and Sell and trad with their Brethren beyond the water, they Should Still Keep hold of the Same covenant chain and enjoy peace &c

But where is the covenant chain of Peace, and it Seem that chain got Rusted and little poling Broken one, is not good for nothing, when, shall you go to be mented and seeking for the pinsers [?] and Shop But you cannot fined it and Now you got to Built it your own, the King of England interfere you Builting you a Shop he says come to me, But you Determent that you shall Built one for your own and the King also Determent that you shall go to him, that created quarrel

it is true that all the Indians Nations has nothing to Do with your father children quarrels we are therefore take upon the consideration with your opinion and with ours agreeable and we take your advise and we shall stand Notual and keep hands Down for Peace with all Sides, &c this is all at Present—

the commissioner

Returned thanks to us for answer we have made—and Dismiss the meetting, immediately after Dismission made preparation Returning for home Every one of the companion that afternoon went five miles to make Retirement for the Night, with good feelling toward Each other there we enjoyed ourselves By united feelling and the Next Day after Blackvest we start on our away till noon we came to a large forest and made stop for a few Days for the purpose [121] of gathering meat timber with vension and hunt for our venisons and provisions for us long our journey toward home

after we Stop at this Place, I went out to hunt or to See whither there was any agam in the about or any Nearer at this place, after I got out Sight of our fire Side But little away, I Saw a Number of dears Running Coming toward me, and they Stoped it not far from me, I have than a chance to shut at one of them, and killed, and the Rest of them Did not get out sight of me and Stop I then made hast toward them, and I made an other Shut at it and killed that too, and took this Dear on my back and carried to our fire Side with one Deer and the other, I made the Rest the Boys to go after the other one, the company was very well please with the two Dear for our Supper and Blackvest, at this time we was nothing to feared and Stayed at this place Several Days, and Start on again toward onondaga there we made a long visit with the onondagas the onondaga Indians wishes us to stay longer as we Did with them, and also or Especially thos that had been long with us at albany But we thought we had Stayed long Enought with them althought we have a great Deal of fine times and with good Dances previous while we Stayed with them they So Kind to us, I have some notions to Stay with them But my companion

would not let me Stay, So had to go with them home at Genesee
River this is in about in the fall the year 1764 [1776] when we
arrived at our old home Stead, and found our people are in good
condition in good health and we Remained Peacably all during
the winter &c

Chapter Two

Commitment to the King's Cause

"the Bargain
is now considerated made"

INTRODUCTION

The Iroquois found it impossible to hold to the course of neutrality they had adopted at German Flats. As the American Revolution grew in intensity, so grew the pressure on North America's
native people to play a role in the conflict. Having failed to crush
the rebellion in its early stages, Britain found it expedient to
approach its old allies, the Six Nations, and ask that they hold
firm to the ancient covenant chain and take up arms to fight
beside British and Loyalist troops against the enemies of the
king.

The rebels as well as the British attempted to secure Indian
allies. Indeed, the British government avowed that it did not
attempt to enlist Indians as allies until the rebels had employed
Indians in their service, an argument that "contains a small
measure of truth" (Wise 1970:188; see also Sosin 1965). However,
the rebels, themselves able to attract only a very small number of
native allies, used to considerable effect as propaganda the British employment of "savages." Even in 1776, when for the most
part Indians on the frontier were still neutral, the Declaration of
Independence complained of British use of "the merciless Indian
Savages" against rebellious Americans.[1] This exaggerated charge
has been followed by a long string of half-truths and outright lies

relative to Indian participation in the conflict, which as Wise (1970:184) attests, "originate in the American national myth."

Wise correctly insists that it is a great misconception to think "that the Indians were instruments to be 'loosed'" or indeed "to write of 'Indians' as if they were one people" (Wise 1970:183).[2] Various Indian groups had different motivations and differing degrees of enthusiasm for entering the whites' family quarrel. It was only in 1777 that the Senecas and some of the other Iroquois chose to move from a position of neutrality and play an active role on the side of the Crown. In this segment of the narrative Blacksnake describes the council where this decision was made.

Taking up the Hatchet

Blacksnake recounts the conference where British representatives convinced the Six Nations, or at least a substantial portion of the confederacy, to agree to take part in the war. Blacksnake is reasonably clear in indicating where the council he has described took place (he says "at the banks of the lake Ontario on the South East side of the lake"). Draper's notes from his interview with the chief indicate that the council was at Oswego, which fits the location given in the narrative—that is, the southeastern shore of Lake Ontario (DM 4-S-17). I will note here, and discuss at some length below, other locations that have been suggested for this council.

Blacksnake reported to Draper (DM 4-S-17) that the Genesee Valley Senecas constructed canoes below the falls of that river (now Rochester, New York) and paddled to the conference. In all, Blacksnake reports two thousand Senecas as attending, more than half the Indians at the council. Draper's notes indicate that Senecas present at the council, in addition to Cornplanter or John O'Bail and Red Jacket, were Kayáhsotha? and Kayę?kwæ·htǫh (Old Smoke). Also present was Cornplanter's elder half-brother, who eventually took the sachem title Kanyotaiyo? or Handsome Lake.

In dealing with the Six Nations, the British representatives used two explicit strategies to draw the confederacy into the conflict. The first was the old alliance, dating back over a century, between the British Crown and the league. The second was purely economic; Britain had the resources to subsidize Iroquois armies in the field. With the disruption of normal trade caused by the war, the motivation to become in effect professional soldiers (some would say mercenaries) must have been great. It also seems possible that questions of land were in the minds of the Iroquois debating whether to join the Crown. In many ways the American rebels represented land-grabbing frontiersmen, while the Crown at best (from the Indian viewpoint) tried to erect a permanent barrier between white and Indian settlement or at worst moved to orderly surrender of native lands with compensation to the holders of aboriginal title.

There was not immediate unanimity about taking up arms alongside the soldiers of the king, however. The old split in the confederacy, dating back to the French wars, appeared again in this council. The Mohawks remained firmly in the British pocket. This nation was always most loyal to the Crown (see Lydekker 1938); its chiefs had visited London as early as 1710 (Bond 1952; Garratt and Robertson 1985). Joseph Brant had just returned from that metropolis, where he had hobnobbed with the like of James Boswell (Boswell 1776). The Mohawk population had embraced the Church of England. Opposing the Mohawk position was that of the Senecas, most distant of the Six Nations from the English government in Albany, who in the past always had been the most willing to shed British blood.

The narrative presents arguments put forward by Brant favoring support of the Crown and by Cornplanter for charting a neutral course, reflecting the long historical relationship of their respective nations, Mohawk and Seneca, and the British Crown. Draper's notes from his interview with Blacksnake record that Handsome Lake and Kayę?kwæ̈·htǫh, the latter in his seventies, "spoke strongly" against taking up the hatchet and that Kayáh-sotha? also opposed going to war (DM 4-S-17). In Blacksnake's narrative, the exchange between Brant and Cornplanter becomes

Joseph Brant or Thayendanegea. Etching published to accompany an
article by James Boswell in *London Magazine* (Boswell 1776; the plate
faces p. 339). Brant was in London from December 1775 to June 1776,
arriving back in North America in July 1776. J. Ross Robertson
Collection, Metropolitan Toronto Library, T15494.

heated. Blacksnake mentioned a "conexionship" between Brant and Cornplanter. This is a fictive kin relationship, based on common membership in the Wolf Clan, rather than an actual blood relationship. Brant addresses Cornplanter using a term Williams has translated as "nephew." If Cornplanter had been a generation younger than Brant, it would have been appropriate for Brant to address his fellow clansman Cornplanter as "nephew" (i.e., sister's son). Recall that in matrilineal societies such as the Iroquois a mother's brother (uncle) enjoyed considerable responsibility for and authority over his sister's son (nephew). But Cornplanter was not a generation younger than Brant, and the appropriate kinship term for Brant to use for Cornplanter would appear to be "younger brother." Hence Brant seems to have been patronizing in his reference to Cornplanter as "nephew," attempting to put Cornplanter in a subordinate position.

The arguments of Brant and his supporters prevailed, and the Senecas agreed to join in the war. Draper records that Blacksnake reported "the British leaders plied *Gien-gwah-toh* [Kayę?-kwǽ htǫh] & others freely with brandy & sugar—& under this influence, they concluded to go with the other nations & join in the war" (DM 4-S-17−18). Draper indicates that all the Six Nations accepted the war belt.[3] Brant took hold of it on behalf of the Mohawks; Kayę?kwǽ htǫh and Kayáhsotha? accepted it for the Senecas. "Then *Jug-ge-te*, or the Fish-Carrier of the Cayugas: Then *Gah-Roon-de-noi-ya*, or the Lying-Nose, of the Onondagas: Then *To-wa-wah-gah-que*, or the *Rail-Carrier* of the Oneidas: Lastly, the war-belt was accepted by *She-gwoi-e-seh*, or the *Dragging-Spear*, of the Tuscaroras" (DM 4-S-19).

Having made the commitment, the Senecas proved as enthusiastic as the Mohawks in the pursuit of the war. Of the other members of the confederacy, however, only the Cayugas seem to have been equally committed. Blacksnake told Draper that "Not many of the Oneidas & Tuscaroras were in attendance" (DM 4-S-19). A majority of the Tuscaroras remained neutral, and a majority of the Oneidas, at least initially, responded to the influence of their New England (and pro-rebellion) missionary Samuel

Kirkland and espoused the rebel cause. It also seems that the majority of the Onondagas remained neutral until the rebels burned their village in 1779.

The council concluded with the traditional ceremony, with each individual striking the war post and singing his personal chant (see Fenton 1978:316). Blacksnake described it to Draper: "Each chief separately would sing the war song, —& dance the war-dance, & strike his hatchet into the war-post, indicating how he intends to strike the Americans. When the chiefs had successively gone through the ceremony, then the warriors followed—going through the same exciting & animating song, dance, and gesticulations" (DM 4-S-21).

The Officials of the Indian Department

Responsibility for securing alliances with various Indian groups lay with the Indian Department. It was under the direction of Guy Carleton, governor of Quebec, that in 1777 the officers in the Indian Service began activities to bring the Iroquois into action on the side of the king. John Butler, who had fled his Mohawk Valley home for Niagara, had in fact been pursuing this course for some time. His activities had been hampered both by restraints from above and by a lack of supplies. The arrival of supplies and the removal of restraints coincided with the return from England of Joseph Brant, Guy Johnson, and Daniel Claus. Although they at times came into conflict with each other, the knowledge, experience, and influence of this group of officials did much to advance the British cause. Johnson did not play a role in the initial recruitment of the Six Nations, however, since he remained in New York City after his return from Europe.

Officials of the Indian Department conducted a series of meetings with the Six Nations in the spring and early summer of 1777. Guy Johnson wrote from New York City saying he had received word from Brant that the Six Nations had committed themselves to the royal cause as early as May 1777 (NYCD, 8:713). Butler met with some Seneca and western Indians at

Niagara on July 11, 1777, and on July 13 Butler took them to Irondequoit, where Butler held a great council that lasted two weeks (Graymont 1972:120). In the meantime Claus and Brant met at Oswego, Claus with a supply of Indian goods and Brant with two hundred Mohawks he had personally recruited. Butler joined them there. Butler learned to his chagrin that Claus was his superior and in command of the Indians. The purpose of all this activity was to gather an Indian army to support the expedition of Lieutenant Colonel Barry St. Leger against the fort at the carrying place between the Mohawk River and Oneida Lake, Fort Stanwix (renamed by the rebels Fort Schuyler). Claus and St. Leger went on with some of the Indians to Fort Stanwix. Butler tarried awhile at Three Rivers (the junction of the Seneca, Oswego, and Oneida rivers) before moving on to Fort Stanwix (this account of these movements follows Graymont 1972:120–28).

One can argue that the experience and abilities of Brant, Butler, and Claus were important in bringing the Iroquois into the war. Brant was certainly important in bringing the Mohawks into line (although his sister Molly may have been even more important). Blacksnake suggests that Brant's urgings were instrumental in bringing over all the Six Nations. The return of Daniel Claus was also of some consequence. Like Butler he had long been close to the Johnsons (he was another son-in-law of Sir William); like Butler he had had long experience in the Indian Service; like Butler he spoke and understood at least one of the Iroquois languages. Another significant fact was action from the British military at long last. Until 1777 British forces in the area had been dormant. All the offensive actions had been undertaken by the rebels. But now red-coated (and green-coated) armies[4] were marching over New York trails. Finally, much-needed supplies were getting through for the use of the Indian Department.

Gifts and Forest Diplomacy

The exchange of gifts at conferences and councils seems to have been a precontact practice; at least it was deeply ingrained in the northeastern North American political process. Often these gifts were wampum belts or strings that proved the sincerity of the speaker who presented them. In some cases wampum belts served as mnemonic devices for recalling past treaties. Such vast quantities of wampum were exchanged at conferences that I suspect most of the belts and strings were recirculated.

Goods other than wampum were on occasion used in diplomatic negotiations. At least some of the presents given to the Indians when treaties were signed were simply a continuance of this custom.

Of course the bulk of the goods presented to the Indians can be viewed as direct compensation for their services. Many goods were direct support for military operations—arms and ammunition. But warfare also kept the men away from their usual hunting, trapping, and trading, and so they expected compensation for this. Of course, in time of war Indians were more susceptible to this type of inducement because warfare had closed their normal trading outlets.

Great powers—rich powers—have always (and certainly still do) subsidized lesser ones to do their fighting for them. It was as true in the forests of North American in the 1770s as in the jungles of Nicaragua in the 1980s.

The Locale of the Council Described by Blacksnake

The most recent, and perhaps most thorough, survey of documents relating to the Iroquois in the American Revolution is that of Barbara Graymont (1972). Because her study is systematic and well documented, her views on the accuracy of this part of Blacksnake's narrative merit careful consideration. She does not accept Oswego as the locale of the conference, although she expresses dismay at the prospect of determining whether Blacksnake is describing the council that took place at Irondequoit between the Senecas and Butler, the later encounter at Oswego, or Butler's final council at Three Rivers: "[Blacksnake's] account is somewhat confused . . . for he seems to describe the taking up of the hatchet at Irondequoit; yet we know that the other tribes of the Six Nations were not there, though a few representatives of these nations may have been present. Nor was there really time for any extended council at Oswego" (Graymont 1972:126).

It is difficult to believe that Blacksnake describes a meeting at Three Rivers, even though "we do not know precisely what happened at the Three Rivers council" (ibid.). Graymont notes that Brant was not at Three Rivers and believes that Blacksnake was not there either: "It is evident from the documents also that Blacksnake was present on the first day of the siege of the fort. He mentioned having traveled there with a group of Indians separate from the main army. From this description, it would seem that he was with Lieutenant Bird's advance party and therefore could not have stayed behind for this council at Three Rivers. It may be that Blacksnake was describing an event he did not personally witness but was told about later, though the manner of narrating would seem to indicate his presence. He also gave the impression that this was the original council at which the Iroquois were recruited and not a later one, as was Three Rivers" (Graymont 1972:127).

Graymont thinks that Blacksnake describes the meeting at Irondequoit, although she does express some reservations about this conclusion (Graymont 1972:120–21). A point she finds distressing is Brant's role in the narrative. Brant was not at Irondequoit: "Blacksnake's confusion is difficult to understand because he came to know Brant well during the war and readily recognized his picture when shown it in 1842" (Graymont 1972:121). She thinks it may have been either that the Mohawk chief Aaron Hill made the speeches Blacksnake attributed to Brant or that the old man or Benjamin Williams simply became confused. As I noted earlier relative to the reported debate between Brant and Red Jacket, Blacksnake did attribute actions to Brant at a time and place when we know the Mohawk was not present.

The possibility remains, however, that the council did take place precisely where Blacksnake locates it—Oswego. A white captive adopted by the Senecas, Mary Jemison, also names that locality as the place of the council. The historians and anthropologists Stone, Beauchamp, Smith, and Wallace have all accepted Oswego as the locale of the council (Stone 1838, 1:187–88; Beauchamp 1905:231; Smith 1946:26–27; Wallace 1970: 132–34). Lyman Draper also supported this view (DM 4-S-17). And Brant was at Oswego.

An argument against Graymont's Irondequoit hypothesis is that Blacksnake does not name the British speaker. During the war Blacksnake served as often with John Butler as he did with Joseph Brant. That he does not name him is perhaps an indication that Blacksnake did not know, or would not come to know, the spokesman for the king's cause. It was perhaps Claus but more likely St. Leger, since an interpreter was required. Both Claus and Butler could speak to the Six Nations in Mohawk.

Graymont argues that there was not time at Oswego for the council as outlined by Blacksnake: "The Indians might well have been addressed by Claus or St. Leger or both at Oswego before they departed; but no council such as Blacksnake described in his 'life' could have taken place there" (Graymont 1972:127).

Graymont's point is well taken. Claus's commentary indicates that he was at Oswego only two nights, July 23 and 24 (NYCD, 8:713), hardly enough time for the deliberations Blacksnake recounts. Blacksnake mentions three days of council followed by an interval of a few days, and then the announcement of the departure for Fort Stanwix. Claus states that he equipped Brant's party at Oswego, but he says the rest of the Indians were to be equipped by Butler at Three Rivers.

This was a time of intense rivalry within the Indian Department, with Claus and Brant aligned on one side and John Butler on the other. Each side complained bitterly about the other, and such feelings have limited the objectivity of their statements. Butler was particularly anxious to defend and enhance his role in bringing in the Six Nations, while Claus belittled the contribution of his subordinate.

Another bit of information in Blacksnake's narrative adds to the confusion. He mentions the arrival at the mouth of the

Niagara River of a ship loaded with goods. Claus brought his supplies with him to Oswego; Butler, however, received his supplies well before the July meetings. It is possible that Blacksnake refers to Claus's goods, but Claus claimed to have brought mainly military supplies—the luxury items ("Ginlings Bells") Blacksnake describes seem to fit better the goods distributed by Butler (Claus's report in NYCD, 9:719). It is possible that Blacksnake said or meant the ship came *from* Niagara rather than to Niagara, bringing to the council (whether at Oswego or Irondequoit or Three Rivers) goods Butler had stored at Niagara.

A Spring Council at Oswego?

There is one other possibility, hinted at in the published record—that Blacksnake is describing a council in the spring of 1777. Brant wrote to Guy Johnson (so Johnson reported in a letter from New York in July 1777) as early as May 1777 that the Six Nations, save the Oneidas, had agreed to act in concert (*"as one Man"*) in support of the British-Loyalist cause (NYCD, 8:713–14).

This hypothesis is supported by Mary Jemison, who describes the council essentially as Blacksnake does and then indicates the passage of some time before the recruitment of the party attacking Fort Stanwix (see Seaver 1824: 74–76).

In most ways Mary Jemison's account substantiates Blacksnake's. While there is no indication that she attended the conference, she notes that the chiefs at first said "that they should not violate it [the agreement of neutrality made with the rebels] by taking up the hatchet against them" (Seaver 1824:74). The British speakers pressed on, emphasizing the wealth and power of the king: "That his rum was as plenty as the water in lake Ontario," that his men were numerous, and that as allies the Indians "should never want for money or goods" (Seaver 1824: 74). The Indians agreed to take up arms, and "as soon as the treaty was finished, the Commissioners made a present to each Indian of a suit of clothes, a brass kettle, a gun and tomahawk, a scalping knife, a quantity of powder and lead, a piece of gold, and promised a bounty on every scalp that should be brought in. . . . Many of the kettles which the Indians received at that time are now in use on the Genesee Flats" (Seaver 1824:75).[5]

The white woman also agrees with Blacksnake about the content of the invitation to go on the Fort Stanwix expedition: "The British sent for the Indians to see them come and whip the rebels; and, at the same time stated that they did not wish to have them fight, but wanted to have them sit down, smoke their pipes, and look on" (Seaver 1824:76).

Additional evidence suggesting a spring council bringing Six Nations commitment is that by June 25 the supposedly pro-neutrality Kayę?kwǽ·htǫh (Old Smoke) was already harassing Fort Stanwix with a party of warriors (DM 4-S-22). It is difficult to understand how this could be *if* the Senecas, and Kayę?-kwǽ·htǫh, did not commit themselves to the British-Loyalist cause until the councils at Niagara, Irondequoit, Oswego, and Three Rivers in July 1977.

But if the council committing the Six Nations to support the king did in fact take place in the spring, as both Blacksnake and Mary Jemison say, we would expect to find greater record of it in the documents. Neither Graymont (1972) nor Smith (1946) reports such a conference, but then records of the July 1777 Oswego (or Niagara-Irondequoit-Oswego-Three Rivers) conference are also very, very scarce, as Stone (1838, 1:187) complained.

Although it is possible that events did not take place at Oswego exactly as Blacksnake outlined them, I do think it likely it was there that the final Seneca decision was made, under the urging of Brant as well as the "Red coat man," to enter the conflict on the British side. The events may not all have taken place at Oswego, but the narrative accurately portrays the pressures being placed on the Senecas and other Iroquois. Certainly the encounter between the prowar Brant and the neutralist Cornplanter as described by Blacksnake makes fine reading.

[121] But in the Spring in the year 1765 [1777] I than was about 16th years of my age, when Messenger arrived at our country [122] and having the authority of the British government, for Notifying to our chiefs or in the head men of our Indians Nations to admittance to his convention at the banks of the lake Ontario on the South East side of the lake

Cornplanter asked the messenger for what object holding a convention with the Indians and the Red coats officers messenger Replied to make arrangement with the father the King of the great Britain

Sachum   we wanted that you should Showed a part of the face what it should be arrangement made with the Indians

Messenger   the father wishes to have arrangement be made for in future time may be appeared Disturb our affairs and wishing to make all understood in Regard such things may a Rise

Sachum   I will give Notice to my people and the chiefs also and we will take up the consideration on the subject in council with all the Six Nations Brethern and if the Indians Chiefs and warriors Should Rested their minds upon the subject and favour to go, we will go and attented the father opened and kindled his convention and would listened and hear what he would say to us and I will now immediately Called and be gather together at our long house, for to hear the general opinion they will make on the Subject

in a few Days Notice Chiefs and warriors got together and at hand to be Decided whither the question will be favoured among the people and it appeared Majority that are willing to attent the Notice, and appoint to go with sent for their attendance the convention at the said appointed place to be held a general convention Considered by British government

the Decision that whosoever wishes to go long they may go young men and young females [123] may also go if they wishes for witnesseth that it may appear when we will meet with the british men for to see what arrangement he is going to make with us,

I was than invited by my uncle to take charge a certain company to keep them long quietly this was in the year 1765 [1777]

So all the chiefs of the Six Nations and the warriors went a long with the chief and and also with our women went a long with us, they were mostly for fear that it might be a Snare going on or Dangerous it might created by Red Coat warriors.

But when we arrived there at the place appointed ground for council fire or convention, immediately after arrival the officers came to us to See what wanted for to Support the Indians with Provisions and with the flood of Rum. they are Some of the amongst the our warriours made use of this indoxicating Drinks, there was several Barrel Delivered to us for us to Drinked for the white man told us to Drinked as much we want of it all free gratus, and the goods if any of us wishes to get for our own use, go and get them, for and from our father gaven to you, and for the same the above gift, our chiefs began to think that the great Britain government is very Rich and Powerfull to his Dominion to force things and kind to his Nation, all things a boundantly provided for his people and for us too and Seval head of Cattle been killed for us to Eat and flour the our female Sect [sex] was very well please for the Kindness we Receive from our white Brethren while in During 2 or 3 Days after our Rest, Commissioner had visited us for to get aquaintance and Notice for to meet together tomorrow at 10, oclock A.M. } { the Readers must excuse me for I do not Regulect on what month or what [124] day the month for I have no larn or to understand English Either I only what I hear from the enterpreter through the Speech By commissioner

commissioner wishing to the chiefs Should be on hand in good Season in the morning So by the understanding, in the morning was be held a meetting or convention after Breakfast we went on to the ground of council fire, and the people got together the commissioner then called to order, he than made inquirer whether was all the Six Nations of the Indians chiefs were all Presents,

Redjackett, we are Suppose to be all in presence Except onondaga Chief were not presents But we are ready to hear your proceeding

Commissioner—I was Send By father of old England to proceed the object the greatest important to be communicated with the Red Brethern in Regard to the King of England Servants a quarrel Existed between America we are therefore would induce us to called upon you to hold a meetting with us in Regard to it, to make arrangement in that it might be in case may make Disturb among you on our account—this is the important Subject that we are considerable Bound to each other to help any in case whatever to assist Each other of the two Brothers, and love Each other and be good obedience to Submission to authority of our father and who is able to support us when we are Distress

But here is American considered our fathers children But Disobedience and Rebellion of our fathers Rules and government

and he therefore Sent a Serval of us to Support our father government and he feeld it is a right for to Corrected them and we feelds appregation to obtained the government, and he want you all the Six Nations and others Indians Nations to turned out and joined with him and gave [125] the American a Dressing and punishment for his Disobedience and violated his laws he is therefore he would called upon you—and to addressing—we are therefore would invited to to you all of the Six Nation and others

who is not yet engagement to Stand face against his father wish
to turn in to correct the Disobedience children and the father of
the old England want you to joined with us to correct Disobedience children—

our father will Support you all the Necessarys Such war utensils gun and powder and leade and Tomahawk and Sharpe Edges
[swords] and provisions and all the stimerations [time rations]
will be well Supply in all times in During the upporation of the
family quarrals

But the father is Rich Every thing is planty around his
country—

and now here american is very poor he has no mean to forced
it forward, and will Soon give it up for has no armorials to force
against British army, and not only well arms But it is great many
in Number of men to against America they cannot Do anything
with the British.

Now here is your father offered you to take his axe and Tomehawk to hold against American and here is the Bucherknife and
Bowieknife that you will also take for to take the American luck
[lock] and sculps [scalps]

and our father will pay So much Each one Sculp in money &c

and here america is very poor he has no means to force it
foward and he will soon given it up, he has no Regularly government [126] first we will go from here to take all the forts Belonging to America the fortstanwix we will take first and wyo ming
[the Wyoming Valley in Pennsylvania] &c these two forts that
Shall take will be Sufficients to Show our fathers stringth

So Adjournded:

Joseph Brant   Cornplanter and Redjackett and Serval others
chiefs and of the head man of the Each Nation of warriors agreed
that they wanted take the consideration on the Subject So
journed, that Day, for the Next morning that they might be able

to give answered which has all Read laid before us in Relation go to waring against the America

at that time I feel Desirious to Exactly Know our in voice will be in generally especial minds in Regard to it, as for my mind in taken Extract the I remember the Promiss once made with american and the Six Nations of Indians

and the Same Day in afternoon we was called up together all men for the object is to take the consideration of the offered has been given to us by the Red coat man, I than Supposed—the chiefs would Refuse the proposition been made to us for it is Reasonable if they Desired for the Promises that has been made Between america and the Six Nations of Indians.

But the Next day called to a council having mat and called to order By Brant meetting holdind to ourselve, Before Rede coat man called

Mr. J Brant came forward and Says that the offered is Reason for all things that the King of the great Britain is the father only If we should Rebel and do nothing for him and Neither for america do nothing for them, we appeared like a sleeping all the chiefs and warriors Excipt our woman folk, they will be crying and wo for us all [127] Because there will no peace for us any how to Either Party if Should be Down and Sleep we shoul be liable to cut our throat by the Red coat man or By america if we by stile I therefore Say and will Say take up the offered By the Red coat man for I shall aurged my people to go and joined the father and help his people and his government this is only way for us to Do But Every Nation speak for themselve

Redjackett }

Says I wish and Desirious to the warriors give liberty to Say Something in Relation to it for its importand that may make mistake moved it may cost us our live I therefore wishes further move to Reconsideration in Regard to it, war is for Depens upon life and property }

Cornplanter or John obail

Says to his people—warriour you must all marked and listen what we have to Say war is war Death is the Death a fight is a hard Business, all I wanted Say to all of you with others Nations which is combined with one Body—

Here is america Says to us, not to lift our hands against to Either Party, because they got in to Difficulty, it is nothing to us, and he also say let him fight it out for his liberty and will Rebel the government of his own Brother in fact we the Indians Nations of Several Differance parts of this continent we Does not Know what is for—and we are a liable to make mistake moved I therefore full Desirious to wait a little while for to heard more the consultation between the two party, it was a good Reason for to hold on a while, let the British say all what he is going to Say to us, we than clear to see where we are a going, very ab to be Decived—

But cornplanter got through Speaking Brant got up on to his feet and Say Nephew, that is called according to his conexionship, to Stop Speaking So planter Did Stop Brant than Said to cornplanter [128] you are a very coward man it is not hardly worth while to take Notice what you have said to our people you have showed you cowardness &c Cornplanter then Says nothing more till Next Day after, the British Council was over, the warriors had great Dail of controversy created amongst themselve Some for Brant and Some for Cornplanter appeared to creat it in two party, Redjackett was there the Same time But he Did not say much of anything in Regard to it

and at this time of our Braved warriors they appeared to be had not like to be called Coward men they began to say we must fight for Some Body that they cannot Beared to be called coward

British was then called up to the council, the warriors then appeared taken more instrest in the matter—

Called to order, Brothers our father in old England loved you as well as white people because he believed we are in one, it was his childrens and he wanted not alowed to have any suffered and any condition whatever as I have said to you before I Repeated once more, a part of his children Rebilion the father Government and he is going to Correction the children now Enemy to their father, the america Done very wrong to their father, Disobeyed the orders which has been given to them, these are therefore they Deserve correction, and the America calculated to Do more wrong to their father, and wishes you to joined not with them, if you Do you may surely Depen upon lost your country—we therefore Say come go long with the father and he will give you all you wants and your children and woman that they Shall not suffered, Such clothing and Provisions During the opperation of the [129] war, with the Rebelous children they will Soon give it up for they are poor and father is very Rich Every thing is Planty nothing to asked whate he Sent it to you, if you take it up now we will furnish you all your wants take it up the Hatched and Sharp adges and paint against the Enemy, if you only obeyed your fathers wishes you will have Every things your Need it, Eat and Drink and ware and money, and wishes now to make up your minde in concerning } {

the wariors than proceeded more in taken the consideration and consulted together and unitedly, and Speaking By the Brave warriors are then willing to go into it, and many of the warriors made a Different Speaches in Relation to the war fairs However they seem to want to be honor to their farther, the old general made our people believed was nor such thing to be Defeated By the poor children of america—

the amongst the warriors Disturb made and appeared to be Divided and the Red coat officers found that Indian warriors are Split and also the female Sect likewise the began to use their influence over the warriors—had considerable Exsitement among them about one Day and an half untill the Ship was landed at the mouth of Niargary fall or at fort george [Fort Niagara6] Brouth in many Small articles for Suppose for the Indians to Bribe with, and to upset the Indians minde, Delivered them a Small Ginlings

Bells and it was curiousity to our femals Eye and the Nois, and orstrich feathers, and the warriors also Never Did see such things and it must curiousity to them likewise, and very well Please with it and Beads was also Delivered to and well Please also with it, for to ware their Nack and they thinks wonderfull things for them to ware that too and all these things was Brought it Before them [130]

and the British also Brought over what the called wampum the produced two called ancient Belt of wampum, one of twenty Rows was called the old covenant between the Indians Nations and the whites whither is so or not I cannot tell nothings about it, But it Did appeared to me, By the whole multitude of Indians Believe what he Did said to us, in general Thing,

The Sachams gotogethered consulted together on the very importand part, to take consideration with whicth Blood belonging to us &c.&c. Cornplanter or John obail, Did not wish to going to it, for many Reasons, they than called on the Iroquois for to have Consultation of the whole matter, whicth is Ready laid before them, to be Earnest feelling toward the Subject of war fair, &c and we than got all to come to the council, not But afew speak at that time and wint and gon into Effect, Because that the British government are very Rich and Kind to us, and made many atemps what good things he will do to us, Because the father love his Red Brotheren, and offers and many good things that they never Did see, before, Such things that, I have been telling Before in Relation to it, of the articles, well it Did looked to me considerable Sight, they therefore passed Revolution that they Should take the King of england men offers us for the majority of the Iroquois ascent feathfull, and the mothers also consent in Regard to it &c

the Cornplanter Spoke and Says, every Brave man Show himself Now hereafter fore we will find are many Dangerous times During the actions of the war, for we will See a many Brave man amongseth american Soldiers whicth we Shall meet, with theirs Sharp adge [131] Stools [swords], I therefore Say you must Stand like good Soldier against your own white Brother Because just as soon as he fined you out that are against him he than will Show you his wit no mercy on you on us, I therefore Say Stand to your Post where is time come Before you But a gard yours be } { Brant was there all time During the convention and he all time favor for great Britain Side in Relation to the offered, whicth the Red coat man, By whicth use his influence to going to Effect By the wishes of great Britain government after our own convention adjourned untill Next Day—Excuse me for I Did not kept minuts for I have no larning only for my tru memerly [true memory] I cannot tell what Day transacted at that time But for the Next Day together at the council

Seat of ground

first called to order By the Red coat man and for our opportunity to answered to him

Joseph Brant Says

our white Brothern will now Ready to hear to us, and will listened what we will say to them, in Regard to the proposition that he has made to us, in Relation to the war affair and I suppose our minde are all settled I therefore would Ready give to them answered in Regard to it, and wishes you to all to say yest or no, most every one say yest at that time, appeared all willing—

J. Brant called to the Commissioner to order for they are Ready for answer they going to give, and says

We the Six Nations of Indians been held a council by ourselve to taken a Deep into consideration of the war affair that we have taken examination of Each Nation to passed its own Revolution in Relation to the war affair, and found Every one [132] of the tribe are ascent and undertaken to take up the offers you have made to us and all the affair we Shall meet before we get throught with it,

Brant Say I now

will turned toward you to British commissioner as I have Said that we have been taken a Deep into the consideration of the war fair if the american people Doing wrong and Disobeying to his fathers Rules, he than is a liable to be punishment—

although we have been communicated with the america commissioner in Relation to your own Brother Difficulties, the american Says the King of England greatly misuse the america, if so he is title from Deserve punishment, But if the america acturally Done or Doing wrong to his father Rules without cause he liable to be punish as I said before— { But we Did know not What made Disturbance between you and america, we are suppose thought its in Deal, it Did not agree with the two country, and is not yet settled and will not settled, they will fight for it, for their liberty and if so as I says we the Six Nations will now take up the offered, for we have supposed the america acturally Disobeyed the fathers laws and if so he is title and Deserved punishment and if the case, we shall therefore would turned out and fight for the King, for father sake for we considered he is the head man of all Nations, of white people, —we are supposed that you are one of his Servant of the King—

we therefore would now take your hand for the Bargan with us and your to Day—we may mis it and we may be Right or wrong— for God Know Regard us, But if we [133] were wrong God will be not on our Side But if were on the Right side we Shall again the Day—whither Right or wrong But if Should be on the wrong side we should Defeated,

But now is your Dudy to give us instruction what first coarse to take, for we think now is your Dudy to appoint what first to Do and we Shall Do, as you Directed to it, for we shall think your protection and our protection to Each other, this is all at Present—

We are therefore now Ready to hear the in truction for the first move we shall make, for the Bargan is now considered made to hand to hand, although this is were not sured whether we were aright to Establish and Revolutions and controled to others minde But there we Shall Do now as we are bind ourselves to Do so, By the consent of the majority of our people &c

The British commissioner I Did not know his name or forgotten Brant called his name Serval times But I do not Reculected now,

But he Receive the answered that Brant made to him

Very good Sir Said he and Thank you all, we will firstly go to Dinner and Drink Rum and sugar, and we Done So that afternoon our head men was a little to much Rum they Did not Do anything untill the Next morning gotogether we were Exspected to be intructed whate Shall be first Place we shall Do or where we Should be the Best course to take &c the commander Says that we Shall make preparation in a few Days to get Ready in and be well prepared [134] for the war attentions and for gathering Military ammunitions, we than when we get Ready and go first to make our force against fortstanwix that will be the first move we will make and take that fort, and if we Receive we good prospect the object we than Shall go to take wyoming, that will be the second Strip when we Do all these things the america than may take Reconsideration that he may Surendered all it once &c,&c, But we Shall be with you all times Said the Rede coat man

Chapter Three

Blacksnake Takes the War Trail

"to Spill the human Blood"

Blacksnake soon learned the truth of his uncle Cornplanter's words: "war is war Death is the Death a fight is a hard business." Testimony in his narrative and from Draper's interview indicates that he fought in almost all the significant engagements between the Senecas and the American rebels during the Revolution. In addition he testifies to frequent small-scale but individually harrowing encounters in the forest. Although frightening and traumatic to those involved, such brief violent actions are usually lost to history because records of them seldom survive. Blacksnake truly spent the years of the Revolution in "a hard business," and it became clear to him that indeed "war is war Death is the Death."

Blacksnake's narrative of combat during the Revolution reflects errors either in his own memory or in Williams's rendering of the account. For the most part the series of battles and encounters he reports cannot with certainty be tied to known historical events. Draper's notes from his interview superficially appear more closely correlated with historically known events, but as I stated before, from Draper's notes it is impossible to differentiate Blacksnake's actual words from Draper's speculation.

In this introduction I will attempt to outline Seneca activity during the Revolution and Blacksnake's role in that activity.

Cornplanter (in Seneca, Kayęthwahkeh, also known as John O'Bail or John Abeel). This portrait was painted by F. Bartoli in New York in 1796. Cornplanter, as Blacksnake's uncle (likely mother's brother), had a heavy influence on the life of the young Seneca. Indeed, Blacksnake was long known to whites as "the Nephew" because of his relationship to Cornplanter. The slight droop in Cornplanter's eyebrow is likely the result of an injury in the carriage accident in 1786 while en route to New York as described later in the narrative. Courtesy of the New-York Historical Society, New York City.

Seneca actions are well documented in the historical record, but Blacksnake has provided a significant expansion of that record. A critical reading of both his testimony and other sources gives a particularly detailed, and particularly human, view of Indian participation in the frontier campaigns of the American Revolution.

The Siege of Fort Stanwix and the Battle of Oriskany

Blacksnake and other Senecas of his generation received their baptism of fire in the bloodiest engagement of the Revolution, considering the number involved. Although they were victorious on the field of Oriskany, the battle was but one element in a campaign that failed to achieve its objective, the capture of Fort Stanwix (renamed Fort Schuyler) at the "carrying place" between Wood Creek (leading to Oneida Lake and Lake Ontario) and the Mohawk River (see map 2).

The combined British-Loyalist-Indian force advancing from the west to capture Fort Stanwix was commanded by Lieutenant Colonel Barry St. Leger, breveted to the rank of brigadier. The expedition was part of a larger plan to isolate New England from the rest of the rebellious colonies. Among St. Leger's troops were regulars from the Eighth and Thirty-fourth regiments of foot, a company of German jaegers (riflemen), and the loyalist corps, the Royal Regiment of New York under the command of Sir John Johnson (Stone 1838, 1:218–20; Graymont 1972:129). John Butler commanded a body of men sometimes called rangers, but they were employed by the Indian Department. The loyalist regiment known as Butler's Rangers was not raised until later in the war (Mathews 1965:42, 175–76). Only eight light pieces composed the train of artillery—two six-pounders, two three-pounders, and four cohorn mortars (NYCD, 8:719). St. Leger was so confident of victory, if Mary Jemison is to be believed, that the Six Nations were asked to go along just to "sit down, smoke their pipes, and look on" (Seaver 1824:76). In numbers the Indian portion of the command probably equaled and may have ex-

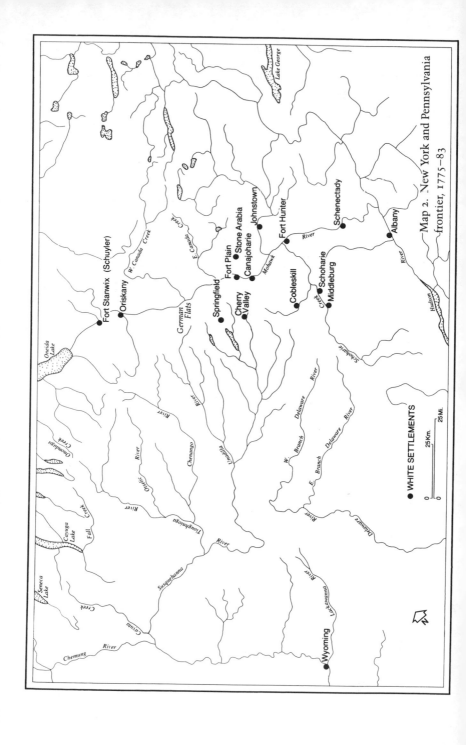

Map 2. New York and Pennsylvania frontier, 1775–83

WHITE SETTLEMENTS

ceeded the white contingent, giving St. Leger something in the order of sixteen hundred fighting men. The Indians were for the most part Senecas and Mohawks but also included other Iroquois as well as Mississaugas from Canada recruited by Daniel Claus (Graymont 1972:130).

Parties of Indians had begun to harass the rebel fort early in the summer of 1777. One of these was led by Old Smoke (Kayę?-kwæ̈·htǫh). This remarkable individual was well on in years, possibly in his seventies or eighties. Despite his age he was active throughout the war, and Blacksnake reports that Old Smoke and Cornplanter served as commanders for the Senecas in the field throughout the Revolution. As a concession to his age, though, on at least some of the campaigns Kayę?kwæ̈·htǫh traveled on horseback rather than on foot (DM 4-S-48).

Old Smoke and his men were hovering about Fort Stanwix when on June 25, 1777, Captain Gregg and Corporal Madison disobeyed orders and left the fort to go hunting for passenger pigeons. Gregg and Madison were shot and scalped at about 10:00 A.M. (Gregg looked at his watch after his assailants departed). A rather romantic tale has Gregg saved by his "faithful dog," who brought rescuers. In reality he was found, still alive, at 3:00 that afternoon, and even though on the next day it was thought his recovery was "doubtful," he survived (Stone 1838, 1:226–27). Blacksnake met Gregg nine years later and was shown where he was scalped (DM 4-S-22).

In groups of four and five, the Indians continued to infest the region about the Fort. On July 3, 1777, a party of berry pickers was fired upon, and two girls were killed. "By the middle of July, . . . large parties of soldiers could venture abroad on the most pressing emergencies; and even one of these was attacked, several of its numbers killed and woun[d]ed, and the officer in command taken prisoner" (Stone 1838, 1:228–29). Daniel Claus sent Captain John Deseronto, a Mohawk chief, accompanied by John Hare of the Indian Department, to raise a small party to reconnoiter the fort. That party returned with five prisoners (one a lieutenant) and four scalps. The prisoners were interrogated and revealed the degree to which the fort had been strengthened over the summer. Claus reported this to St. Leger, who still had the opportunity to strengthen his artillery train. But St. Leger declined to wait, "making little of the prisoner's intelligence" (NYCD, 8:719).

The vanguard of St. Leger's force did not reach Fort Stanwix until August 2. Under the command of Lieutenant John Bird of the Eighth Foot, and including a body of Indians under Brant, it found that the rebels had closed twenty miles of Wood Creek by felling trees. This was the route St. Leger was to use to bring up his meager artillery. Captain Gilbert Tice of the Indian Department entered the fort on August 3 under a flag of truce. His "Proffer of protection if the Garrison wou'd Surrender . . . was Rejected with distain" according to a member of the garrison (Lowenthal 1983:26).

The body of St. Leger's army straggled in to surround the fort on August 3, 4, and 5. A large portion was diverted to clear Wood Creek and to cut twenty-five miles of road through the forest so that the eight little guns and mortars could be brought up (NYCD, 8:720–21).

Warning came on August 5 from Molly Brant, Joseph's sister, who had not yet fled the Mohawk Valley, that General Nicholas Herkimer was advancing with a rebel force of eight hundred Mohawk Valley militiamen to relieve the seven-hundred-man Fort Stanwix garrison (Graymont 1972:129–31). Reflecting the divisiveness of the conflict on the Mohawk Valley population, Herkimer's brother, brother-in-law, and nephew were all serving in the British Indian Department (Swiggett 1933:83). Also accompanying Herkimer was a group of Oneidas, willing to shed the blood of their elder brothers in the league in support of their New England missionary and his rebellious cause.

St. Leger could not or would not spare his regulars to meet the rebel militia. Instead he dispatched four hundred Indians, the light company of Johnson's Royal Greens, and Butler with the Indian officers to meet the oncoming force. In an incredible display of military ineptitude, Herkimer's force pressed on in a disorganized column lacking scouts, an advance guard, flankers,

or any customary protection. Sir John Johnson had nominal command of the Loyalist-Indian force, but Joseph Brant is given credit
for picking the battlefield. The rebel forces were caught as they
were jammed together on a causeway over a narrow creek surrounded by marshy ground in a ravine six miles from the fort.
Daniel Claus's description of the battle does little to convey the
intensity of the conflict, which was often hand to hand:

> They therefore on the 6th marched on, to the number of upwards
> of 800, with security and carelessness. When within 6 miles of the
> Fort they were waylayed by our party, surprised, briskly attacked
> and after a little resistance, repulsed and defeated; leaving up-
> wards of 500 killed on the spot, among which were their principal
> officers and ringleaders, their General [Herkimer] was shot thro'
> the knee, and a few days after died of an amputation. (Claus in
> NYCD, 8:721).

The first volley caused many casualties in the main body and
led the rear guard to abandon the field. They were pursued and
slaughtered by Brant's Mohawks. The remainder of the force did
not panic (or perhaps did not run because there was no escape),
and a daylong battle ensued, with British and Indians withdraw-
ing to their plundered camp (the sortie from the fort is discussed
below). Although the rebel force temporarily left the field, it
withdrew to lick a near-mortal wound.

All commentators agree that the battle was a bloody one.
Perhaps as close an estimate as can be reached of the rebel casualties is Wallace's (1970:135) tally of two hundred to four hundred killed. Graymont finds the British claims of inflicting five
hundred deaths credible (1972:137–38). Even Wallace's lower
estimate is an astounding 25 percent of the American force.
Wallace's estimate of Indian-Loyalist losses is clearly too high—
he believes two hundred were killed (Wallace 1970:135). The
Senecas bore much of the brunt of the fighting, yet according to
Blacksnake (DM 4-S-24), they lost only thirty-five men, including
five chiefs. He gauged the losses of all other Indians engaged as
being fewer than the Seneca total. Claus provided an even lower

report of Indian-Loyalist losses: "We lost Capt Hare and Wilson of the Indians, Captn Lieut McDonald of Sir John's Regt 2 or 3 privates and 32 Indians, among which were severl Seneka chiefs killed. Captn Watts, Lieut Singleton of Sir John's regt and 33 Indians wounded" (Claus in NYCD, 8:721). Blacksnake listed for Draper the Seneca chiefs who were killed at Oriskany: "*Hasque-sah-ah,* or the Axe-Carrier—*Dah-wah-de-ho,* or *Things-on-or-beside-the-Stump—Gah-nah-a-ge,* or Black Feather-Tail—*Dah-gai-ownd,* or Branch of a Tree—*Dah-oh-joe-doh,* or Fish Lapper (i.e., the-tail-laps-over-the-head.). . . . One Seneca chief, *Hah-no-gwus,* or the *Grease-Skimmer,* received a severe sword cut across the nose & face, & another cut on the back of his head, —he recovered" (DM 4-S-24–25).

An interesting footnote to the Oriskany battle is that Red Jacket and three others are reported to have fled at the sound of the first fire, returning to their homes on the Genesee. Possibly because it was his first experience in battle, Red Jacket was not chastised for this exhibition of cowardice (DM 4-S-24).

Herkimer had asked for a sally from the fort to aid his "advance." This was executed by Colonel Marinus Willett with two hundred men and a fieldpiece. They got as far as the Indian encampment, where they captured Lieutenant Singleton and a private of Johnson's regiment and "totally Fouled & plundered . . . [the encampment] of as much Baggage as the Soldiers coud carry" (Lowenthal 1983:31). The raiding party returned to the fort immediately and, according to the Fort Stanwix journalist William Colbraith (Lowenthal 1983:31), "brought in a Number of Blanketts, Brass Kettles, Powder and Ball, a Variety of Clothes and Indian Trinketts and hard Cash, together with four Scalps the Indians had lately taken, being entirely fresh and left in their Camp. Two of the Scalps Taken are supposed to be those of the Girls [of the berry-picking party], being neatly Dressed and the Hair platted. . . . Four Colours were also taken & Immediately hoisted on our Flag Staff under the Continental Flagg, as Trophies of Victory." Colonel Willett's son claimed that the expedition surprised Sir John Johnson, forcing him to leave in such haste that he lost his coat, and that twenty-one wagonloads of booty, including five flags, were captured (Willett 1831:53–55).

This booty was the net gain of the sortie from the fort, which had no effect on the battle being waged at Oriskany. Willett is reported to have been jubilant at the results of his enterprise, but as Graymont (1972:136) has so aptly stated, "General Herkimer must have wondered."

Claus perhaps overstates the effects of this sally, noting that the rebels "took away the Indian packs, with their cloaths, wampum and silver work, 'they having gone in their shirts, or naked, to action;' and . . . they returned with their spoil, taking with them Lieut Singleton and a private of Sir John's Reg who lay wounded in the Indian Camp. The disappointment was rather greater to the Indians than their loss, for they had nothing to cover themselves at night, or against the weather, & nothing in our Camp to supply them till I got to Oswego" (Claus in NYCD, 8:721).

Four rebel officers remained in Indian hands after the battle of Oriskany. British efforts to gain the release of these prisoners were rebuffed. Shortly after sunrise on the morning after the battle they were forced to run the gauntlet—that is, to run between two rows of warriors armed with clubs, knives, swords, and axes. There exist numerous accounts of prisoners who did this with little or no injury; one suspects this was because of sentiments that the prisoner's life should be spared and that he would be adopted into Indian society. Indeed, it is tempting to interpret the running of the gauntlet in these cases as a rite of passage allowing the captive to be reborn and incorporated into his new homeland. The mood of the Senecas after Oriskany was not so charitable, however. Losses suffered in the previous day's battle had been too great, even though far greater damage had been inflicted on the enemy, for the Indians to resist the temptation to take further revenge. All four prisoners were killed while running the gauntlet (DM 4-S-25–26).

While some American historians (cf. Stone 1838) have claimed Oriskany as a rebel victory, it is difficult to follow their argument.

The Mohawk Valley militia did in fact temporarily hold the field, but their advance had been halted, and the badly mauled column limped back home. They did not lift the siege, and it was mainly the strength of the fortifications and the light weight of the British artillery that led St. Leger to abandon his mission.

After the defeat of the rebels at Oriskany St. Leger sent John Butler under a flag of truce with another demand that the fort surrender. He was led blindfolded into the fort. Its commander, Colonel Peter Gansevoort, refused to surrender (Graymont 1972: 143). Blacksnake told Draper that the Seneca name for the officer carrying the message into the fort was O,so-ownd or Turkey (DM 4-s-26). If Draper's notes are correct this may be a clue to Butler's Indian name, but it could also be the name of Gilbert Tice.

Old Smoke and Brant wanted to follow the retreating rebel militia into the Mohawk Valley (Graymont 1972:136). Claus and Sir John Johnson agreed on the value of this foray. Johnson approached St. Leger, "but the Brig said he could not spare the men, and disapproved of it" (NYCD, 8:721).

The siege of Fort Stanwix continued until August 22, when St. Leger decided to withdraw. By this time many of the Indians had already concluded that the attack was fruitless and returned home. The expedition simply lacked sufficient artillery and other resources to carry out a successful siege against Fort Stanwix's defenses (Claus in NYCD, 8:721–22). Despite the victory at Oriskany, Herkimer's men inflicted no inconsiderable losses on the Indians. The Senecas had at most a thousand fighting men. The loss of more than thirty in a single day's combat was a substantial cost for the community. Mary Jemison testified to the impact of the battle on the Senecas. "Our Indians alone had thirty-six killed, and a great number wounded. Our town exhibited a scene of real sorrow and distress, when our warriors returned and recounted their misfortunes, and stated the real loss they had sustained in the engagement. The mourning was excessive, and was expressed by the most doleful yells, shrieks, and howlings, and by inimitable gesticulations" (Seaver 1824:77).

The Senecas had endured what was perhaps the bloodiest fight of the Revolution. They had fought courageously and sustained heavy losses, and they had inflicted far heavier losses on their foes. It is nothing short of incredible that racist (no milder word seems appropriate) historians ignore this battle and later ones in assessing the mettle of the Indian warriors. If on other fronts the Loyalists, the British, and the Germans had fought for the Crown with the effectiveness of the Iroquoian-speaking forces in New York, the outcome of the Revolution might have been far different.

Mohawk Valley Raids: 1777–78

Although St. Leger retreated, the Indians and their Loyalist allies almost immediately began to raid settlements in the Mohawk Valley. Among the first to be driven from their homes, though, were Indian allies of both sides. The participation of the Oneidas in Herkimer's army infuriated their brethren in the league. "The Six Nation Indians, after the action, burnt their houses, destroyed their fields, crops &c killed and carried away their Cattle." The Oneidas in turn "revenged upon Joseph's Sister [Molly Brant] and her family (living in the Upper Mohawk Town [Canajoharie]) on Joseph's account, robbing them of cash, cloaths, cattle &c and driving them from their home." Mohawks, "poor women & children whose husbands were in the King's service," were driven from both the Upper and Lower Towns, Canajoharie and Fort Hunter (NYCD, 8:725). Rebels were enthusiastic participants in driving the Mohawks from the valley and looting and occupying their homes, for as Graymont (1972:147) has noted, "many of these Indians lived in far better circumstances than their white neighbors who were only too glad of the opportunity to raise their standard of living at the Mohawks' expense." White loyalists suffered similar treatment (Mathews 1965:47).

An initial raid, while the Fort Stanwix siege was under way, was led by a Loyalist named McDonald in the Schoharie Valley. The combined Indian-Loyalist force was repulsed by a detachment of cavalry under Colonel John Harper supported by local militia. Two of the rebel horsemen were killed (Graymont 1972:

47; Simms 1845:243–48); Indian-Loyalist losses are not clear. If Blacksnake's narrative is true, though, his father in all likelihood died in that brief skirmish. It is quite possible that Blacksnake meant Schoharie Creek when he spoke of "one of the Branches of the mohawk River where my father bones now Remained."[1]

In the narrative Blacksnake precedes and follows the report of his father's death with mention of an attack or attacks on one or two rebel settlements or forts. Like some other segments in the narrative, it is impossible to tie these accounts to known historical events with any certainty or even reasonable probability. One can be certain that some episodes in the narrative are not in correct chronological order, and it is possible that some of the violent episodes in this chapter constitute the merging of experiences from two or more combats and also that Blacksnake repeated to Williams in different words two descriptions of a single battle, hence causing it to appear in the narrative twice. A conservative, safe, and reasonable course would be simply to present the narrative as it stands and avoid the difficult if not impossible task of relating it to the historical record we know from other sources. However, it is equally difficult to resist the temptation to try to correlate descriptions in the narrative with historical events. Others who have used the Blacksnake manuscript (i.e., Graymont 1972; Wallace 1970) have been unable to overcome this temptation. The conclusions presented here differ from those of Wallace and Graymont; readers are of course free to arrive at yet other conclusions.

A guide to the period is provided in table 1, which summarizes my view of the correlation between the narrative and known historical events. There are many raids and battles that do not appear in table 1, so a substantial number of alternative interpretations are possible. An important point illustrated in the table is that if the information Draper gathered in his interview with Blacksnake relates to reality, he was present at several major engagements besides those described in the narrative. It is also possible that he was present at other Revolutionary War battles on the frontier that for some reason did not come to be mentioned or identified in Draper's notes of his interview with Blacksnake.

My guess is that the references in the narrative that bracket Blacksnake's mention of his father's death refer to the same raid, one not discussed in Draper's interview with Blacksnake. I think that the town "destroyed . . . on west side Near of albany" refers to the same engagement as that at "the fort ga doh ga," and that this is the battle of Cobleskill on May 30, 1778. Cobleskill was the only major engagement between the Fort Stanwix campaign and the Wyoming campaign, and Simms (1845:277) reports that the invading force was "mostly" Senecas and Mohawks.

Aware of the presence of Indians and Loyalists, a detachment of thirty to forty regulars under Captain Patrick and fifteen militiamen commanded by Captain Christian Brown encountered twenty or so Indians near the house of George Warner. The Indians retreated, drawing the rebels into a trap laid by Joseph Brant, who had as many as three hundred Indians and Loyalists under his command. Brown is said to have urged caution, advice that Patrick ignored. Patrick did not survive the battle to give his side of the story. Suffering several casualties and realizing the size of their opposition, the rebels retreated, pursued by the Indians in a running fight. One of Patrick's lieutenants is reported "to have been spared, by giving a masonic sign to Brant" (Simms 1845:276).[2] Five retreating rebels took refuge in George Warner's house, which was set on fire. Two attempted to escape and were killed, while the other three succumbed to the flames. Total rebel losses are reported to have been twenty-two killed, a half-dozen wounded, and two captured. After the battle the Indians and Loyalists destroyed houses and outbuildings in the settlement, twenty in all (Simms 1845:272–78).

Admittedly, an attempt to tie the description in the narrative to the Cobleskill engagement is tenuous. Arguments can be put forward against this. Cobleskill was unfortified, yet Blacksnake speaks of a fort. Blacksnake reports that after the battle "we then Retreated for winter," whereas Cobleskill was fought in the spring and was followed by further fighting. Also, Brant con-

Table 1: Proposed Correlation of
Blacksnake's Narrative with Historical Events

	Historical Events	
Date	Place, Event, or Battle	Pages (from 16-F)
August 1777	Oriskany, Fort Stanwix Siege[a]	134–37
August 1777	Schoharie	138–39
—	—	139–44
May 1778	Cobleskill	138–39
July 1778	Wyoming[a]	144–47[c]
September 1778	Wyalusing, Susquehanna Valley	147–50
November 1778	Cherry Valley[a]	—
July 1779	Fort Freeland[a·]	—
August–September 1779	Sullivan's invasion of Seneca country[a]	194–96
August 1779	Brodhead's invasion, Allegheny River[d]	150–53
Winter 1779–80	Fort Niagara[a]	196–99
August 1780	Canajoharie[a]	—
October 1780	Schoharie Valley[a]	—
—	—	213–16, 155–56

[a]Draper's notes from his interview with Blacksnake indicate that Black-snake was present at these events.
[b]It is possible that Blacksnake was not present at this action.

Blacksnake's Narrative	
Date Given in MS	Geographical Location Named in MS
—	—
1765 (after Fort Stanwix)	Branch of the Mohawk River[b]
March, 1768	Genesee River
Spring 1766, summer 1767	West of Albany; fort called gah doh ga
Three months after March 1768	Da,a,i,Dah,a
Unclear; either after harvest 1768 or after spring 1769	Delaware Nation on the Susquehanna
—	—
—	—
Spring 1770	Seneca country
While Blacksnake was gone to Wyoming and other places	Allegheny River
Winter 1770–71	fortgeorge
—	—
—	—
1770 or 1771	Allegheny River in Pennsylvania[d]

[c]This segment is ascribed to Cherry Valley by Graymont (1972:188) and Draper (DM 4-s-83–94).
[d]Blacksnake was not present at these actions.

tinued to raid in the Mohawk drainage after Cobleskill, where-
as we know Blacksnake fought at Wyoming in Pennsylvania.
The last anomaly can be explained by the fact that Brant and
Major John Butler met at Tioga as Butler was journeying to the
Wyoming Valley (Graymont 1972:166). Possibly Blacksnake and
other Senecas joined Butler's forces there.

Support for the ascription of Cobleskill is that it is the only
major engagement between Oriskany and Wyoming and that
Blacksnake's description of the fight is not incompatible with the
running battle at Cobleskill. If Blacksnake was not at Cobleskill,
this description is probably best assumed to represent Cherry
Valley.

The Forest Encounter: March 1778 (?)

A lengthy portion of the narrative is taken up describing an incident that took place in the spring of 1778 before the Cobleskill
battle, or possibly in the spring of 1779. Blacksnake was hunting
in the woods near the falls of the Genesee (at what probably is
now Rochester, New York, but possibly Letchworth State Park)
when on returning to camp he was attacked by twenty-five to
thirty whites (one would guess that he exaggerates). He had heard
their whistles but did not see them until he was within fifty yards
of his camp. As he saw the whites they fired at him, but all the
shots missed. Blacksnake then gave the war whoop (the second
manuscript says "the Indians wisils" [DM 16-F-187]) and bounded
toward the enemy. The Seneca war whoop has been rather pon-
derously described by Morgan (1851:272): "It was a prolonged
sound upon a high note, with a decadence near the end, followed
by an abrupt and explosive conclusion."

Blacksnake's cry brought aid from the camp, and he pursued
the fleeing whites. He took one captive, using his musket barrel
to parry a sword stroke. Leaving the captive with another Seneca
he continued the pursuit, even though his musket was broken.
The three fleeing whites emptied their muskets, and through
pure bluff (his only functional weapon was a tomahawk) Blacksnake convinced them he had others with him and took them
prisoner. By this time aid had arrived, and when one of the

captives refused to march Blacksnake gave orders to kill him. One of Blacksnake's party tomahawked the stubborn and foolish frontiersman (DM 16-F-188).

The party with its three white captives spotted the fires of the remainder of the party Blacksnake had encountered. The narrative provides a brief but vivid account of the forced march across the Genesee and northward to the supposed safety of the Seneca country. Upon reaching the home of an elderly Seneca couple, the Senecas thought they had escaped the whites who were pursuing them. This feeling of security proved ill founded, for no sooner had Blacksnake returned to his home village than he heard that the elderly couple had been killed and the woman scalped. Blacksnake led a party in fruitless pursuit of the murderers. Returning home to find another family murdered, he set out again, and this party discovered the tracks of shoes (rather than moccasins), which convinced Blacksnake that it was in fact whites who were the killers.

With this raiding party active in the area, the Senecas posted sentries at their settlements, but the whites slipped away to return whence they came. It is difficult to tell the origins of this group. It may have been a scouting party of the kind that were being sent from Fort Pitt to keep watch on the frontier and give warning of impending attacks. It is also possible that it was a group of settlers on an unofficial raid.

We are given no clue to the fate of Blacksnake's three prisoners. It seems likely that they would have been made to run the gauntlet. Having survived this (as most captives did), they may have been adopted and kept in the Seneca village, or they may have been sent to the British post at Niagara. It is likely that they eventually ended up at Fort Niagara and probably remained there until the end of hostilities.

Wyoming: July 1778

Perhaps the most one-sided action of the war was the engagement at Wyoming. Here Major John Butler led a force of 464 Indians and 110 Rangers to attack the settlement and the series of forts in this valley on the Pennsylvania frontier (Cartwright 1876:30–31). The "head leaders" of the Senecas were Cornplanter and Old Smoke (DM 4-s-27). The detachment arrived at Wyoming on June 30, 1778, and on the next day persuaded Wintermoot's Fort and Jenkin's Fort to surrender. Forty Fort refused to follow suit and on July 3 sent a force of over four hundred to attack the invaders. Under the command of Colonel Zebulon Butler and Colonel Nathan Dennison, the rebels fired three volleys before coming within effective range of the Indians and Loyalists. The Indians fired first, followed by the Rangers, and devastated the rebel ranks. The Indians then outflanked their opponents, who panicked. As happens with inexperienced troops, the retreat became a rout and over three hundred were killed. Indian-Loyalist losses were fewer than ten. Blacksnake told Draper that five Senecas, two Cayugas, and an Onondaga were killed (DM 4-s-28). On July 4, Forty Fort and the remaining Wyoming stockades surrendered. The invaders destroyed the eight forts and one thousand houses in the valley. No civilians were harmed (Graymont 1972:167–72; Swiggett 1933:127–33).

One cannot be certain which incidents in the Blacksnake narrative refer to this battle. The section presented below under the heading Wyoming is a good candidate, but it may well refer to the Cherry Valley battle in November 1778. The place name in the narrative, "Da,a,i,Dah,a," appears to be neither the name Draper recorded for Wyoming, "*Ski-an-do-wa*" (DM 4-s-29), nor the one he reports for Cherry Valley "*Ki-e-ton-geh*" (DM 4-s-30). The name Draper elicited for Wyoming appears to be the Iroquois name for that locale—"Skehandowana" or "Tsanandowa" (Donehoo 1928:259). That for Cherry Valley resembles the "Ka-ri-ton'-ga" reported by Beauchamp (1907:173) as an Onondaga (?) name for Cherry Valley. Graymont (1972:188) sees this passage in the narrative as descriptive of Cherry Valley, and Draper (DM 4-s-83–84), in his notes from his interview with the aged chief, also presents this view. But Draper's testimony should not be considered conclusive. It is possible that the old man became confused trying to recall and clarify something he had dictated five years earlier. And it is possible that the notes reflect Draper's thoughts rather than the reports of his informant. This is the major fault of Draper's notes of his interview with Blacksnake—they are interspersed with his own hypotheses and conclusions.

Supporting the Cherry Valley hypothesis is the beginning of the narrative, which does not suggest an army venturing out of a fort to meet an invading force. It is in fact suggestive of Cherry Valley, where Captain Walter Butler split his force to invade the settlement. But at Wyoming the Indians fought on the left, separate from the Rangers, which is not completely incompatible with Blacksnake's description.

The second version of the narrative further confuses the issue. It contains only a brief account of the engagement presented here and follows this with an account of a battle that is identified as Wyoming. But this second battle is clearly the Seneca action against the troops who had burned several Delaware towns. It seems possible that Williams or Blacksnake became confused by the fact that a commanding officer, Nathan Dennison, and most soldiers on this expedition were from Wyoming (Wallace 1970: 138). It is true that the casualties reported for this second engagement are more suggestive of Wyoming than of the relatively minor battle at Wyalusing. However, all other circumstances in the description, and the fact that Blacksnake and Williams do not refer to it as Wyoming in the first narrative, support the hypothesis that this second action is the engagement at Wyalusing on September 29, 1778.

The bulk of this section of the narrative—that is, the section I believe describes the battle of Wyoming—is devoted to Blacksnake's description of hand-to-hand combat with several soldiers. Blacksnake emerged victorious from these exciting fights, having killed the several foes—more than three—he encountered. In his interview, Draper (DM 4-S-81) reports that Blacksnake claimed to have killed ten during the Revolution—three at Oriskany, *five* at Wyoming, and two elsewhere. Earlier in the notes of the interview is a claim that Blacksnake killed two during the raid on Canajoharie in August 1780 (DM 4-S-46). If these recollections are true, then the passage being discussed must describe the Wyoming battle. Also, at Wyoming over three hundred rebel soldiers perished. At Cherry Valley only sixteen combatants were killed (Graymont 1972:189). While not impossible, it seems unlikely that a quarter of these would have been done in by Blacksnake.

Additional support for believing that the engagement below is Wyoming is provided by Blacksnake's statement that he returned home in the harvest season. Cherry Valley was fought in November—following that engagement Blacksnake returned home to a snow-covered village. The sequence presented in the narrative—a battled followed by a return home to harvest crops, followed by a summons from the Delawares to help repel an invasion—fits well with the Wyoming encounter in July followed by the September action against the invaders on the Chemung.

His statement, "So we Stayed at home peaceably all the fall and the winter till the Spring," is distressing. It may represent the intentions of the Senecas, for as he points out in his next paragraph, he was present in the engagement at Wyalusing in September. He was also at Cherry Valley in November.

A key to resolving the site of the battle is the identity of "general Duckey," who commands the British and Loyalists. Perhaps because *t* and *d* are a single phoneme in Seneca, Williams frequently confuses the two in the narrative. Given the nature of Williams's spelling, it is reasonable to conclude that the name intended is "Turkey." Unfortunately, we have two conflicting pieces of evidence suggesting who this Turkey might be. Draper in his interview with Blacksnake arrived at the conclusion that John Butler was known as Sug-au-tah or the Lodging Tree. Sug-au-tah had a son, Dux,e,a, whom Draper believes must be Walter Butler. O,so-ownd,[3] Turkey, is reported to have been "an officer in *Sug-au-tah's* regiment," and Draper thinks he is "Capt. John McDonald," also known as Captain John McDonell (DM 4-S-23). I should emphasize that these are Draper's conclusions. Conflicting evidence is provided by a letter from Abraham

H. Casler to Draper dated October 30, 1848 (DM 16-F-225). "The Gov. says Captain Bird was their [Wyoming] and commanded in conjunction with John Butler . . . he says the Indian name of Butler was Turkey that of Bird was Tuck Shell." If John Butler and Turkey are the same, then the narrative below is probably Wyoming, since John Butler was there and not at Cherry Valley.

Although portions of this segment of the narrative may involve confusion, by Blacksnake or his recorder, of Wyoming with other encounters, I think most of the incidents described took place at Wyoming. But whether they happened there or not, the narration provides a glimpse of the hand-to-hand combat at which the Iroquois warrior excelled.

When Lyman Draper interviewed Blacksnake, he directed many of his questions toward myths that had grown up around the name Wyoming. Blacksnake confirmed the absence of Brant (many popular histories depicted a bloodthirsty Brant murdering women and children). He also denied any truth to the myth of the Seneca "queen" who is supposed to have tomahawked fifteen to twenty prisoners. A reconnoitering expedition by Cornplanter and several other Senecas is recorded in Draper's notes. They crept up on a hill that overlooked Forty Fort to count its garrison. As he does in several other places, Blacksnake remarks on Red Jacket's distaste for battle, reporting that he remained "behind the main body of Indians—yet within long shooting distance, & still to be in no great personal danger" (DM 4-S-29). We can only regret that Draper did not ask for or record Blacksnake's actions in the battle—the difficulties in reaching conclusions about the correct interpretation of the Williams manuscript might have been alleviated.

Wyalusing: September 1778

The American troops who capitulated at Wyoming had agreed to lay down their arms for the "present contest" (Graymont 1972:171). The Senecas soon learned the value of such promises (though one could argue that the Indians and Loyalists broke their promise that "the private property of the Inhabitants [of

Wyoming] shall be preserved entire to them"). The very soldiers who agreed to lay down their arms in the Wyoming Valley were within two months marching up the Susquehanna burning Indian villages and killing and scalping Indians (Wallace 1970:138–39).

Colonel Thomas Hartley, who commanded the forces on the northern frontiers of Pennsylvania, set out from Fort Muncey on September 21, 1778, with a force of 200 to 250 infantry and seventeen "horse" (this was a pet idea of Hartley's, and they probably served as mounted infantry). Hartley's force advanced through difficult country: "The Difficulties in Crossing the Alps . . . could not have been greater than those our men experienced" (PA, 7:5).

On September 26 his advance party killed "a very important Indian Chief" (PA, 7:5) and scalped him. They advanced with the Indians fleeing before them and burned the abandoned towns of Sheshequin and Tioga. They captured a number of prisoners, one of whom suggested that Walter Butler, Colonel John Butler's son, was in the neighborhood with upward of three hundred men. They decided not to advance to Chemung but instead retreated, taking with them "fifty or sixty Head of Horned Cattle and some Horses they got there, beside several other articles our People brought with them in Cannoes" (PA, 6:773).

Late at night on September 28, Hartley's forces arrived at Wyalusing. Hartley reported his men "much worn down—our Whiskey & Flour was gone" (PA, 7:7). The men tarried the next morning until 11:00 cooking some beef they had slaughtered. Finally under way, the force came under attack. Hartley reported that the Indians advanced too rapidly, allowing his force to nearly surround them. Hartley lost four killed and ten wounded; he reported that the Indians left ten dead on the field and that their losses must have been three times his own (PA, 7:7–8). The Indians followed the retreating force to Wyoming, where on October 3 they "kill'd & scalped 3 men, who had imprudently left the Garrison at Wioming to go in search of Potatoes" (PA, 7:7–8).

Blacksnake participated in this battle. He tells of the arrival of a messenger reporting invaders into the Delaware country (Sheshequin and Tioga were Delaware or mixed villages). Hartley's force was apparently observed from its departure (he was so informed by the prisoners he captured), giving the Indians time to send messengers to the Senecas, but not allowing enough time for John Butler (Ducky) or Brant to come from "fortgeorge" (meaning Fort Niagara).

Blacksnake's description of the engagement is the least credible portion of his narrative. The numbers and casualties involved are much too great for this battle. Indeed it seems possible that Williams got his notes mixed up and has combined with this engagement portions of Blacksnake's account of the battle of Wyoming or Oriskany. It was at Wyoming that Blacksnake "slained most than another times" (presumably, killed more than in other battles). The phrasing at the end of the narrative is reminiscent of the end of Blacksnake's description of the Oriskany battle.

In the narrative Blacksnake suggests that Captain Pollard (Captain Pollet) and "Young King" were along, although in his discussion with Draper of the affair at Wyoming he indicated these two were too young to be fighting at that time (DM 4-s-28). The reference to Young King is easy to understand—it is likely that Williams has here become confused because Old Smoke and Young King, uncle and nephew, respectively, bore the same Seneca name, Kayę?kwæ·htǫh. Williams would have known Young King under that name.

In the second version of his narrative, not included here, Blacksnake indicates that at this time the Delawares were "Enexted" to the Six Nations, "But not in full conexionship &c." This refers to the status of women given to the Delawares, the old semidependent status from which they had moved in the previous two decades.

Cherry Valley: November 1778

Blacksnake was to participate in yet another major engagement in 1778. The rebels in New York had long been concerned about the exposed position of the settlement at Cherry Valley, but the blow did not come until November 1778. Although the attack was expected, the luckless settlement found itself in the hands of "a criminally incompetent commander" (Graymont 1972:186). Five days before the attack an Oneida Indian brought word that "a Large Boddy of the Enemy who ware Collected on the Susquehanna and Ware Desird to attack this place" (ibid.), yet the commander, Colonel Ichabod Alden, still refused to allow the inhabitants of the valley to collect in the fort. He and his officers in fact did not live in the fort but instead slept at the Wells House, more comfortable accommodations away from their men.

The Indian-Loyalist force had command problems of its own. The personal conflict between Brant and the Butlers flared up again. John Butler was not present, but his son Walter Butler, a captain in his father's regiment of Rangers, had command of the white portion of the force.[4] It is reported that the conflict between Brant and Butler was so intense that Brant was stopped from leaving the expedition only by the pleas of its Indian members that he remain with the force. The ninety Loyalists Brant had under his command chose not to serve under Butler and left (Graymont 1972:183–84). One must remember that the source of these allegations against young Butler is Daniel Claus, who harbored no love for the Butler family.

Butler marched on Cherry Valley with a force of 520 men. Of these 150 were Rangers, 50 were British Army regulars of the Eighth Foot, and 320 were Indians. Cornplanter was the leading Seneca; Old Smoke was not along (DM 4-s-33). The Indians were in an angry mood. They had been falsely accused of atrocities at Wyoming. Moreover, the troops they had allowed to go free had in a matter of months taken the field against them, burning their villages and killing and scalping their people. Many seem to have felt that retaliation was in order.

Red Jacket, though, lacked enthusiasm. It is reported that near Tioga he announced that the year was too far advanced for carrying on warfare. He and three others turned back (DM 4-s-31).[5]

Butler had detailed knowledge of the disposition of the garrison in Cherry Valley. Cornplanter, Brant, and forty other Indians had surprised an advance party and taken four prisoners

including Adam Hunter, who knew Butler and had Loyalist lean-
ings. He provided Butler with valuable intelligence (Graymont
1972:186; DM 4-S-31).

The attack did not proceed as Butler had planned, however.
Captain John McDonell and fifty Rangers were to cut off the
Wells House, where the officers of the garrison were lodged.
Instead, the fight broke out earlier than planned because of a
chance encounter with two woodcutters. The Indians rushed
ahead. Indians under Little Beard attacked the Wells House, killing Colonel Alden, five other officers, and a number of men of
other ranks. Civilians in the Wells House were also killed. Blacksnake did not participate in the attack on the Wells House (DM
4-S-32).[6] Butler and the Rangers and regulars moved to engage
the garrison and keep them penned in the fort while the Indians
fanned out through the settlement and burned it. In the action
civilians were killed, despite the efforts of British-Loyalist and
Indian commanders. Sixteen rebel soldiers and twice that number of civilians were killed, and seventy were marched off as
captives (forty of these were soon released). Almost two hundred
of the inhabitants of the valley escaped death or capture, but no
buildings other than the fort were left standing (Graymont 1972:
189–90). The burning continued all day November 11 and into
the morning of November 12. One of young Butler's goals in
taking prisoners was to negotiate an exchange for his mother,
who was held prisoner by the rebels.

Blacksnake's narrative lacks any description that can be clearly identified as Cherry Valley. The chain of events in the narrative becomes broken and confused—it seems likely that a description of Cherry Valley may have existed at one time but that
in preparing the final manuscripts Williams lost that portion.

Fort Freeland: July 1779

The protracted war, drawing men away from their homes for long
periods from early spring to late fall, began to adversely affect the
Seneca economy. The food supply was shrinking frighteningly.

As early as December 1777 Old Smoke complained that the Fort Stanwix campaign had reduced the harvest through neglect of fields during the summer. Similar causes led to a worse crop in 1778, so that by summer 1779 most of the cattle in the Indian country had been eaten, and there were reports that people were reduced to a hunting and gathering existence (Graymont 1972: 203).[7]

It was a desire to obtain much-needed supplies that led Cornplanter with 120 Senecas and Cayugas and Captain John McDonell with fifty Rangers and some regulars of the King's Eighth into the Susquehanna Valley in July 1779. Blacksnake told Lyman Draper that Seneca participants included Cornplanter (as commander), Jack Berry, Mary Jemison's husband Hiokatoo (Hi-yu-dau-goo), Handsome Lake (Con-ne-u-e-sut), Farmer's Brother, Little Beard, and others (DM 4-s-33).[8]

The force approached Fort Freeland at about sundown according to Blacksnake. He reported that the Indians first killed sheep, found in a pen, for provisions (DM 4-s-33–34). The fort was garrisoned by only thirty soldiers and sheltered fifty women and children. Surrender was the prudent course chosen.

The Indian-Loyalist force then turned to meet a relief expedition, possibly eighty strong (Graymont 1972:202), under the command of Captain Hawkins Boon (PA, 7:597). It was defeated, and Boon and several of his men were killed; one Indian fatality was reported, contradicting Blacksnake's testimony to Draper that "the Indians lost none killed" (DM 4-s-34). The expedition then "burnt thirty miles of a close-settled country, which inhabitants had abandoned" (Cartwright 1876:37).

The expedition killed sixteen men and took thirty others back to Niagara as prisoners (as usual, women and children were left unharmed) (PA, 7:610). This blow caused panic on the Pennsylvania frontier. Petitions were circulated asking that General John Sullivan's army, then embarking on a major expedition into Seneca country, return to defend the frontier. When Sullivan did not offer his army for this purpose, some suggested court action against him. A militia officer reported the country nothing but "Disolation, fire & smoak" (Wallace 1970: 140–41).

The Fort Freeland expedition garnered 116 head of cattle, and McDonell reached Niagara with 62 of these. Some were lost on the journey back, but most were siphoned off to the Indian towns (Graymont 1972:203).

There seems to be nothing in Blacksnake's narrative that we can tie to this expedition.

Sullivan's Invasion: August 1779

The Battle of Newtown. At the same time that McDonell and Cornplanter led their forces against Fort Freeland, a massive army was gathering for a ponderous and destructive drive into the heart of Seneca territory. The expedition was supported by a congressional appropriation of £32,743⅓ (New York 1929:9). Command was given to Major General John Sullivan, who began organizing the campaign as early as May 7, 1779. By June 23 he was at Wyoming, but he dallied there for six weeks while gathering his forces and supplies. Finally on July 31 he set out for Tioga with fifteen hundred men (see map 1). He burned Chemung, an Indian town of thirty buildings, on August 13, but a skirmish with about twenty Delawares cost him ten killed and twelve wounded. On August 19 the town of Owegea was burned, and junction was finally made with General James Clinton's force of fifteen hundred, who had marched from the Mohawk and descended the Unadilla and Susquehanna rivers, burning Tuscarora villages on the way. Sullivan assumed command of the force, for the most part consisting of regulars of the Continental Army and as experienced, well armed, and well equipped as any force the rebellious colonies were capable of putting into the field. In fact, Washington complained, "The force actually detached left the Army so weak that I am persuaded every officer of reflection . . . was uneasy for the consequences" (New York 1929:122). Artillery included four six-pounders, four three-pounders, two howitzers, and a cohorn mortar. On its first day of march (August 26) the force moved three miles.

The Indians lacked the numbers to successfully resist such a force, and the British command, although they had been warned of the impending invasion since April, were unable or unwilling to commit sufficient resources to assist them effectively. None-theless the Iroquois, supported by John Butler and his Rangers, made a valiant attempt to defend their homeland.

As early as May 20, Major John Butler had moved with a portion of his Rangers to the Seneca village of Canadasaga, Old Smoke's home village (DM 4-S-36), on the lower portion of Seneca Lake. This village, following the destruction of Onondaga,[9] was "the present Council Fire of the five Nations" (New York 1929:89). While Butler remained there watching the enemy and worrying about the scarcity of food, McDonell launched his expedition against Fort Freeland and Joseph Brant led a force against Minisink. Brant's initial thrust burned the settlement but netted only four scalps and three prisoners because, as Brant complained, of "the many Forts . . . into which they were always ready to run like ground Hogs" (New York 1929:108). The next day the militia gathered and caught Brant by surprise. He rallied, however, coming up in the rear of the enemy, and managed to kill about forty, with his own losses being three killed and ten wounded. Despite this the mission was viewed as disappoint-ing—no cattle were taken.

Butler with two hundred Rangers and regulars and perhaps six hundred Indians was at Catherine's Town, fourteen miles from Sullivan's army, on August 26.[10] Here, "strongly seconded" by Joseph Brant, he urged a retreat while harassing the enemy army as it advanced. However, "the Delawares had pointed out a Place where they said the Enemy ought to be opposed, & the Senecas & others in consequence of this, were obstinately determined to meet them in a Body, and I of course was obliged to comply" (Butler in New York 1929:136). Blacksnake named Hoch-ha-dunk, who could speak English, as the Delaware leader. The Senecas were led by Old Smoke, compelled to ride a horse be-cause of his age, and Cornplanter. Others present included Farm-er's Brother, Jack Berry, Little Beard, Handsome Lake, and Red Jacket (DM 4-S-35).

On August 28 the Indian-Loyalist force constructed a breastwork of felled trees. They were close enough so the American forces heard the ringing of their axes. They were not attacked and again took up their positions the next day. The Indian-Loyalist lines extended from a ridge abutting the Chemung River, across the route to the Indian village of Newton to a large hill on the northeast side of Baldwin Creek (on some maps Butler's Creek). Or at least that is how Butler claimed the line was supposed to run—he reported that the Indians on his left (the north end of his line) pulled back well to the west and south of the creek, enabling the enemy to outflank the meager force.

Sullivan commenced his attack at 2:00 P.M. on August 29. He used his artillery against the breastwork, and the shells from the cohorn and howitzers burst behind the Indian-Loyalist army, giving the impression that they were surrounded. Blacksnake told Draper that this led Old Smoke, Brant, and Cornplanter to change the Indian line (DM 4-S-36). Poor's Brigade took advantage of the opening on the left flank, putting the Indians and Loyalists in a most precarious position. Retreat was their only option. As Blacksnake later admitted, "The Indians did not manage well" (DM 4-S-36).

Butler estimated that he lost ten killed and twelve wounded in the battle (New York 1929:137), but the Americans reported finding fourteen enemy bodies on the field, leading some to judge the Indian-Loyalist casualties as considerably higher. The Americans lost four killed and thirty-eight wounded (Graymont 1972: 213).

Red Jacket was said to have been the first to retire. Later he killed a cow with his tomahawk, presenting his bloody ax as proof that he had killed an American. Much to Red Jacket's discomfort the ruse was discovered, and the incident was to haunt him later in his life (DM 4-S-36–37).

The Newtown battle was the only large-scale Indian-Loyalist resistance to the invasion. Cornplanter urged a stand at Canadaigua, but too many men were involved in evacuating women and children from the Seneca villages to assemble a force of respectable size to oppose Sullivan. The Senecas did not regroup and prepare to fight again until after they had retreated beyond the Genesee. By then, however, Sullivan felt his forces had advanced to the limit his supplies allowed and had begun to retreat back to the Susquehanna.

Seneca and Cayuga Villages. Sullivan's army thus marched unopposed to the north and west, burning all the towns in its path and destroying the crops growing in the fields. The numerous journals kept by participants in this campaign give us a view of Seneca culture at this time.

Sullivan claimed to have destroyed forty towns—Seneca, Cayuga, and Delaware. He felt that a "moderate computation" of the amount of maize destroyed was 160,000 bushels. Although his destructive work was thorough and extensive, he exaggerated in claiming that "there is not a single town left in the country of the Five nations" (Cook 1887:303).

Maize was the Senecas' principal crop. One officer called it "the best corn that Ever I saw (some of the Stalks grew 16 feet high)" (Cook 1887:27). Considerable variety had been incorporated in their diet as domesticates were added to the maize, beans, squash, and sunflowers that they had raised aboriginally. Sullivan's army is reported to have destroyed "Corn, Beans, peas, Squashes Potates, Inions, turnips, Cabage, Cowcumbers, watermilions, Carrots, parsnips &c." in addition to "mush milions" (Cook 1887:90). The army destroyed extensive apple and peach orchards near almost every Indian town they burned. One report indicates that a single Cayuga orchard had 1,500 peach trees (Cook 1887:113), although 150 seems a more likely figure (see Cook 1887:143). Domesticated animals also provided food for the Senecas—cattle, hogs, and poultry were found, as was hay meant to feed horses and cattle (Cook 1887:74, 98, 173).

Some of the Senecas still resided in houses consisting of a pole frame covered with bark, but many occupied much more substantial dwellings. Sullivan noted that the houses in Little Beard's Town (Genesee Castle), "the grand capital of the Indian country," were "mostly large and elegant" (Cook 1887:300–301).

Lieutenant Colonel Adam Hubley noted that Kendaia was "neat and well-improved," that houses in Honeoye were chiefly [of] hewn logs," and that Kanadalaugua's houses were "well finished, chiefly of hewn plank" (Cook 1887:159–61). Big Tree's house was constructed entirely of cedar (Cook 1887:98). For the most part Indians still used smoke holes in the roof to vent smoke from their fires, but some had chimneys, particularly in the town of Canadaigua (Cook 1887:204, 217).

The towns were for the most part small; most had fewer than thirty houses. Sullivan gives the size of Canadasaga as fifty houses, and Genesee Castle consisted of 128. The towns generally lacked fortifications, although Canadasaga (Seneca Castle) had "the ruins of a Stockage fort & block house" (Cook 1887:74). This was a remnant of the French War (see SWJP, 9:457–59).

The booty obtained in these towns was considerable. At Chemung the fleeing Indians left behind "a Quanitity of striped Linning deer Skins, Bear Skins, Kettles, plates, Knives, Ladles, and a number of articles of Varyous kinds, which the Soldiours soon maid themselves masters of" (Cook 1887:139). In another town the invaders found "great quantities of furniture" including feather beds (Cook 1887:89, 187). From the same town the soldiers obtained "a large quantity of pewter" (Cook 1887:173).

In one town the army found "a dog . . . hung up, with a string of wampum round his neck, on a tree, curiously decorated and trimmed. On inquiry, I was informed that it was a custom amongst the savages before they went to war to offer this as a sacrifice to Mars, the God of War, and praying that he might strengthen them. In return for those favours, they promise to present him with the skin for a tobacco pouch" (Cook 1887:160). Others report these sacrifices were found in several towns, the dogs being hung on poles twelve to fifteen feet high. They report that the dogs were sacrificed in pairs, one to be a jacket and the other a tobacco pouch for "their Imaginary god." The sacrifices had been made upon hearing of the defeat at the battle of Newtown (Cook 1887:76).

Later historical evidence ties the sacrifice of two white dogs (or one) to the Seneca midwinter ceremony (see Tooker 1970). The dogs were sacrificed to the two brothers—Sapling and Flint—who created the world with its good and evil aspects. The Senecas have two major religious ceremonies, midwinter and green corn, the latter held at the end of August. It is possible that the dog sacrifices were part of the green corn ceremony in 1779, either as a traditional rite that died out by the time for which we have more detailed accounts of Seneca ritual or as an extraordinary feature of the ceremony in an extraordinary year.

Among the booty taken from the houses were masks of the False Face Society: "We found in one of their houses an image which I think might be worshipped without any breach of the second commandment—not having its likeness in the heavens above or in the earth beneath, &c" (Cook 1887:187). A False Face mask captured by the Sullivan army was later exhibited in a museum in Philadelphia (Fenton 1956:350).

A number of commentators mention ornate graves near one village. These are described as "butifully painted on Boxes they build over the grave of plank hewn out of Timber" (Cook 1887: 217). Another journalist described a tomb in the same cemetery: "The body was laid on the surface of the earth in a Shroud or Garment, then a large Casement made very neat with bords something larger than the body & about 4 foot high put over the body as it lay on the earth and the outside & top was painted very curious with great many Coulours, in each end of the Casement was a small hole where the friends of the Deceased or any body might see the corps when they pleased, then over all was built a large shed of bark so as to prevent the rain from coming on the Vault" (Cook 1887:29). This manner of disposal of the dead seems to have been unusual. Other journal entries indicate burial (the soldiers opened the graves), and in Genesee Castle some bodies were cremated (Cook 1887:26, 99, 142).

Atrocities. The army Sullivan led into the Seneca country had little love for Indians. Scalping Indians was the accepted custom—no one even suggested it should not be done. The army went beyond this practice, however. An Indian woman was murdered not in the heat of battle but in cold blood long afterward (Cook 1887:12, 49). Two dead Indians were skinned to make leggings for a lieutenant and major of the First New Jersey Regiment—the lieutenant casually mentions it in his journal (Cook 1887:8, 244). A crippled Indian boy and an Indian woman were locked in a house that was then burned (Cook 1887:13). Sullivan does deserve credit for preserving the life of the century-old Tuscarora or Cayuga woman found at Catherine's Town.

Boyd's Party. After the battle of Newtown the Senecas offered no resistance to the advancing army. Instead they fled before it, often leaving kettles on the fires as the advance guard of Sullivan's force entered the town. It was not until Sullivan approached the Genesee that the Senecas again prepared to resist the massive army invading their homeland. Sullivan's maps were poor, and he was searching for Genesee Castle. To find it, on September 12 he ordered Lieutenant Thomas Boyd of Daniel Morgan's Rifle Regiment to reconnoiter. Boyd took with him twenty-six volunteers, mostly riflemen but including Honyose, an Oneida chief. Sullivan later noted that this was "a much larger number than I had thought of sending, and by no means so likely to answer the purpose as that which had been directed" (Cook 1887:300).

Boyd's party, after killing two Senecas, stumbled into a large party of Indians waiting to ambush Sullivan's army. His men on each flank made their escape, but the sixteen in the center could not. Thirteen were killed in combat, and the Oneida Honyose was killed shortly after his capture (Seaver 1824:79–80). Blacksnake witnessed this. Honyose was recognized by his own brother, Gah-ne-gi-e-song, "the Lemonade," who reminded Honyose he had tried to persuade him to fight for the Crown and "said he would not kill him—the Senecas might do as they pleased." Little Beard killed Honyose with a sword (DM 4-s-37–38). Lieutenant Boyd and Michael Parker, another rifleman, were captured and taken to be tortured. The prospects of ambushing the entire enemy army were disrupted, however, and the Indians and Loyalists abandoned the field leaving their packs behind (Graymont 1972:217).

When Sullivan's men captured Genesee Castle they found the remains of Boyd and his companion: "The bodies of Lieut Boyd and the other his fellow sufferer mangled in a most inhuman and barbarous manner having plucked their nails out by the roots, tied them to trees and whipped them with Prickly Ash, whilst the rest threw darts at them, stabbed them with spears, cut out their tongues, and likewise cut off their heads" (Cook 1887: 112). Blacksnake told Draper that he "recollects nothing of Boyd and Parker being captured, nor of their fate" (DM 4-s-38).

Results of the Invasion. Sullivan, upon reaching Genesee Castle, faced about and retreated homeward, completing his appointed task of devastation on the way back. The Iroquois, in the meantime, huddled about Niagara drawing British rations from that post. Blacksnake reports that the Iroquois camp stretched eight miles above Fort Niagara, "presenting the appearance of one continued Indian village from Fort Niagara to Lewiston" (DM 4-s-40). Mary Jemison has described her reactions to the work of Sullivan's men: "We all returned, but what were our feelings when we found that there was not a mouthful of any kind of sustenance left, not even enough to keep a child one day from perishing from hunger" (Seaver 1824:83). The destruction of food resources was particularly damaging because

the succeeding winter . . . was the most severe that I have witnessed since my remembrance. The snow fell about five feet deep, and remained so for a long time, and the weather was extremely cold; so much so indeed, that almost all the game upon which the Indians depended for subsistence, perished, and reduced them almost to a state of starvation through that and three or four succeeding years. When the snow melted in the spring, deer were found dead upon the ground in vast numbers; and other animals, of every description, perished from the cold also, and were found dead, in multitudes. Many of our people barely escaped with their lives, and some actually died of hunger and freezing. (Seaver 1824: 84)

Sullivan (and Brodhead driving up the Allegheny River—see below) failed to destroy all the Seneca villages, however. Blacksnake's home village of Conawagus, just a few miles from Genesee Castle, was not touched. Mary Jemison moved to the upper Genesee where corn still grew in Gardow Flats (Seaver 1824:83). Sullivan's drive inflicted few casualties on the Senecas. There was the problem of sustaining the Iroquois warriors and their families over the winter, but when spring came they were ready to move into the field again. As one of Sullivan's officers noted, "The nests are destroyed, but the birds are still on the wing" (Cook 1887:101). The next July Guy Johnson numbered loyal Iroquois warriors at 1,200. Of these 830 were out raiding rebel settlements (NYCD, 8:797).

Blacksnake's Account. There are some errors (or ambiguities) in Blacksnake's account of the invasion. The action did not take place in the spring as he implies. It is possible that Joseph Brant was conferring with the Loyalists at Fort Niagara ("fort george" in the narrative), but it is certain, as is confirmed in Draper's notes (DM 4-S-35−36), that Brant was with the Indians at Newtown. Also at Newtown were John Butler, Walter Butler, and John McDonell.

However, Blacksnake's narrative clearly indicates the two actions. He accurately, if briefly, describes the Indian position at the Newtown battle, then goes on to describe the encounter with Lieutenant Boyd's detachment and the capture of the Oneida Honyose.

Brodhead's Invasion: August 1779

While Sullivan's army was putting the torch to Seneca villages and towns as far west as the Genesee, similar treatment was being given Seneca towns on the Allegheny. Blacksnake vividly reports an incident on the Allegheny that, unlike most of the narrative, is not an event he himself saw. Instead the text relates the experiences of Redeye, who had a narrow escape from the forces of Colonel Daniel Brodhead, marching up the Allegheny River from Pittsburgh in August and September 1779. The Sullivan invasion occupied Blacksnake and his neighbors at that time.

The Brodhead expedition was planned as a diversion in favor of Sullivan's major thrust up the Susquehanna to the Genesee (Cook 1887:306), although some unrealistic plans suggested that the two forces could meet in the Seneca country and push on to Niagara (New York 1929:12). Brodhead burned eleven towns on the Allegheny River and French Creek, destroying a total of 165 houses, "some of which were large enough for the accommodation of three or four Indian families." Brodhead claimed to have destroyed over five hundred acres of crops and collected "30 m. Dollars" in plunder (Cook 1887:308). The Brodhead expedition left Pittsburgh on August 11 and returned on September 14.

Brodhead's report to George Washington is of interest because it provides an account of the incident involving Redeye that Blacksnake included in his narrative and described to Draper.

At ten miles on this side the town [Conewango—now Warren, Pennsylvania], one of the advanced [g]uards consisting of fifteen White men, including the spies & eight Delaware Indians, under the command of Lieut. Hardin of the 8th Penn'a Reg't, whom I have before recommended to your Excellency for his great bravery and skill as a partisan, discovered between thirty & Forty warriors coming down the Allegheny River in seven Canoes. These warriors having likewise discovered some of the Troops, immediately landed stript off their shirts & prepared for action, and the advanced Guard immediately began the attack—All the troops except one column & Flankers being in the narrows between the River and high hill were immediately prepared to receive the enemy, which being done, I went forward to discover the Enemy, & six of them retreating over the River without arms, at the same time the rest ran away leaving their Canoes, Blankets, Shirts, provision and eight Guns, beside five dead and by the signs of Blood, several went off wounded, only two of my men & one of the Delaware Indians (Narrowland) were wounded & so slightly that they are already recovered & fit for action. (Cook 1887:307–8).

As Brodhead advanced up the Allegheny the Indians fled before him. From Cornplanter Peak on the east side of the river, they watched the Americans destroy a town already appropriately named Burnt House (Fenton 1945:108).

Although Brodhead claimed that none of his men were killed on this expedition, Seneca sources report otherwise. Blacksnake reported that Halftown, an Allegheny Seneca, had been fighting with the forces against Sullivan but hurried home to oppose Brodhead. He raised some forty warriors to accompany him. He found that Brodhead had retreated, but four stragglers were caught and killed near Burnt House (DM 4-S-42–43). Traditions recorded among twentieth-century residents of Burnt House (the Cornplanter Grant) tell of heavier casualties among Brodhead's force: "In the night they descended on Brodhead's advance guard and killed six, whose graves on the [Cornplanter] Grant the Cornplanters of today [1941] still show. Farther up-river, at Jimersontown [Allegany Reservation, New York], just south of Salamanca, the Indians surrounded the advanced party, who entrenched themselves. Twelve soldiers were killed and buried there" (Deardorff 1941:6–7).

Fort Niagara: Winter 1779–80

After the devastation of their country by the rebel invasions, the bulk of the Senecas, Cayugas, and Onondagas clustered about Fort Niagara. The British encouraged the refugees to move to those settlements left untouched or to go into the wilderness to subsist by hunting and gathering, for they did not have the resources to feed the more than 5,000 Indians gathered round the fort in late September. By late November 2,900 remained (Graymont 1972:220–22).

In February there arrived at the encampment four messengers from Philip Schuyler. These were the seventy-three-year-old Oneida Skenandon; another Oneida, Good Peter; and two Mohawks friendly to the rebel cause, Little Abraham and White Hans. After presenting Guy Johnson with a letter from Schuyler concerning exchange of prisoners, the delegation met with the Indians gathered around the fort. They presented wampum belts and called on the Indians to return to a neutral stance. After deliberating overnight, Old Smoke and Aaron Hill, a Mohawk, contemptuously returned the wampum belts. Johnson threw the four messengers in jail, where Little Abraham died. The other three remained there until they agreed to fight on the side of the king (Graymont 1972:225–28).

In this segment of the narrative Blacksnake also indicates the injustice he felt was done the Onondaga Indians in the destruction of their villages. Until the American invasion (a glorified looting expedition), these people had been largely neutral.

He also describes the resettlement the following spring, with the dependence upon the British for hoes and other implements and utensils. It was the decisions the Senecas made in locating their settlements at this time that determined the sites of Seneca reservations first established in 1797, some of which the Senecas continue to occupy today.

Blacksnake discussed this resettlement of the Senecas with Draper. This story of resettlement (DM 4-S-78–79) has considerable importance for events subsequently discussed in Blacksnake's narrative and hence is worth quoting in full (see map 1).

Seneca Settlements. —The Senecas after the destruction of their towns in the Genesee Valley spent the winter of 1779–80 in the neighborhood of Fort Niagara. In the spring of 1780 they divided, some went to Tonewanda [Tonawanda] (*Blacksnake* went there, & remained 2 years—then went to Alleghany)—Tonewanda was then an old Indian settlement, —others went to Cattaraugus, also an old Seneca settlement, —others settled on Buffalo creek, then for the first time settled—& not much settled till after the treaty of

1784: Others then went to the Old Alleghany settlement [Burnt House of the Cornplanter Grant], where Cornplanter subsequently settled—which had been mostly abandoned at the taking up of the hatchet & removed to Niagara, to be more convenient to participate in the war—now in spring of 1780, these returned, accompanied by others. In 1782, *Blacksnake* went to the Alleghany settlement to reside, & soon after *Cornplanter*, Con,ne,di,yeu [Handsome Lake] & others.

Canajoharie: August 1780

The fears expressed by one of Sullivan's officers, that the Sullivan and Brodhead expeditions left the "birds still on the wing" (Cook 1887:101), were amply demonstrated in the spring and summer of 1780. Numerous war parties, including one in April under Joseph Brant that captured Captain Alexander Harper and thirteen others making maple sugar, set out from Niagara to the white settlements in early spring. From Canada Sir John Johnson came south into the Mohawk Valley in May with a Loyalist-Indian force. Joseph Brant was in the field again with a force including pro British Oneidas and Tuscaroras and burned the Oneida village of Kanowalohale in late July 1780 (Graymont 1972:229–35).

Blacksnake does not seem to have participated in any of the actions (DM 4-S-43). He may have helped burn the Oneida town, but he makes no mention of it. If in fact he did not, he may have joined Brant soon after and seems to have been a member of the strong force that appeared on August 2, 1780, in the heart of the Mohawk Valley at Canajoharie. Draper's interview indicates this, but some doubt is cast on this conclusion by Blacksnake's assertion that "Turkey" and one hundred British and Loyalists were present. Stone (1838:95) reports that this expedition was entirely an Indian one. In other respects the events conform to those outlined by Stone.

The Indians, including Old Smoke, Cornplanter, Red Jacket, Farmer's Brother, Little Beard, Handsome Lake, Jack Berry, Hiokatoo, and other Senecas as well as Brant, ignored the population huddled in Fort Plain (or Fort Plank). Some trapped in the settlement were captured or killed while attempting to flee.

The most dramatic incident in this battle was the encounter between Cornplanter and his father, John Abeel (or O'Bail). Abeel had fathered the famous Seneca warrior and chief while trading on the Genesee. When he was a child Cornplanter's mother had introduced him to Abeel. After Cornplanter married he journeyed to see his father, but the white man did not respond with gifts as Cornplanter had expected (Parker 1927). However, Cornplanter still exhibited the kindness an Indian felt due his kinsman when he recognized the old man during the burning of Canajoharie. Cornplanter apologized to his father for having burned his house and gave the old man the option of returning to the Indian country to be supported by his son or being immediately released. Abeel chose the latter. Blacksnake reported, "At a council of leaders, it was agreed to let old O'Bail & most of the other prisoners go free—which was accordingly done, as a compliment to Cornplanter" (DM 4-S-44–45).

Following Mary Jemison's account (Seaver 1824:84–85), Stone (1838, 2:126–38) indicates that this incident took place on Sir John Johnson's autumn expedition against Schoharie. Later scholars have accepted Blacksnake's testimony on the topic as recorded by Draper (Wallace 1970:145; Graymont 1972:236).

The raid on Canajoharie netted fifty to sixty prisoners and destroyed fifty-three houses, a like number of barns, a gristmill, a church, and two forts. An additional twenty houses were destroyed at Norman's Kill (Stone 1838, 2:96). The destruction of Canajoharie and Norman's Kill is indicative of the Indian-Loyalist raiding that both preceded and followed Sullivan's punitive thrust into the Seneca country.

After the destruction of Canajoharie, Cornplanter, his nephew Blacksnake, and some thirty others decided to search for some good horses to take home. They found some about twenty miles southeast of Canajoharie. Eight persons were killed (two of them by Blacksnake), two prisoners were taken, and "Several good horses & colts were secured—*Blacksnake* got a fine one" (DM 4-S-45—46).

Schoharie: October 1780

In the fall of 1780 Sir John Johnson took the field in an expedition "comparable in size and destructiveness to Sullivan's of the year before" (Wallace 1970:145—46). The force consisted of three companies of Johnson's Royal Greens (the Royal Regiment of New York, Johnson's Royal Greens, which at this time actually wore red uniforms), two hundred Butler's Rangers, a company of British regulars, and a company of German jaegers (light infantry armed with short hunting rifles). This force gathered at Lachine, outside Montreal. From there they traveled by water to Oswego and then overland to Tioga, where they were joined by the Indian contingent and more Loyalists, including John Butler and some of his Rangers (Swiggett 1933:233).[11] The force carried with it two mortars and a "grasshopper," a brass three-pounder. The strength of the force was somewhere between 800 and 1,500 (Stone 1838, 2:105—6).

Blacksnake reports that the large force rapidly consumed its provisions. Horses were killed for food, even the one used by the aged Old Smoke. Indian hunters were sent out, and considerable numbers of ducks were killed, but these were not sufficient to feed the army. The last horse was eaten two days before they reached Schoharie (DM 4-S-48).

On October 16 the army entered the Schoharie Valley. The force slipped past the upper fort, but by midmorning they were discovered. They invested the middle fort (at Middleburgh), but three attempts by Johnson to communiate with the middle fort to induce its surrender were violently rebuffed—the officer bearing the flag of truce was fired upon. Although Johnson gave up his attempt to capture the fort, he laid waste the valley. The force moved down the valley past the lower fort to the vicinity of Fort Hunter on the Mohawk, burning every rebel house and barn on the way.

Blacksnake recalled that he and his uncles, Cornplanter and

Handsome Lake, along with five other Seneca warriors, invaded a house to find that the inhabitants had fled leaving their breakfast on the table. The Indians had not eaten for two days. Blacksnake and his companions "didn't wait to sit down" but "snatched and devoured what they wanted to satisfy the cravings of hunger." Refreshed, the group went on to burst into a fort, "the gates were not fastened," and capture ten people hiding in the houses within (DM 4-s-51–52). I have found no evidence to confirm this claim of Blacksnake's.

All the next day was spent ravaging the neighborhood of Fort Hunter. That evening a portion of the force crossed to the north bank of the Mohawk. On October 18 the two divisions marched up the river, burning as they advanced. Caughnawaga and Stone Arabia were burned.

On October 19 a small force sallied forth from Fort Paris under Colonel Brown. By this time Johnson, with most of his force, was on the north bank. Brown and at least forty of his men perished in the ensuing battle (Stone 1838, 2:116). The day was spent pillaging, and late in the afternoon Johnson gathered his weary army at Klock's Field. Here his force was caught by General Robert Van Rensselaer and the Claverack, Albany, and Schenectady militia. The forces clashed, and at twilight, although it is claimed (Stone 1838, 2:121–22) that the British-Loyalist-Indian forces were disorganized and in flight, Van Rensselaer also chose to retire from the field. The next day Van Rensselaer did not pursue Johnson, although the latter's actions have been called (by the unabashedly pro-American Stone [1838, 2:125] "rather a flight than a retreat." Whether flying or retreating, Johnson's forces—specifically Brant, Cornplanter, Blacksnake, other Indians, and some Rangers—captured three officers and fifty-three men of other ranks who had marched out from Fort Schuyler to destroy Johnson's boats on Onondaga Lake (Stone 1838, 2:124; DM 4-s-56).

The devastation wreaked by this campaign was tremendous. At least 150,000 bushels of grain were destroyed—nearly the same amount Sullivan claimed to have destroyed in the Indian country the year before. Two hundred houses were burned. Governor George Clinton lamented that Schenectady was now the western frontier of the state of New York (Graymont 1972:238–39).

Hudson's Rescue of the White Captive

It appears that the raid into the Schoharie Valley under Sir John Johnson was Blacksnake's last military experience in the Revolution. Indians, including many Senecas, were in the field fighting in 1781 and 1782, but no evidence in the narrative or in Draper's interview suggests that Blacksnake fought in any of these actions. The narrative does contain one final episode relating to warfare and captives, but here again we have an event Blacksnake did not witness. Also, because of the confused state of the narrative, it is difficult to locate this episode in space and time. While it is possible that it took place late in the Revolution, it also seems possible that Blacksnake is here telling the story of actions during the old French War, shortly after his birth.

When Draper interviewed Blacksnake he questioned him about this event, and he records that "the affair of 25 or 30 Indians destroying a small American party between Pittsburgh & Harrisburgh—a prisoner taken whom Capt. Hudson rescued—was some 79 miles east of Pittsburgh (DM 4-S-84). This location corresponds to the home of the rescued white, however, and may not be the site of the rescue.

An Indian known as Captain Hudson or John Hudson (both Captain and John were used frequently as first names for Indians at this time) freed a captive during the French and Indian War. The so-called *Historical Collection of the State of Pennsylvania* (I am indebted to a marginal note by Draper for this reference) gives testimony from a court case:

> Personally appeared, &c., &c., &c., George Woods, and saith, that about 12th or 13th of June, 1756, he was taken by Indians in the settlement of the Tuscarora, in the county aforesaid [of Mifflin,] [author's brackets] and that the wife of John Grey and his daughter Jane, and others, were taken at same time; —that they were all

carried to the Kittanning town on the Allegheny river, —and there
divided among the Indians, —and some time in the month of July
then next, the said Indians delivered me, together with Jane Grey,
to a certain Indian named John Hutson; which said Indian took me
and the said Jane Grey to Pittsburgh, then in possession of the
French; and after some days the Indian Hutson delivered me to the
French governor Mons. Duquesne; from which time I found out
the said Indian called John Hutson, who informed me that little
Jane Grey was then a fine big girl, and lived near Sir William
Johnson's . . . Dated June 1789—never sworn to. (Day 1843:384–
95)

This John Hudson was To·nihokæ·ʔwęh, "Open Door," one of
the eight Seneca sachems (Harris 1903:390). This title was later
held by Ely S. Parker—Morgan's informant, United States Army
general, and commissioner of Indian affairs. In an undocumented
statement that rings true, Harris (1903:390) points out that Hudson's second son was also known as Captain (or John) Hudson.
This second son was "Hah-yen-de-seh," which Harris renders as
"Dragging Wood" or "Hemlock Carrier." Blacksnake told Draper
that "*Hi-en-de-sa, or the Wood-Drawer, commonly called Captain Hudson* was a Seneca—lived originally on the Genesee:
Died at Franklin, Pa. about 20 years ago" (DM 4-S-84). Harris
(1903:390) notes that the younger Hudson "in the first campaigns of the Revolution . . . won rank as a chieftain of note. It is
impossible to distinguish between the deeds of the old sachem
and those of his son in the early years of the war."

Both the elder and the younger Hudsons remained in touch
with George Woods (the white captive delivered to Pittsburgh)
and his family. A son of George Woods, Harry, became a lieutenant in the Bedford Rangers. As a member of this unit Harry Woods
ventured forth on an expedition in the spring of 1781, under the
command of Captain John Boyd, the elder brother of Thomas
Boyd, killed on the Sullivan expedition, and of William Boyd,
who had been killed at Brandywine. Also in the party was a
handsome youngster named Horatio Jones. This expedition was

ambushed on a foggy June morning, and Boyd, Jones, and several others were captured. Boyd's men had stumbled on a party of almost one hundred warriors led by the younger Hudson and Shongo (Ga-nee-songo) and a detachment of Rangers commanded by Lieutenant Robert Nelles.

Harry Woods was showing the better part of valor and fleeing the field with an empty rifle when he heard, "No hurt you Woods! No hurt you Woods!" His pursuer was the younger Hudson, who had recognized the son of his father's friend. Hudson allowed Woods and two other rangers to escape (Harris 1903: 393–95).

Blacksnake's narrative does not appear to refer to this encounter between the younger Hudson and Harry Woods. If it does not refer to the incident involving the elder Hudson and George Woods, then a third white owes his life to the Hudsons.

A bit of confusion is added to the matter by Peter Crouse's letter to Lyman Draper. Draper, after his interview with Blacksnake, had written to Crouse with further questions. He asked, "Was *Capt. Hudson* on any of the above campaigns—if so, which? What was his Indian name?" (DM 16-F-232). Crouse, who had been interpreter for Draper's interview with Blacksnake, replied, "Captain *Hudson* was at the battle of Oheesky [Oriskany], Ski-an-do-wa [Wyoming], Ki-e-ton-geh [Cherry Valley] & he was there when Cornplanters father was taken [Canajoharie] & the lime incident occurred [Johnson's Schoharie Valley campaign]—his Indian name *Sa-go-yes*—he died soon after the Revolutionary war & he had rather his idea that he died at Oswego" (DM 16-F-234). It is possible, then, that a third Captain Hudson fought in the Revolution, although I believe this passage refers to the elder Hudson. "Sa-go-yes" may either be Hudson's name before he assumed the sachemship or may represent an error on Crouse's part—Draper's next question, not answered in Crouse's letter, concerned "Sa-go-yes."

Both Hudson, with his facility for languages, and the white captive play roles later in Blacksnake's narrative.

The narrative that follows provides a glimpse of this violent period in Seneca history. As I have indicated, this long section is open to varied interpretations. I hope that this lengthy introduction to the narrative will help readers interpret the material. It should also fill in some of the gaps in Blacksnake's narrative as presented by Benjamin Williams.

[Fort Stanwix Siege and Oriskany]

[134] which we got Ready in a few Days and we meet again, on the ground of Sembly the commander called to order and Set his Big Cannon fire three times and all the captains and other offices Brought on many good things to make us good feelling, and they march Round Several times when they got throught. Says to us that we shall go the Next Day for we are Ready to perform and toward fortstanwix, and we was intructed to go there or near at the forts and we must wait upon which may later or behind Either army, this is the advice we got from them So we start at all the warriors and went on a few mils when we Retire for to wait it the Rest of the company there we Stayed over night Next Day about at noon we all got together, for to ascertain the Number of us that who are engaged to go the whites company went an other Rout we agreed to meet them Near forstanwix we went on that afternoon and trallute [traveled] Several Days we Reach it at the Place where appoint it place to stop, at the Same Day the British army Reach it the Same so we could communicate Each other in the Evenning at near forstanwix in the Next morning [135] Early of the Day the British officers undertooke to go into the fort, for the purpose of to see the situation and ascertain the Number of them and how it could be taken &c But first orders we have to help his men to Built it Kind a Brush and trees for preventing that it should happen the american may certain come upon us throught the Night Near the forstanwix So we went on to work But during in the afternoon our British officer went to the america fort for to have communicated with the officers on the importand affairs in pretention of settlement if possible, But the same time object is to see what going on in side of the fort, But while our officer going toward or approaching Near the gate of fort, and the Enemie took our officer and Blindfuled [blindfolded him] and lead him into the gate, and conversed with the officers and stayed quarter of an hour, and they let him out the gate, and let him come to us and from us that

the americans will not surrender and Rather firght an [fight on and not] to given up they fort or possesions, During this the america fire they cannon at us, and the British party began to fire at them the same time

But while maken the preparation for Battle the news came from the Enemies that we must wait till they are Ready about 2 Days we was notice that we now take up the arms, there was Six thousand men arrived of american to meet with us, so our head man made further arrangement in preparing for Battle with them—

our chiefs commander and others officers concluded the we should march about 3 miles off from our camps to on the choice ground where and we must Shed our [136] whites Brothers and ourselves Blood over the Earth and the Bodies of the Deade one will forever laid Down, for the cause of obtaining the British government, the most object is going off three miles from the tents, for to keep the Stinking the Deade Bodies off from the tents So we march out to the chose ground, when we got them, about the second Day morning from the time our British officer was Blindfulled before going into the fortstamwix—then we have met the Enemey at the Place appointed Near a Small creek, where had the Six thousand men, that they 3 cannon and we have none, But Tomehawks and afew guns amongst us, But agreed to firght with Tomehawk Skulling [scalping] Knife as we approach to a firghting we had preparate to make one fire and Run amongst them we So, while we Doing of it, feels no more to Kill the Beast, and killed most all, the americans army, only a few white man Escape from us there I have seen many norrow places and close to hand to be Kill by the Speare in the End of muskett [i.e., bayo-nets], that I had to Denfended mysilfe By my hands and Exsive-tive [excessive?] act, During all the afternoon, But take tome-hawk and knifes and Swords to cut Down men with it, there I have Seen the most Dead Bodies all it over that I never Did see, and never will again I thought at that time the Blood Shed a Stream Running Down on the Decending ground During the

whites Brothers and ourselves Blood
over the Earth and the Bodeis of the Deade one will
former laid Down, for the cause of obtaining
the British government, the most object is going
off three miles from the tents, for to Keep the
Stinking the Deade Bodeis off from the tents
So we moved out to the chosen ground, when
we got there, about the Second Day morning
from the time our British officer was Blind
pulled, before going into the fort stanwix —
then we have met the Enemys at the Place
appointed Near a Small creek, when had
the Six thousand men, that they I can now
and we have none, But Tomehawks and
few guns amongst us, But agreed to fight
with Tomehawk Skalting Knife as we approach
to a fighting we had preparate to make one
fire and then amongst them we So, while
we doing of it, feels no more to Kill the
Beast, and killed most all, the american
army, only a few white man Escape from us
then I have seen many norrow places and
close to hard to be Kill By the Speare in the
End of musket, that I had to Denfender myself
By my hands and Exivition act, during all
the afternoon, But take Tomehawk and
knifes and Swards to cut Down with
with it, then I have seen the most Dead
Bodeis all it once that I never did see, and
never will again I thought at that time
the Blood Shed a Stream Running Down on the
Decending ground during the afternoon, and
yet Some turning crying for help, But
have no mercy on to be Spared for them
But as to the Distress of the senecas only
30 Kill at that time, and I have took prisoners
at that time, and Some others took prisoners
too, But that they was Kill By cluting & Running
thought a certain Distance and they were not

"Forstanwix Battle." Blacksnake expresses his feelings about the hard-fought battle of Oriskany. Page from the memoirs of Governor Blacksnake, Joseph Brant Papers, Draper Manuscripts (16-F-136). Courtesy of the State Historical Society of Wisconsin.

afternoon, and yet some living crying for help, But have no mercy on to be spared for them But as to the Distress of the Senecas only 30 kill at that time, and I have took prisoners at that time, and Some others took prisoners too, But they was Kill By Clubing & Running through a certain Distance and they ware not [137] one Escape they ware all put to Death by that way clubing them, and we never undertake to Barrying them, So many of them, we only Covered up with Brushes, &c after we a Rested a little, after this we met together with the British generals, and he formed us that the great Britain has Sent a large army to assisted us, and with ship load of men for us, that they ware coming upon the Mohawk River, and want it us to go with them to meet those ware coming upon the River, So we went on to the Bank of the River and stayed there a little while and the general ordered us to go home and see our families this was a few Days after the fortstanwix Battle we Returned for our families by the orders of the British general, we then went an toward home there was considerable in the way of geting homes whicth we might avoid truble and avoid fortstan-wix for fair that we might be tacked [attacked] without prepara-tion for them—

[Mohawk Valley Raids: 1777–78]

But than we Kept Right on a Noying to our Enemies till we had abattle or Rather Destroyed a town on west side Near of albany this is in the Spring in the year 1766 [1778?]—at this time I was chose to be taken a charge of a certain army of the Indians

My father was one of the Seneca Chief that who was kill By america warriors Immediately after the fortstanwix battle on the one of the Branches of the mohawk River where my father bones now Remained,

My mother was than live and she married again in a few year after my father was Killed, that whose She married to By the name was Jackson [138] and She Bear a Boy By him, now living at what called old town on the Allegany Reservation on the catta-raugus county state of new york—

My mother was than live 20 years aftcr my father was kill in the year 1765 [1777?], { and all his mains and uncle cornplanter Being so convidentual in me, and noted young man and given me Some Kind of office, or I have Some thing to Do over the people at that time.

Next summer in the year 1767 [1778?] I made the first move to go and attacked a fort belonging to america, what the Indians called for the fort gah doh ga the English name I did not know, But we had agood firght there, and had use the means which we use to use it as we had done before, Battle of any way taken the adventages, as I say before that we have note got Sevision [not got permission] to fire guns, But only Knife and tomehawks, and Run Right amongst them, and cut Down men and I have Killed how many I could not telled for I pay no attention or to Kept it, account of it, its was great many for I never have it at all my Battles to think about Kepting account what ID Killed at one time

But I have thought of its many that it was great sinfull by the sight of God. Oh I Do think so, it is Bad Enought to Spill the human Blood But again might Doing in honour for protected our own country and So &c where all the Indians Nations was Built forever, But our Battle [139] was finish Before we made our Return we then Retreated for the winter in the year 1767 [1778?], we Replace ourselve, at Near home for our Hunting till Spring, Some of those which ware family went on home But when we got Ready and hunt Deers and Bears and Elks and other garms—for Provisions preparing for the Next for to play upon, and for our childrens and for the old folks, whicth we have to provide for, all their wants, whicth we always maken preparation for them before we to leave them—

[*The Forest Encounter: March 1778* (?)]. about in the month of march we the Several of us make Returned from hunting for home In the year 1768 [1778?], when we on the away for home we had make a Stop at the about 3 miles from the Genesee falls Near

the bank of the Genesee River for the Purpos of Retiring for
geting our Diners that we have had to carried on our Backage
[baggage] with Dryed venision, &c we went and strock of fire for
to cook Some venision for Diners &c But in During in acting
Building a fire, I took my gun and Step it out upon the Bank of the
River, for the purpos of that I may fined Some waterfowl, to Shoot
at, for the object is to Save the feathers for the Dresses or making
crown to ware on my head when I am injoying at home, &c

I was about 80 Rods from where we all Stoped I heard of Some
Body wisiled [whistled] or made Such Sound on the left Side of
me within afew Rods of me I listened for Some time for hear
more [140] But hear no more I wheel Back to our fires, till I got
about 10 Rods from folks or Near Enought So Near that they may
Some of them see me as I was coming toward them I than heard
again, Such a Sound that heard before right behind me I turned
and look Backword as soon as I look Back they fired at me But not
any one touch me, of their Bad ball, and when after their fired I
than Saw 25 or 30 men with well armed men I just give the hoped
I than made a Jump toward them, and I Run with all I might
persuid them as I was Running my gun lock strock on the leam
[limb] of the tree and Broked So my gun was good for nothing, But
Kapted [kept] in my hand, But the anemy fired once more before I
over took them, the first one I came to him he wheel Round
about and Drawed his Sword and was going to laid over me, and
while on the motion—I lift it up my gun Barrel he track [struck]
that and broked and [in] two, in this momant I took him as my
prisioner and took his armunision [arms and ammunition] away
from him and other Indian Brother came upon the run I told him
to take this prisioner and him he Did so I run on after the other
ones that who got away, I than had nothing But tomehawk, I than
persued on the other about one mile I over my indian I Run by
him and To go about amile I over took the other three white men
Running Before me, and, I hollao to them and they fined me a
lone, they wheel [141] Right Round about and Discharge their
guns at me, But I Did not Know where or what came of their Balls

never touch me, But at this time or a momant they might Kill me just as well as not, for I fined this they are to much for me to Stand it against them. But feel like Death althought I made out to mak Indian a whoop and also made a Signs thought that Some Body with Near me I than made an other Signs as I was approach them, that is if they give me up their armunisions that they will be Save their lives and they Did So, when I came to them, So tooke them and the armunisions, But at this time I have nothing But Tomehawk, I have not got Beneficial to Defent myself with

But took one of his arm and on his hands the other and told them is Presioners and they much go long with me at this time the others 3 Indians come to us I told them these 3 whites man Shall be save, and I want it them take a long and I take one with me, But one of them Refuses to go, or to come a long and the other two they advise him to go a long with them, he talk to them a while I Did not larnt them what he said, But I told him to come right a long he Shoked his head and Sign he made that he Rather Die than to go I feel sorrow for him I want it him the Best of the three But he made again that he Rather Die than to go, &c I than Say to the Indian that they Killit I than told to Save the other two, and took them a long Back with us, about 3 miles to our camp, when we got Back to the camp we Eat a little, we than picked up our backages and went Down the River about a half a mile [142] a plac where we could Built a float [raft] for to cross the River, with it—for the River was considerable hight, So we went at it and Builted a Cobble [couple] of them So to carried all of us in crossing the River 20 men of us So we cross it Save, and went about one mile from the River we made Retirement, for the Night, after we Regulated in the Night, we have watches Sent them Back to the River, to watch whither our anemy have following us or persuad [pursued] our track, in During the Night—

But toward in the morning, the watchment [watchmen] Discovered was fire light about half a mile below on the other side of the River we Exspected much be those company that who escaped from us is following us about Braking Day light we made a

Started it a long the 3 prisioners we traveled on very fast, &c and Kept 3 Indians as far half a mile behind us—for to hear by them, if our anemy still following us or not for fear that they may continue followed us—But also oursilve [ourselves] continue traveralling all Day made no stops, But we Did not get home that Night althought we travereled after Dark some time for to get in as far as we could, when come to stop some time in the Night made no fire just laid right Down and with out fire that Night is favourable—and we covered oursilve up with skins and furs &c and we laid over night very comfotable throught the night, in the morning we started on, we exspected that we shall at home about noon, we got Some dryed venison with us that could be Eating as we go a long [143] without Stoping for fear our anemy over hulled the persuer, But we got home at that Day, the first house we came to it there we found But old folk are home that house the young Indian was gon away from home, and the Boys also and the young Squaw also ware gone, But the od Squaw and the old man, and made a Stoped little while there for to have the old folk conversed with them, and we start on for home that afternoon we got home I thought there we escape from the anemy after we got at home we heard from the old folk that they was murdered by the yankeys, &c and old squaw was taken her skull [scalp] and gon off with it I than supposed that the anemy must kept very closed to our hills [heels] But we escape from them, what made me think So because no longer after we got home to take man a pipe and fill with his tobaco and Snoke it up or got Done snoking before we hear that the old folk was murdered by who was followed us I feel no Dobt out it.

But this three Prisioners that we bring home with us who I got them well Secured But about ten of us put out and persued them that who has been murdered [those who had murdered] the old folk as far as we track it [them]—in the Night came Rain, So Dark that could not go on and had stoped for that night, was very waet, till the next morning we could not tracked them no more, and we had oblidge to go Back and quit them and go home when we got home once more, there we Saw another family was all killed and by who we cannot larnt, only we supposed this must be Done in the night—and all we could tracked them [144] was Bare foot it But for one about half a mile, there I found a Shoe tracks I than Says to my men that I found the white man track they must be the ones that whose murderer of those family that night, the white man ware Shoes, the Indians ware mukinsin [moccasins], by these are very Easily tell white track and the indians in general I therefore was well convidence that white warriors murdered this family at this time we are oblidge to watched or Gard Stations in Different Places Every Night, for some time So they Did not come any more

[Wyoming: July 1778]

about 3 months after this we was to go with army of 300 men by the commander of general Duckey [Turkey] British officer was called or Rather notice to be aready such atime and to be met with them such aplac [a place] and Such a Day and to be made a further arrangements and instruction is to be given us whicth Should be perform after we should arrived, at what called by the Indians, Da,a,i,Dah,A, I Did not know what, the English name of the Plac the Town where we are going to fight, But in our appointment was up we was Ready and went to a plac appoint it, is to be met with general Duckey and his army we was than intructed what we Shall Do By general advise, we was to go on one side of the Town or village, and they was to go on the other Side of Said village and they was also to attack first and make Draw the anemy attention from us so we Should come behind the anemy hills, and put our tomehawk on Back side of their heads, &c &c [145] and let this be the understanding so a greed on party, So Depart it one party went in one Rout [route] and the other went an Difference Rout—But Some how we got there first about 2 hours before them But when we arrived there and Send Report to the villege whether other were there or not But we Did Receive any Reports for about 2 hours at the time we sent for it, the

Report was that we must now go Near to the villege and watching the opportunity according foregoing understanding So we
approached to the villege as we got there the fight was commanced on the other Side of the villege, and we Did not have any
opportunity or to see only hear the gun fire holloo I than Says to
my men that we will never Do any thing, Esl we go the momant I
than give orders to march on and Run and take all the live if posible, and Showed their Braveness I gave them in good incouraged
So Started have Said nothing more untill we got through the
Battle—

But as for mysilfe what I Done During the actions of this
Battle—as I Start when all the Rest Start from But I Did not see of
the Rest of them for some time after I got into the amongs the in
the village, first man I came to him I fire it at him and kill em But
in the Next one I just took the Butt end of my gun over head
Down he went mind him no more about it Exspected him Dead,
But in the third one I took him the same a way thought I may
take his Skull as I Drawd my knife to his head and lookin back
and saw this the sam man that I butt him over, just come to me,
and Drawed his gun and appointed to me and was so Near to
Sprong at him and he fire the [146] gun at me But just as he fire
there was the Indian behind him I give the war whoop just touch
my clothes with his Ball never Draw no Blood out of me, I had me
knife in hand I just Drawed upon his throat and cut it Down he go
the second time I says to mysilfe now I guest Stayed Down and
off again for another one, I run I saw a cobble [couple of] Indian
wound it, and they are at able to go on I Run on farther and tell to
other Indian to go Back and take care the Indian and Did so, I
went to other Stret there was some more for me to Do I just than
took my tomehawk and Strok one and to another and so on Dont
minde anything about criing woman and children and men some
just Diing some fighting and all Shap there was not many gun
fired that fight, and Did not last great while another I Did not
know how many I kill, only I kill some many and I have gon By
very norrow places to be Kill mysilfe

and we got throught fighting we gether together—and the
general Duckey ordered us to go and Distroyed all the villege for
the people they were all most Distroyed anyhow and take the
goods and cattle horses and sheeps and what ever provisions and
take all a long and By this mian [means] subdued them and never
was up a gain, there was very a few Escape from us at that time,
and being so taken their property by the whites But as for mysilfe
about taken kind of property I Did not because I think bad a
Enouth to kill men and Distroyed their village [147] and the
Bodies was laid there when we a way from this Plac there was no
such Prisioners has been save, and the children a few was left I
know what came of them we left them there un take care off just
as the general was orders to Do no more But we left here and went
back for home to genisee River Near avone [Conawagus] when
we got home about the time to harvest what a little corn has been
planted By our Squaw and children So we Stayed at home peacably all the fall and the winter till the Spring 1769—we have a
Small Battle with a few of us some time go off of some settlements and small villages that we use to go and fight with them
and alway have advages ot them and Kill them as many as we
could By that a way considerable so and By the By the British
officer had to us and called us to go a certain plac with him and
his Small company to Destroyed we have Done that away often

[Wyalusing: September 1778]

till we heard from the messinger Send from Delaware Nation of
Susquihannah, for to let the Six Nations know that the american
throop [troops] are coming to Distroyed the habitents of the
Delaware tribes of Indians and they also wishes us to protect
them, in very Short time Notice and put us Great Deal of truble
in our minds for we could not have a time Enouth to Send a
messinger to called upon general Duckey and Joseph Brant Both
was at fortgeorge [Fort Niagara] made us feell very unhappy—

But Cornplanter and RedJackett and mysilf governor Blacksnake captain Pollet [Pollard] and captain Young [King—really

Old Smoke] and Several other chiefs of [148] the Six Nations put their head together and consulted in Regard the Notice just received and we all a greed that we Shall go and assist the Delaware Such a Short tirm Notice, that we Should have to Do all we cant for them if possible to Save them or to Save Nation &c

So we went on made the preparation for it, in Short Notice, made 1 thusand men and gether together 1 thusand men of Indians only But are Brave man all of them and was Ready to go, we had to go without general Duckey and Brant, or any of the head quarters, and we feel Distitude provisions and the means to go to with it But we all agreed that we shall go—So Started on the Run a Part away in order to meet general Potter from Pennsylvania of Wyoming with in five Days, we Deavours to get there in time we travaled on the way five Days before we arrived among the Delaware Settlement we than larnt that the Potter had 3,,000 men with him, and we are only about 1,,400 to Stand against Potter of the 3,,000 men and of well arm—So all this we consulted together what course we Shall Do, finally fined ourselve could not avoid it, we Stand fight or Surroundered—So we appointed the commanders and captains, and also all came bind together that we Shall fight with tomehawk that we Shall fight till all Killed, So Did not any that night we are not because we are afread But council and encouraging in the Early in the Morning was all Ready to go to choce ground where is calculated to contact with the 3,000 men But suppose messingers Report may Received from general Potter and we wait it for some [149] time and Did not came So we went on the ground in moment we appeared Potter began to fire upon us, to commanded to contact together, when the fired I commanded a Shase of the warriors I give the war hoop orders to go and amongst the anemy But fire once and Run the way we Slain was a wicked But feel no mercy just took the tomehawks and knifes and Swords with we might During the action of fighting to commanced about 9 oclock A.M. and till and 2 oclock in the afternoon—all we could tell in our party was mark on our hands and faces But fears nothing I feel thought to Die there as with as any other plac about 4 hours very hard fight Potter begin to Retreat at that time I slained most than another times in During the action, and the after Battle was over we Suppose the american about 2,000 Kill and Rest Run never leaved it them wounded Kill as we go a long only those are able to Run they ascape, But the Six Nations 5 Kill and great many wounded—

at that time we not Did not use mush guns mostly we use with Tomehawk & swords &c the way we to do, go and Run amongs them and give them no chance to fire their guns

as for myself the way I took my Tomahawk & sword and go among the anemy and Nock Down and cut with my sword and cut man Down two and our as went But than I went after took place that show Blood spiled on the ground that I ever Did see Such a large Body of Dead Bodies at this time we Have took the Bodies Barried as many as we could in comended to Barried with Brcess [branches] and other stoff to covered the Bodies [150] the Next morning we had truble to Barried the Dead Bodies into hips of the Dead Bodies we was than gethern together that whos was then at that time

[Here follows an undecipherable paragraph which has been crossed out. It seems to be the same as the paragraph below.]

Cornplanter and Redjackett and Young Kings [i.e., Old Smoke] and mysilfe and all the Six Nations or Leading men of that time was at mitted in Battle

But the six Nation was at an hand only Joseph Brant was not there

[Sullivan's Invasion: August 1779]

[194] About in the Spring in the year 1770 some of our fellow men was out East hunting they come cross it the American stroop [troops] are coming on to Genesee River to attack the six Nations, according to the titing [tidings] that they bring us that

stroop will not be able to get on to the River about 5 Days, the calculated what truble they have to get long with their armmanisions throught the wilderness to contain with, at this time Joseph Brand [Brant] was at fort george in Council with the British officers for the purpose of making calculation and we will not have a time to sent brand & others for our assistan or our protection so we must stand the ground, so we made the preparation for to meet the anemy and on such place where we shall meet them, So the watchmant tell us that anemy are coming such Place, so we started with 300 men Early In morning we travesalled on towart seneca Lake all Day we Did not get there till Next Day at noon, when we come to seneca Lake we Divided our men some goes upon the hill about 30 men and another men Goes a Rounded the hill and I went upon the hill when we got upon top the hill and we saw the american troop were coming on toward the the other Company we than immidiatly March Down hill to meet our men, after we got Down Saw american had more men we ware of, So we concluded to stand back for we are not able to stand against them till we get better [195] Chance, that this time america had commanded fire their gun and cannon at us But we stood back and Kap Runing backword till Night we than made Retirement for the Night, the american troop made Retirement for the Night about one mile from us, their general not known by name, Next Day morning the america warriours began to approach towart us and fired at us, at this time we begin to wake and cheer up so we a start it to approach them about half a mile we come to a small Swamp to go throught we saw the anemy was Coming on great body of men we frighten and we wheel Right back again throught this little swamp and stop in the Edge of this swamp, the enemy after us thought they had to cut Road throught this Swamp, so we stood proper Distain where they are coming out the swamp, while we stood there, saw the enemy coming behind us about fifty men, some of the Indians company hollowed to the head quarter to fire once, then we Run against them and went amongst them with force and slain them with Tomehawk and swords upon them and Distroyed them all not one escape, one of uniada [Oneida] Indian among the whites army and took him as prisonner for afew manut, one of the seneca Chief slain him with tomhawke and kill him, because this uniada Indian had Indian Skull [scalp] tide on his belt the most consaquant of his Death his life was not spared, after this we went on toward the head of the seneca lake where it was afew Indians families Live there, But they was all kill by the whites where I supposed this uniada Indian got the skull, so we pass long toward [196] Geniseeo, we came out to the River where Now called mountmoris [Mount Morris], there was stood 2500 men of the six Nations was Ready to meet american to have it Battle But the american was gon back toward New york So we Did not have any fight there.

[Brodhead's Invasion: August 1779]

[150] while we are gon to wyoming and other places to war with our own america whites Brothers

Captain Redeyes and anothers Indians was with Redeye about ten of them together following Down stream on the Allegenny River with Bark canoes and hunting furs, Redeyes and his comrates was Down about five miles below Brokenstraw now called warrent county Pennsylvania they had been camp out on the [151] Bank of the River, Captain Redeye took his Rifle and walk it Down on the Bank the River, about quarter of a mile from his camp there he saw a company of men of war, and count them, how many it was the company they was about 500 men in the company and they saw him and he Run Back to his camp, they fire it at him But not toucth him the Ball, But he Rum as fast as he could, then they put after him about 50 of them, But he Rather out Rum them—as soon as he got into their camp he told his comrate that the whites company are coming close to hand that they had Better Run soon as possible So they start it and Run for their lives, some Run up the River, and Redeye and 3 others went with him and got into their Bark canoe and put cross the River

But before Reaching Crossing, the company come upon them and fire it and this 3 Indians was Kill in the River while crossing and Redeye jump it out the canoe into water and Dove in the water as far as he could go under water but the company kept fire gun at him as far as they see him.

But he made out cross the River life as soon as he got out the water and Run to the first tree and got behind that—till water drin from him—and made out Escape from them—But the whites company kept pursued him up the River,

Captain Redeye Kept it going Day and Night untill he came up to now called Cornplanter Reservations [Burnt House] at that time and at that place was no Regular settlement only a few Indians family Stop it there for to Rase some [152] corn that year 1769 [1779] the Indians and women and children made than prepared themselves for to get out, away from Danger of their anemy that are coming up the River—that Redeye urge his people to get Ready as soon as posible and also made all the Indians to march up the River, and they took Backages with Some provisions and vinisions, and the young one and get them a way as soon as posible, for the Danger near at hand of the 500 men are coming to Distroyed them So they got away, and left all those unmoveable Such Crops on the ground and come in to state new york and made a stop at now Cold Spring [Allegany Reservation] and made retirement for a few days and sent messnger over to Genesee River immedially and to the head quarter to let them know the disturbantes and the persons that who was Kill at the time Redeye was first drove from hunting &c&c. when Redeye first got up at Cold Spring and his company Buried their corn and vinsions under the ground you have seen the hold frequently a long side the River like potatoe holds when the Indians has been Buried up their provisions and cooking utenstial those Indians wandering about in the woods or in when is having forest &c. till uncle Cornplanter and Red Jacket and myself come over to protect them, when we got down to Cornplanter now Reserved in Pa [i.e., Burnt House] where the Redeye had it corn that season the whites has been there, and cut all the corn and throw the River, so that we could not have any Redeye should come back and the whites ware gone down again and we persued them as far as warren Pennsylvania [153] and see nothing of them so we returned a gain and called upon all the Indians and we went long up stream and over to Genesee River and down home at avone about winter sit in.

[Fort Niagara: Winter 1779–80]

[196] Afew Days afterward the Messinger arrived from fortgeorge, the words is send to us our wars is Displayed take Place, we than held a general council of the six Nations in order to calculate what course Shall we pursued &c the Revolutions is to go to fortgeorge in order to find out the facts of the wars Department unanorously [unanimously] agreed, in this council That I govirnor Blacksnake & uncle Cornplanter [or] John Obail Redjackett and others chiefs commanders of the armies of the six Nations, and the warriors all agreed to go to fortgeorge, this was in the fall the year 1770 [1779] very man take his Nabsac [knapsack] with Indian Bread calculated to last on the away journey toward fortgeorge our families was laft at home on genesee River, and part of the warriors stayed at home for the protection the Indians at home and the Rest of us all went for fort George, I see nothing on my journey worthwhile to say any thing about it, when we arrived at fortgeorge Joseph Brand was there and all the generals, and others officers in wars, I immidiately visited to onondaga this was immidiately after corn harvest when I arrived at onondaga [camp], I saw But afew onondagas Indians, there was most all gon and taken as prisoners taken by white people in force taken to fortstanwix and one Indians family was Distroyed Intirely and the Indians town was Burnt and afew Indians was ascape the time other Indians [197] was taken I called them together for the purposed of getting unformation from them concerning of wars affair, for I Did know once that the onondaga

Indians was Stand Natol [neutral] taken no part of the two parties and to larnt all the circimstances Being Taken so and injured them by the white and the consaquancis

They told me in council that the whites Rather accuse these onondaga Indians might have some hand in with the Senecas & others tribes of Indians being waring against american But very much mistaken, in fact is injured them without cuase, they arent people about war But the onondaga tell me that the white people thinks that onondaga Indians might anoying to the whites settlement by slaying by, I, than considerate the white were very wrong By making prisonners of these Indians, while they are not guilty of the accuse laid upon them, I immiediately Return to fortgeorge, for the winter is about set in immiediately after my arrival at fortgeorge, we was called a council by the British general and appointment made and the time a Day, the Expiration the hour, we went and meet with them

Says to us, I Received a letter from washington, Stated in letter he has Now Defeated and Raise his flagg for pease and he Shall hereafter also obeded [obey] our father king of the great Bratain &c your shall therefore Remained here this winter and injoyed yoursefves and Eat and Drink and Enouth to ware and Be Merry for our againing Day &c&c A few Days afterward four messinger arrived from fortstanwix this four Messingers was an Indians chiefs from unida [Oneida], they had to come out with Snow Shoes, the snow was so Deep, But they are so Strongly Diserous to make pease for the Six Nations and the americans

[198] These messingers called to open council with the six Nations, so the Nation let the council opened for them and to let them atmitted to forwarded their object

They say in council, that we are truly sent by general george washington for the purpose, that your might perfecly understand the war is now over and Decleared pease for the Great Britain is now Defeated and no more war &c we believed not, what they said to us how can we believe general just has been said that the

america has now Defeate and Declared peace, &c and this merican missingers said the great Britain is now Defeated and he
Declared peace, we Did not believed such thing &c our officers
took these four unida chiefs in prisonment in the Jial for several
months at fortgeorge jial, they stayed till the Snow began to go off
and melt it a way in the spring 1771 [1780].

About in the month of March in the year 1771 the six Nation
met together for to consulted Each other, and they concluded to
have a general council with the British officers for to making
arrignment for the spring work that we may plant some corn So
we met in council we will Now ask you what shold we so this
Spring, Said Cornplanter to British chief British chief answere
Said to us to selected our own Location wherever we may choce
in Regard to wars, say nothing about it the council Dismissed,
The Next Day met the Six Nations of Indians together again for
the purpose of selection of the lands where we Shall Settled So we
pass the Resolution that we Shall go and settled on Buffalo creek
that will be our own ground to Rest upon and to Remain the
whole of the Six Nation. So we begin to make preparation to go
on to it, So started Every family had their own [199] choce for
their homes when we come to Buffalo Creek, about in the month
of April Several of us went back to fortgeorge to get lots of hoes
for to work with, on land, plant corn, Brak up Sod with hoes had
no plought or cattle or work horses So we have to Do the best way
we could about planting a things, so we got the hoes, the British
government furnishes us and some mone [more] hunting utan-
dual [utensils] furnishes us that time, and at this time these four
unida Indians was in the jail was Discharge, ang gon back home
without we given them answered with which they prepared in
council &c&c

[Hudson's Rescue of the White Captive]

[213] PS induring the Revolutionery in the year 1770 or 1771
companied with cornplanter & captain Strong, Captain hudson

and Several warriors as they Sailed Down Stream on the allegany
River in the State of Pennsylvania as they Sailed between Moho-
non & Kittaining Saw Several Smokes out the among havy forest
and landed to the shore [214] and got out the Bark canoes and
went up on top the Bank—and Saw quiet Large number of the
company of Deleware Indians, by their Experience was making a
prepration, burning of the prisonner onto Stake, the Deleware
come out where the Seneca was Stood and wanted to know any of
them could understand their language, and it happen that Captain John Hudson could understand three Difference lanaguages
with his own he can talk Deleware and English lanaguage, So
made enabled them to communicated with them, first he wanted
them to go and journed with them Burning their white prisoner,
and this Delewares could not any of them understand English
lanaguage, and this hudson he goes to the prisoner asked him
whither he wishes to be Delivered from this cruel Death answered yes if posible Said the prisoner So Captain John Hudson
went and talk with the Delewares and use his influance to let the
prisioner go and use good reasons for it, he laid the Rules before
them, and Captain Hudson Know all those things being one of
the chiefs of the Seneca Nation and had influance over his people
and others Nations So the Delewares consulted among themselves and concluded to let the Captain Hudson have the prisioner So he Received very kindly and untied from the post and
unbounded and Set him free to captain Hudson, by the time
Hudson told the prisioner to go along with him for he Shall be
Save and Delivered to his friends if the prisioner Know where his,
friends is So Hudson Rescued the white man from the stake and
being burning to Death and the company Start on Down Stream
with the prisonner, as Soon as they got out Sight of the Deleware
camp and Stoped for to make arrignment to making escap from
this Delewars for fear that they might Rise Enemy against [215]
them being taken away from their prisonner. this prisonner told
Hudson that his friends lives on the Road leading from Pittsburgh to Philadelphia in Distance about 3 Days traval from Pittsburgh Said the prisonner—Hudson than told the prisonner that

he must go along with him and he will go a Straight Course if he cant to Stroke Near where the prisioners friends live, the prisioner Replied that he would be very glad after he make home once more and See his friend So captain Hudson turn Round to his comrates and to them go your away toward home and Start from before Day go upon the land Do not let the Delewares Indians see you as you going up the River for fear that they may become Enemy to us we must avoid if we could as posible and I will go with this prisioner and I will Delivered By his friends and I will Returned as soon as I cant go there, and back again, to our country this was happened at the Place what they called by the Seneca—hr-de-ga

Cornplanter [or] John obail than Say to the company we now go from here till a bout time when we think about atime a,cock Crow than we will Start and I will lead you all the Direct away going back toward home if we See any thing in our away, that will hurd us we will try to Subdue them But we will go home as Soon as we could go on conveniently &c the Next morning about atime cock crow we a Rise and put cross the River with Bark canoes, and we Reached on the East side the Shore of the River and got out and Shove our canoes middle of the River let them go Down Stream—and the Captain Hudson bid them farwell and pass Some their own away of ceremony their away of parting their friends than put off with the prisoner behind him, with a great Rejoicing Captain Hudson had three pieces of dry vension about as big as Goose Eggs [216] Each one But he was calculated to get some as they going along, the first Day they have found nothing in their away to be benefited or to keep [?] them, and the Night over took them they lie out without fire they Dars not to have it because that there may be found by their Enemy therefore they lie out without fire, Some under tree they lie very comfortable till Day Brake, they a Rise and went on their course with out any thing to Eat that morning, it happen about noon or Some afternoon they come cross Several tribs of Indians, they are about making preparation to Retirement for the afternoon they it happen come to the Nearst one Hudson begin to talk with them So found that they was the Same tribe that he was himselfe and the Rest of the companies they are Some others tribe and every tribe has one built very long fire well very good Captain Hudson & his partner Eat with them they Some Dryed vension To Same article that they had where Started from the River

they Stayed with them all the afternoon and part in the Night, that Evening, Captain Hudson heard Some the conversation a mong the others tribe concerning of the hudson prisoner that him, and the controversy was so increasing that he was feard that they might take his prisoner away from him according to appearance athings, So he made up his minde what to Do to Escape from them and get out their reach So Mr. Hudson tells his company what Indians about him and about his feared that they may take him and, himself too So he tells that they must put out the first opportunity as Soon as become Dark in the Evening Mr. Hudson tell the Indians that He must go visit to the another Indians fires, about 20 Rods in Distants and he pretended to come back, and stay with them During Night &c

[155]So they let him go, So they went, about half away from the two fires, Mr Hudson tell his Friend to go such a place Discribe when he will meet him and he very still and Stay there till Captain Hudson come So they part it the prisoner went according to the Direction and Stop and Mr Hudson went to camp, and tell them merely come to See them how they geting a long &c&c and he told them that he wanted to go to Next fire and see how they geting a long and prospect their objects &c So he stayed afew moments and went on To his friend is, and than they went on toward another fire, and Captain Hudson managed the same he Did the first fire, and so they went pass two fires Mr Hudson then said to company that they must try to get out the

other Indians company for feells unsafe to be with any longer, so they put out a certain Direction in the Darkest time in the Night Mr. Hudson his courst by guard with Star althought was clouder that Night and they travelled all Night long for feared that they may taken by these Indians

But however they Escape from the Danger appeared things, according to the conversation &c

So they travelled on till noon they came cross a small Deer Shot that & killed it: Captain Hudson taked the whole Deer on his back carried Some unknownit Place or Gulf where they stop and built the fire and Rosted the Deer and they stayed all the afternoon—

just at Night started on about half a mile and stoped retirment for the Night lying Down side of the tree with out fire and about middle of the Night rain Desented put them truble in Sleeping for want of Sleeping So they have to Beared suffering By Rain till Day light and Start on their courst till Night on 3th Day on the fouth Day of their journey in the afternoon they came to where it appeared cattle tracks, and that give them satisfaction the habi-tants cant Be great away off So they approaching toward on they Direct courst till come to improvements [156] and this young man So much cheerfull and gladness prospect seeing his Friends

Captain Hudson than ordered to Stop on plain Sight of cabbin he then to his friend or to the prisoner, Says to him give me your hand So give it and tooke his hand and said to the young man you will now go you away and see your Friends and Remember me who Rescued you in the hands of who passes your sentance to be put you to Death by fire the works of the hands of Delewares Nation, not only myself But Remember all to the Seneca Nation for I am Seneca chiefe I therefore say to you to remember my Nation your and firght no more against me Said the Hudson and they parted young men went one way and captain Hudson went on one away so pass on—this prisoner not known his name although his children now Residing about sixty or seventy miles from Pittsbourgh a Stone house on their primisses on the laft hand side the Road come from Pittsbought the family was very wealther family he supposed

Chapter Four

Negotiating Peace

"great Britain
has no More any to Do with you"

The British-American Peace Settlement and Indian Lands

The Indian allies who had so faithfully served the British Crown were abandoned by the Shelburne government that negotiated peace with the new American states. The peace agreement, the Treaty of Paris, conveyed to the Americans sovereignty over lands south of the Great Lakes as far west as the Mississippi. This was a coldly cynical political move, ignoring His Majesty's allies, who were now clearly expendable in the view of the London government.

It was with great regret and great reluctance that the members of the Indian Department and other officials dealing with the Indians informed them of the treaty, and they chose to mislead them as to its terms and consequences. When Sir John Johnson informed the Iroquois and the Hurons of the settlement in late July 1783, he hedged about the actual terms and gave the impression that the line established in the Fort Stanwix treaty of 1768 would be respected by the Americans.

Indians in northeastern North America viewed the 1768 Fort Stanwix line as establishing a permanent boundary between whites and Indians in North America. The 1768 Fort Stanwix treaty reserved lands north and west of the Ohio for Indian occupation. When the Indians learned of the contents of the settlement ending the Revolution, they were astounded. The British government had given away lands to which the British had never established title—lands west of the 1768 line.

The Attempt for Indian Unity at Sandusky: 1783

In response to this situation thirty-six Indian nations gathered at Sandusky, Ohio, in September 1783. Besides the Six Nations, this council was attended by the Wyandot, Shawnee, Ottawa, Pottawatomi, Ojibwa, Mingo, Cherokee, and Creek Indians. There is no evidence that Blacksnake was at this gathering. The British Indian agent, Alexander McKee, and others from the Indian Department were present. The council dealt with the return of prisoners taken in the Revolution, but its other major concern was the maintenance of the 1768 boundary line. McKee told the assembled Indians that "you are not to believe, or even think that . . . the [Treaty of Paris] Line . . . was meant to deprive you of an extent of country, of which the right of Soil belongs to, and is in yourselves as Sole Proprieters, as far as the boundary Line agree upon . . . in 1768, at Fort Stanwix" (MHC, 20:177). To ensure a united front to defend the 1768 treaty line, Joseph Brant told the assembled Indians, "We the Six Nations with this belt bind your Hearts and minds with ours, that there may be never hereafter a separation between us, for our Interests are alike, nor should anything ever be done but by the voice of the whole as we make but one with you" (MHC, 20:179–80).

Smith (1946:63) has stated that this Sandusky conference established a confederacy "which was not crushed until the success of Wayne in 1794," and he says "the Iroquois were the leaders in forming it and the heads of it, once it was formed." He greatly overstates the case both for the durability of the confederacy and for the importance of "Iroquois" leadership. As is outlined below, the confederacy proved short-lived indeed. Also, while in different circumstances a more unified and powerful Iroquois League might have been able to dominate the western nations, in 1783 there was no chance of this happening.

The Indians' position in 1783 was a difficult one. The British had ceded their lands, and the tribes could not count on the Crown as a source of arms and ammunition in case of further hostilities. The Indians faced war-weary and debt-ridden, but very ambitious, very land-hungry, and very ruthless American states. Although at Sandusky the Indian nations proclaimed that they would act as one to maintain the Fort Stanwix 1768 line, the Americans proceeded to exert selective pressure on various members of the confederacy to break the alliance. This they effectively did, for within a year the Americans negotiated a treaty of sorts with the Six Nations at Fort Stanwix. This was the first step in driving the Indians from north of the Ohio.

The Treaty of Fort Stanwix: 1784

Officials from New York, Pennsylvania, and the central government called the Six Nations to a council at Fort Stanwix. Among those attending was Blacksnake, who has provided us with his account of the proceedings.

The Americans had their difficulties. The fledgling nation had yet to work out the relationship between the central government and the individual states. The Congress, New York, and Pennsylvania all felt they had interests in lands held or claimed by the Six Nations. In 1784 representatives of all three met separately with representatives of the Six Nations to talk about peace and land. Thus the meetings at Fort Stanwix were a tripartite affair. One can well imagine the confusion engendered for the native delegation by the unresolved and competitive nature of the evolving American political structure.

The Indians had wanted to meet not at Fort Stanwix but rather at Niagara, a traditional place for councils. Because on American insistence the negotiations were held at Fort Stanwix, the western Indians refused to participate. Time was to prove the lack of wisdom shown by those Indians who went to Fort Stanwix in meeting so far from the seat of Indian power.

First, the New York commissioners met with Joseph Brant

and others. The parties agreed to the return of prisoners. Brant granted that land cessions might be possible in the future but was adamant that those present were not empowered to make such cessions. It is possible that Brant's reaction to the British-American peace agreement (the Treaty of Paris) was as violent as Blacksnake has described in the narrative. Smith (1946:70) states that Brant believed no land cessions would take place when he left the negotiations.

Next, the Indians met with commissioners and representatives of the congressional government. The initial address on behalf of the United States was given by the Marquis de Lafayette. He set the tone the Americans maintained during the proceedings—that Iroquois territory belonged to the Americans by right of conquest. He chastised the Iroquois who took up arms against their brothers, the Americans, and their father, the king of France. This conquest theory was pure bluff on the part of the Americans. They had only a piece of paper, the Treaty of Paris, to give them any claim to Iroquois territory. There were no American troops on Iroquois soil west of Fort Stanwix. It has been said (Stone 1838, 2:243–44; Graymont 1972:273–76) that Red Jacket made an eloquent refutation of Lafayette's speech, but the story may well be apocryphal.

The arrogant congressional commissioners were determined that land cessions be made. These officials—Oliver Wolcott, Richard Butler, and Arthur Lee—bullied both the New York delegation and the Six Nations. The former were excluded from the council ground by force. The representatives of the latter were forced to cede claims to all lands outside New York State and west of Buffalo Creek (note Blacksnake's description of lands reserved for the Six Nations in his narrative). This land cession by the Six Nations at Fort Stanwix was contrary to the speeches of the Sandusky council and later pronouncements. Thus the Fort Stanwix treaty of 1784 was the first crack in the "confederacy" Brant proclaimed so confidently at Sandusky. That the agreement reached at Fort Stanwix in 1784 involved improper procedures was irrelevant, for the United States acted as if it were

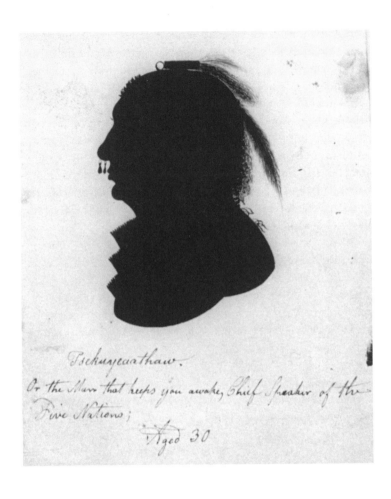

Tsekuyeaathaw Or the Man that keeps you awake. Probably Red
Jacket, about 1790 (Perot Silhouette Collection [book B, p. 31]). Red
Jacket's distaste for battle figures prominently in Blacksnake's
narrative, but also emphasized are his oratorical skills. Courtesy of the
Historical Society of Pennsylvania.

a valid treaty. The only way the Senecas and other Iroquois could have abrogated the treaty was to go to war. Lacking firm British support and without British arms, they found this impossible.

To add insult to the considerable injury of this treaty, six of the chiefs, including the Mohawk Aaron Hill, were kept as hostages pending the return of Americans held captive in the Indian country. Joseph Brant complained that the Mohawks had long ago returned their captives (Stone 1838, 2:245–46).

Following the meeting of the congressional commissioners with the Indians, Pennsylvania officials met with the Six Nations representatives and for $5,000 purchased lands claimed by the Six Nations within that state west of the 1768 line. Compared with the earlier agreement with the United States authorities, this has been labeled "a much more amicable transaction" (Wallace 1970:152).

Brant, who was in Quebec preparing for a journey to England, postponed his trip when he heard the terms of the treaty (he made the journey the next year). It has been claimed that the harsh terms of the Fort Stanwix treaty in fact "drove the Mohawk leader, Joseph Brant, back to the British" (Jones 1982:152). The participants at Fort Stanwix later claimed they had intended to sign not an agreement, but only a pledge to take the proposals home for consideration (Wallace 1970:152). At Buffalo Creek the council refused to ratify the treaty (Graymont 1972:284).

The 1784 Fort Stanwix treaty greatly heightened the resentment and distrust of the western Indians toward the Six Nations. A century of haughty Iroquois domination of their neighbors had not prepared either the Six Nations or the Ohio Valley and upper Great Lakes Indians for the close cooperation in a confederacy needed to face the expansionist United States. But the independent Iroquois action in negotiating the 1784 Fort Stanwix agreement was far worse than previous treatment accorded the western Indians by the Six Nations. The Fort Stanwix treaty of 1784 signaled that "the once imperial Iroquois confederacy [had been forced to] resign from the hegemony of Indian politics in the North" (Downes 1940:292).

Having effectively severed the alliance between the Iroquois and the western Indians, the United States commissioners worked at fragmenting the western confederacy still more. At Fort McIntosh in January 1785, they dictated their terms to the Wyandots, Delawares, Ojibwas, and Ottawas. At Fort Finney in Janury 1786, the Shawnees were persuaded to make peace and cede land. The confederacy of the Iroquois and western Indians denied the validity of the treaties of Stanwix, McIntosh, and Finney, but the confederacy itself was split. As the Americans pushed north and west of the Ohio, war was inevitable, but no Seneca warriors were able to aid the confederates to the west (see Downes 1940:293–98).

Brant Secures Land in Canada

In contrast to the Senecas, who still resided in a fairly remote section of the frontier, even before the Revolution the Mohawks had lived in villages completely surrounded by whites. These Mohawk lands lay east of the 1768 Fort Stanwix line and had been lost to the rebels during the Revolution. In any case it is doubtful that Joseph Brant would have led his people to live under the "yanky" government, even if it were possible. Instead he negotiated with the British authorities for land in Canada where his people might settle.

The initial grant of land was on the Bay of Quinte, and John Deseronto and his faction of the Mohawks (the Mohawks from Fort Hunter) found this land to their liking. The Senecas pointed out to Brant that in the event of hostilities with the Americans it would be advantageous for his followers to live near them, so Brant sought lands closer to the Niagara frontier. On October 25, 1784, Governor Frederick Haldimand of Canada granted to "the Mohawk Indians . . . and others of the Six Nations, who have either lost their settlements within the Territory of the American States, or wish to retire from them to the British" a tract of land six miles on each side of the Grand River from the mouth to the head (Graymont 1972:299). The "head" proved to be a line running from Burlington Bay to the Thames, however. The British purchased this tract from the Mississaugas for the Six Nations.

Brant announced the availability of these lands at the council at Buffalo Creek that Blacksnake describes. It must have taken place after the Fort Stanwix meeting in 1784 but before spring planting in 1785, for the great majority of those moving to the Grand River had already done so by spring 1785.

Blacksnake errs in suggesting that Brant had come back from England for this council. Brant had left the Fort Stanwix negotiations with the intention of going to England but delayed his plans upon hearing the outcome of those negotiations (Smith 1946:71).

According to Blacksnake's narrative, Brant announced that lands had been reserved for "all the 13 Nations." It is likely that Brant was including in his thirteen nations various refugee groups and allies of the Six Nations, such as the Delawares, Tuteloes, and Nanticokes. It certainly is not a reference to the Seven Nations of Canada (and the Six Nations of New York). The Seven Nations was a late confederacy made up of the Caughnawaga, St. Regis, Oka, Nipissing, Mississauga, Saulteur, and Algonkin Indians. These peoples already had lands reserved for them under the Crown, however, and did not settle on the Grand River.

Blacksnake's description of this council illustrates both the customary overnight delay before answering a proposition and the influence women (with "feemail Edvise") exerted in decision making.

The current tribal distribution of the Iroquois reflects the decisions made at Buffalo Creek that Blacksnake records. The Mohawks, except for those who had emigrated to the St. Lawrence a century earlier and those following Deseronto to the Bay of Quinte, are found on the Grand River. The Tuscaroras are found both there and at their reservation near Lewiston, New York. Some Cayugas live on the Grand River, while those who chose to remain in New York State still reside among the Senecas, although they lack land rights on New York State Seneca reservations. Blacksnake errs with respect to the Onondagas—a portion of them moved to the Grand while others remain on their reservation outside Syracuse. The Cayugas and Senecas around Sandusky have since removed to Oklahoma. Most of the Oneidas who remained in New York later removed to Ontario, near London, and to Wisconsin, near Green Bay. The Senecas remain in New York State.

Of the 1,600 Iroquois settling on the Grand, 450 were Mohawk, 380 Cayuga, 200 Onondaga, 125 Tuscarora, and 47 Seneca, and there were 31 "Senecas from the West"—probably around Sandusky (Johnston 1964:xl, 52).

The Journey to See Washington

The decade that followed the Fort Stanwix treaty was one of intensive negotiations for the Senecas. They were unhappy about the lands relinquished in that treaty, particularly the lands west of Buffalo Creek, which included the settlement at Cattaraugus. The Senecas, especially Cornplanter, held frequent consultations with American officials to change these terms. Although unsuccessful in these efforts until the Canandaigua negotiations of 1794, these same Senecas came under intense pressure from the Americans to bring the western nations to the peace table. The perils of dealing with the western Indians are outlined in later sections.

The narrative describes a journey by Cornplanter and Blacksnake to see George Washington. The old man's memory has failed him here, and he has merged at least two journeys Cornplanter made to the seat of the central government. In 1786 Cornplanter and "five associates" (including Blacksnake?) visited the Continental Congress in New York City. Blacksnake told Draper the other four were "*Kog-ga-do-wa* of Tonnewanda—*Che-wah-ya—To-doin-jo-wa*, or Split World, & *Jo-nah-hah*, of Cattaraugus" (DM 4-s-22). The group first journeyed to Pittsburgh, where they were joined by Richard Butler, whom Cornplanter trusted. Cornplanter's wife and sons remained in Pittsburgh. From there Cornplanter, Butler, and the others went to Philadelphia and then by coach to New York City, meeting with an accident on the way in which Cornplanter was injured (Jennings et al. 1984, reel 38, April 25, 1786; Abrams 1965:62; Sublett 1965:88). Cornplanter addressed the Congress on May 2, inquiring about the Treaty of Paris. On May 5, 1786, David Ramsay replied that England had ceded the western lands to the United States. He gave assurances against white encroachment on Indian lands, and Cornplanter agreed to use his influence with the western Indians (Coe 1968:203–5; Continental Congress 1904–37, 30:225, 234–36). They could not have met Washington, for he was spending that year as a gentleman farmer at Mount Vernon (Washington 1925, 3:53–57).

It is possible that Blacksnake spent part of the next summer (1787) with the commission surveying the line between New York and Pennsylvania. "Tiowaniss" met the party on July 4, 1787, and accompanied them "while most of the New York–Pennsylvania line was surveyed" (Coe 1968:292–93). Deardorff has argued that Blacksnake was not yet known as Thę́·wǫ·nyaʔs, so this may have been someone else (Kent and Deardorff 1960: 455).

The Senecas were persuaded to confirm the Fort Stanwix treaty at Fort Harmar in 1789. In the meantime their eastern lands were eroded first by the Livingston leasing scheme (declared invalid) and later by the Phelps and Gorham purchase. The continued unhappiness with the western line established at Fort Stanwix and confirmed at Fort Harmar and anger that Phelps had failed to live up to his promises with respect to his purchases led Cornplanter to journey again to the seat of the United States government late in 1790.

The capital was now in Philadelphia, and the United States was functioning under a new constitution with George Washington as its president. The visiting delegation of Indians, including Cornplanter, Halftown, and New Arrow (Captain Strong), met with Washington. Although all three signed the addresses to "Destroytown" (Washington's Seneca name), the phrasing and personal references suggest that Cornplanter delivered the speeches. Joseph Nicholson acted as interpreter.

Cornplanter complained of the Fort Stanwix treaty and asked for its revision: "You then told us that we were in your hand, and that, by closing it, you could crush us to nothing, and you demanded from us a great country, as the price of that peace which you had offered us; as if our want of strength had destroyed our rights; . . . but your anger against us must, by this time, be cooled; and, although our strength has not increased, nor your power become less, we ask you to consider calmly, Were the terms dictated to us by your commissioners reasonable and just?" (ASP, IA, 1:14). He noted that one of its signatories had contemplated suicide in the traditional Iroquois manner, by eating a poisonous root (see Fenton 1941c, 1986b), rather than face another war. This chief "has said he will retire to the Chateaugay, eat of the fatal root, and sleep with his fathers, in peace" (ASP, IA, 1:141). Cornplanter himself was in fear for his life because of his role in the treaty making: "The great God, and not men, has preserved the Cornplanter from the hands of his own nation" (ibid.). He confessed confusion over who had a right to negotiate for Indian lands and complained that Phelps had not lived up to his bargain. "For this land, Phelps agreed to pay us ten thousand dollars in hand, and one thousand a year for ever. He paid us two thousand and five hundred dollars in hand . . . and . . . last spring . . . he offered us no more than five hundred dollars, and insisted that he agreed with us for that sum, to be paid yearly" (ibid.).

Washington assured the Senecas that past injustices had been due to a weak central government and would not be repeated. He insisted, however, that treaties negotiated (dictated would be a better word) in the past must stand. He promised to protect Indian lands (ASP, IA, 1:142–43).

It seems likely that incorporated in this segment of the narrative are events that occurred at later dates. Blacksnake reports that while he was in Philadelphia his portrait was painted or drawn. I believe this was done by John Trumbull while Blacksnake was there as part of the 1792 delegation to the seat of federal government (see Abler 1987 and chap. 5 below). Blacksnake also reports receiving a medal from Washington. We know that Blacksnake possessed a "Seasons Medal" whose reverse read "SECOND PRESIDENCY OF GEO. WASHINGTON, MDCCXCVI" (Rose 1983:9–10; Prucha 1971:89). It could not have been presented to Blacksnake until 1798 or later, for the first of these medals were shipped from London in July 1798 (Prucha 1971:90). There were three variations of the Seasons Medal, each with a different scene on the reverse (see Jester 1961:152; Prucha 1971: 89). The one presented to Blacksnake was the variant depicting a spinning wheel (Aldrich 1905–7:383).

Blacksnake's narrative gives remarkable detail, but the details seem to emanate from both the 1786 and 1790 delegations. The route followed to New York seems to be the 1786 journey, although it was Richard Butler, not Joseph Dickerson (Nicholson?), who accompanied them from Pittsburgh. The details he remembers concerning the journey—meeting the white man whom Captain Hudson had freed, the fears shown by white children, the obtaining of white clothing, and so forth—most likely occurred on this trip. The descriptions of meetings with Washington show a remarkable memory of later events, even though they took place in Philadelphia, not New York City. The content of the speeches as remembered by Blacksnake is remarkably similar to that recorded in the American State Papers (see appendixes 3 and 4). Blacksnake even recalls the month it took Washington to reply to Cornplanter's message—Cornplanter delivered his speech on December 1, 1790, and Washington replied on December 29 (ASP, IA, 1:142–3).

[199] About in the month of august in the year 1771 [1784] Washington has sent Delegation to us for the purpose of making treaty with us, one white man and one unida chief on the united States they Notify us that washington wishes us to hold a council with him at fortsanwix so we took the consideration on the subject whither the six Nation would agree to go or not, with the controversy among us there was three chiefs was willing and favour of going to go the following names Cornplanter, Brand & Redjackett and myself and others of the Different tribes that are willing to Delegates to fortstanwix—to make out 40 Indians all together that are willing to go and appointment made for us to astart on So, we went took us 7 days to get there, about two Days after we got there open the council with unidas their prepared for peace, we give No answered, till the Second Day from commencement, about 8 o clock in the A.M. when the american officer got up in council, and Said, I was sent by general washington for the purpose of open the council with you all the six Nations of Indians as Brothers and be peace and to let you Know that we and the [200] great Britain is now Defeated and now Settled between him & the american and the British give up his claim a certain portion of this continent and the people that who are fought for him all his title and signed over to us we therefore called upon you to council to make treaty with you and be peace for we Do not wish to set ourselves & you anoying each other any longer, the great Britain has no More any to Do with you for we have Divided all the lands and lakes to East to west to ocean to ocean one half of lak onterio and lake Erie and so on up to lake supereiro so Direct on to the ocean—and we have pass Receipts and written contract between him & merican and also a letter for you to this fact said he to us So he hand over this letter to Brand— Brand took it on his hand and Read it a few lines and begun to sweare and stamp Down and turn Right faces Roun to word us

and, says we are Decieve by the King of the great Britain we are therefore will not stay here another manuit we will go back and we will not give up our lands as British Did, so we left the ground went back to our camps, there we hold privet council by ourselve for to Exorted each other for the Best course to pursued in Regard to it; Brand pass his Resolution that is to go on continue fighting for his Right—for he is willing to Die for his Right and contry with america, cornplanter was not satisfied the language which the america use in council and he wanted to Relized and talk with them more about it in concerning So Redjackett wanted to go & see the washington and myself the same feelling to understand more on the subject more about it and to Rehear with washington proposition because I have been communication with [201] washington before and I know very near his feeling in Relation making atreaty with us, So they ware with controversy all the afternoon and all Night, the warriours says nothing just Listening, Some of the unida young womans Stayed with us that Night that who was on the part of the american side, and they understand is the controversy and Resotution Brand made finally toward the morning Brand called the Rest of the chiefs they are coward that give them incourage to go on But these unida women Rise about Day Brak and went back to their camps and told their chiefs what had been Said by During the Night in Relation warfear So the unida chiefs had come over to see Brand and to make him understand the proposition washington has going to make with the six Nation of Indians, that is to let Six Nation may live and give them a certain purporation tract of lands for the Six Nation May live on and be peace if they only hear from washington this Edvise, unida give Edvise to the Six Nations took the offer Brand than cold off his ambisions and he than said I will now granted with you all and I will Departed with you and go to the King of Great Britain and I will make him good for all Deceiving that he Done to us and you cornplanter & Redjackett & others go & see washington to transact with washington and Do not let him cheat you or Deceiving you in making treaty with washington and I will Do what I could with the King—so Brand

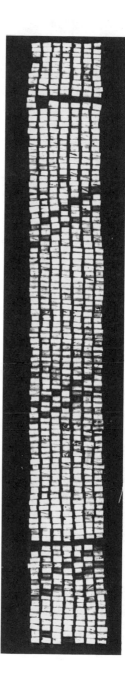

Fort Stanwix treaty belt (NYSM Catalog no. 37415). Clarke (1931: 92) reports that this belt was presented by the Six Nations at the treaty of Fort Stanwix, October 22, 1784. It was once owned by Peter Gansevoort, who had commanded Fort Stanwix during the 1777 siege. It was given to the New York State Museum by his granddaughter, Mrs. Abraham Lansing (Catherine Gansevoort Lansing) in 1918. The belt is 39.4 centimeters long and 5.1 centimeters wide. Photograph courtesy of The New York State Museum, The University of the State of New York.

left us on this ground on the same Day—and the Next was called to the council so we went and the american proposed to the Six Nation washington has sent him to treat the Indians Brothren he will therefore would come and see them by good will [202] I will Now presented as washington would Do with you word for word if you Stop Noying me I will give you a land that was good, cornplanter got up and said we ask you nothing as having us aland for we have alands without you But we will hear you Said the Cornplanter—answered you will be always Noying to my Indians.

I will not Do anything with you if you agree with me to stop it Setting our people to fighting

Said the white man to the Indians, I therefore will now Represented to you, that you shall live & be peace, and will be Distant independent Nation and you Shall have it tract of land sufficient to make Residence of you all the Six Nation and I will give you the Discription as follow

the particulars Places and the beginning about one mile below fortgeorge, from the first creek come out to lake at the mouth of the creek to beginning and Run along the lake shore till come up to the mouth of the Niagara River and Run up the River on the south side of the River and took in the grant Island so it Run up to about 8 miles below the mouth of the Buffalo creek to the corner, and thence Southwordly till come to the allegany River about 2 miles below the mouth of the Olean Creek or point And Crosses the River about 5 or 6 miles on the South side the River to the corner, and thence Northeastwardly tooken in Genesee River come out Near unida on North side of it there is made a corner and thence Place to beginning this is the Discription that he has made in this council to us.

We not granted to that offer the first Day untill about 4 or 5 days afterward before cornplanter given his consent if the Rest of [203] the chiefs would consented and take the Deed that tract of land, which that white man has been given us an offer for our settlement in the Difficulty, and this controversy Desided upon a good condision that is to take that Deed and to take with us leaved to our people to say Grant and Received the offered or not.

that white man had agree to it for us to Do so so the council was Dismiss come home to Buffalo creek in the month of october 1771.

[157] immediately after we are a rested, and called to opened the council to Related the Subject before our people assambly for the purpose of taken the consideration of the treaty [158] Which we have been making with Washington and the Situation of the tract of land Reserved for the Six Nations to make their Residance, and transfered the lanaguage communicating with Washington in concerning making a settlement with all the Difficulty in his councils at New York &c at this time   Joseph Brant got Back from England Mr Brant wishes to the people to take his load off his Back, before our Back empided So the warriors let him go on to tell us what he Done with Great Britain

Joseph Brant Said he

I have been making Reserved land in Camada Sufficence to Reside all the 13 Nations and the land was Described and Satuation commance on at the mouth of Grand River 12 miles wide and as long as the head of the River, which purpose of all the Difference of the Indians Nations would be sufficient for their Residance and hunting Ground and fishing Rivers and Creeks and all waters privillages and traping privillages in the pons, &c,, and 300,,000 of Gold money already paid over to us—and a Large quatity of goods provided for us By Great Britain anually annuity to be paid by agent appointed By British government pay able at fort george without Duty paid for our Goods transportation crossing Recrossing on Niagara River into our side,

all these offered was Recieve by our people and and signed the stipulation of the great Britain treaty with the 13 Nations of Indians Reside in Cannada and to gether with the Indians Residing in Eastern states

So on the part of the Indians was than satisfied on the part of Great Britain treaty with the 13 Nations of Indians &c

So closed and Journed council till Next Day &c—Joseph Brant was than Rather wanted the Six Nations would go over to Cannada to make parmanant home together with all the Indians Nations to form their own Custom Draditions of the Difference tribes of Indians &c [159] and their Regulations, and to live once more indepentante government &c

the Six Nations Rather Refuse to Do so the Next Day the question was then Rises about Removal to Cannada the wisest middle age Indians woman than called upon them to see what they say on the subject of Removal to Cannada to make parminent home forever it was left By them to whither we will go or not So the women Decided to let the Six Nations Remianed on South Side of the line Between America & Great Britain for it may be in future time the cannadian may be obligde to Removed or it may Drove off their lands, So the cannadian might have a share with us &c,, and if we Should be Droved off or Deprived off our lands we Shall have a Share with them we therefore would be justice for us to Gant all whatever given unto us, be no possility &c one woman or squaw yet living this Day She is about 18 years older than Gov Blacksnake that she was one of the committees of feemal party at that time So we have took together with feemail Edvise and with our own So Decided not go to Cannada at Present (Cornplanters sister) [insertion, not by Williams]

this was held a council at Blackrock on 3th Day from commence the council was adjourned for Next Day 4th day Brant ask the Six Nation whither they wanted have a right to take their choce the country of the two, that is they have for canada some for Staying in the States.

Brant wishes to have apart of all the Nations would go to Canada some Remained as he Said before the Mohawk chief than arose and Said my people Shall go to Canada with King Brant he was belong to Mohawk himself So of course his people would go

with him where ever he will go, the Cayugas was Divided Some
gone back to yutica about four families, Some Remained amongst
the senecas at Buffalo & some went with Brant over to Canada
and some went up the lake to Sanduska Settled there,

The tuscaroras was also Divided Some gone over to Canada
[160] Some Remained on our side of the Bondy [boundary] Settled
at Near Lewistown about 7 miles below Niagra fall where they
made permanent home to form their own customs of their Nation

and also the Senecas was Divided into those part Some gone
over to canada with Joseph Brant & Some went up the lake to
sanduska and settled there their perminent home to injoying of
their own privillages and custom of their own coucils and wor-
ships a large number of families Remained at Buffalo Cattaraugus & and and an allegany River and on Genesee River Several
thousand of souls of Senecas Remained in State of Newyork

the oneidas they went back to their old home Stead But afew
gone over to Canada

Onondagos they had Remained where they now live at present to injoy themself of their own privillidges on their own land

So every Nations have Saperated all Directions for theirs Residence Differance countrys the Senecas was the head one of all Six
Nations of Indians Residing with in the State of Newyork

[203] Immediately after our arrival at home our peace makers
called to open the General council, for the purpose of making the
Explanation to them, what stransected at the fortstanwix council and to what offer was made by General washington to the six
Nation &c So Notufiy them all quarters and the appointment
Made, the Expiration of the appointment all come to council, So
they met in the council Cornplanter, J. Obail & Redjackett &

Young King Several others of the peace makers of the Difference Nations of Indians

Cornplanter, J. Obail & Redjackett Tooke the Stand and pass the Blessing of which they alway Do before commencement of speaking to any great impartand Subject

that the our maker guard them Save home &c after this ceremony is pass by, and they went on Given the interpretation of the language which been use at fortstanwix council and all the stransection is Done between the two parties washington & Six Nations of Indians and the Explanation of the Discriptions of their Deeds, it was in written Down on pease of the Skin, tooke them two Days before fearly they understanded all of it, they then the third day consulted among themselves on the subject [204] and they come to the conclusion that Deed and the offer that was made by General washington they will not take it or Received, and also pass their Resolutions to keep continue war—for they are not willing to give up their Rights of the Soil while they considerate actualy all belong to them they Did not Known whither washington or any other white man has any Right to Deed to us any lands the same time the land is belonging to the Indians, we therefore are willing to suffered for the consaquance of it, onless the washington would give us the Better offered that he has here tofor made we will than take another consideration on it if it is the case,

So the Delegation appointed Redjackett & Cornplanter, J. Obail & myself Blacksnake was the proper ones, and young King Several other chiefs of the Six Nation

these Delegations now appointed for the purpose of to take this Deed of lands back to washington and for us to tell washington what Resolution is pass in our council in the month of october 1771 [1784] that is the Resolution is to continuince war &c&c

So we made the praperation to Start before Snow fall this fall So Start afew Days after and Started Several families Started with us So we went on the lake shore as far as to the a small village or settlement what was called Erie and from that to South So got on the stream on franck creek and on what now called midvill and so on Down to the mouth of the franck creek, there was But afew whites families live at the mouth and we made astop with them for they are some acquantance with the Indians and they are a good people and visited Each other among the Indians as will as among [205] their own kind folk, while we was there and Building our Bark canoes for us to sailed Down the River with it we Soon got Ready to go Down and went about 7 mile what now called Big sandy Creek and we stayed there over winter withe Several Indians families to be Neithbors Each other in camping for winter hunting and injoying that way and for our support throught the winter

In the Early of the Spring in the year 1772 [1786 or later] the Delegations Started for washington the first Place we went to Pittsburgh for to see a certain man there, for their interpreter at washington that who is well understand Seneca & Cayuga languages he is a white man his name is Joseph Dickinson

when we arrived at Pittsburgh we made inquiries where Joseph Dickinson is Cornplanter wanted to see him, J. Dickinson soon appeared and communicated with him, in Relation of war fear, and he told us that there is one or two come back from Down the River, that had with army when he went Down, But when he came alone his men was all Distroyed by the westhern Indians of Several Differance tribes of Indians, this man was sent by General washington for to make a treaty and peace to war no more, But those Indians Refuse and Distroyed his army and But very afew ascape and just got into a town this morning and this man on his away to washington on Business—after we Larnt this Distressfull feeling we feel become Disirious to see them, so we invited Mr Dickinson to go with us and see these two men—and we went & see them and we had communicate with them for we had a good interpreter with us, Easy to understand Each of us— and so enabled him to tell us what his Business is and [206] told us the same story Mr. Dickinson has Been telling us &c Cornplanter told him what our Business is, that we are now on away to washington for the purpose of making a treaty of all the Different tribes of Indians, and the Six Nation and american people and all the Native [?] Indians wish to make atreaty by the help of washington the white man wishes us than to wait for him five Days he will be a Ready by that time so he would be one of the compenion with us to washington, So we told him we would for we are feel glad to Do So, so wait it five Days he was Ready to start it all together on foot as we went a long on the Road on the away to Philadelphia found But few inhabitants on the away side of the Road But that generally the families leave their cabins as soon as they see us coming on toward them they had to Run cross lots some times this white man was with us hollow at them for them to come Back for we are not going to hurd them any at all But they will Run a way from us they are fraid of an Indians, I suppose because that we are look So Savage people uncivilized appearance of things when we are engaged to go to war, most every family we come to they Run or hids themselves away from our Sight for feared that we would hurd them, while we are traveling During 67 Days on our journey

Mr Dickinson the interpreter Say to the company that he would go away his so that the Next family we will come to it he will have the conversation with the family so not have them to Run when we come, so we may have pass compriment with them and not be so fearfull toward us &c Cornplanter told Dickinson that he wish he would Do so and we also may want bread to buy from them for he think we are needed [207] and also may have better acquantance with them I told the company I feel Desirious to go with Mr. Dickinson the family will not freared of me for I am Young and not bad looking fellow uncle Cornplanter told me I may go with Dickinson So we went on forward til we came to the Next house was no body live in it we went on by till Next house and Dickinson went into entered the house and Istoot Near at the Door till Dickinson called me in I went in I saw the gentleman & his wife and children, I made the offer to shake hands with the gentleman and Receive & his wife also But the children Refused they cry Right out I told them that I am not going to hurd them but friend to them and wish them they should feel the Same toward me for I am feel friendship with them all for the wars is now close we therefore outh to feel sorrow Now what is now Ready Done by human being for we are now on the away to see washington for the purpose of making a treaty withe the Different Nation of Indians and be peace for all mankind &c

So this family give us all the Bread that they could posible spared and some meat with out charge anything what they let us have, and they invited us by the family to stay with them over night, So we Did the Next morning, they wish us to stay til Blackvest So we agreed to stay he than went on told the story that was happen about 3 year ago, he says 25 30 Indians Distroyed the Small army by the Indians about one half away from this to harrisburght and it was But very afew ascape and he was one of them, and one of the own officers was taken prisonner by the Indians and was Kapt among the Indians for about 2 months than one of the Indian captain Rescured the white man this man was wealthy man this Indians captain name was Captain Hudson and this captain Hudson tooke this white man, and Delivered Near this white mans house [208] and this captain Hudson told the prisoner to go you a way and Remember me So the Indian left this white man This white man came home to his friends unrespected him ever be seen again the man yet leiven &c our Blackvest about called So have leave the conversation with him—after Blackvest we Start on about 3 Days traveral before we arrived a Small village about 30 miles from Philadelphia and we Start it this gentleman house that who was with us from Pittsburgh he called us into certain Room we all went in, by ourselves and soon after Rested this gentleman folks came in this Room and the our interpreter was with them and the gentleman tell us throught interpreter, that he wanted us to Stay with him about 8 or 10

Days at his house, for he is calculated to get clothes made for us white people clothes and Fashion and on his own Expence

and we wanted to know of what the Reason of it he says that it may prevent the whites families being So afraid of us, because being Dress Indian Style Cornplanter, J. Obail & Redjackett Young King & myselfe consent Staying till we get the clothes is made up, while we Remained in this place Received many good time with this people by hunting Deer and foxes chasing by Dogs, and the people of the habitant got acquanted with us and we Did to them and live peacably and hapy injoying with them and the good living while Remained at his house at the time our clothes is all made up and Suit Every man his own coat and colors been taken choice at the time cutting the clothes Every man sent it very well we Stayed this Place 10 Days, till we Start on again with all the company this gentleman went along with us, and Dickinson the interpreter of the Six Nation of Indians the habitand on the Road they appeared contented with us and not So fearfull as they has been before we got [209] other clothes on and feel more apeacably with white on the Road between Philadelphia and the Place where we got the clothes, took us 2 Days traveral to arrival at Philadelphia there we are to Stop according to the orders from the head quarter we had to wait about 10 Days before we hear from washington and larnt where he is and when he will be at Newyork &c while we Stayed this city Cornplanter and myselfe was called to acertain St and house and with our interpreter So we went one Morning, there we Saw Gentleman wishes us to let them Drawn our likeness, and they would give us other Great men likeness or paying for it if we choce, uncle cornplanter consent, So I will of cours I would So went on to work potriat about at the time our potriat Done, our company was Ready to Start for Newyork city So we went on Broad the coach or carriages and went toward Newyork, while was Riding During the Day our coach which I was in & cornplanter and one of this two white man was in the same coach Capsize this while man was some hurd by falling against his face on the ground & Broke his

The Young Sachem / a young Chief of the / Six Nations. Painted by
John Trumbull, Philadelphia, 1792. It has been suggested, somewhat
tenuously, that this might be Blacksnake (Abler 1987). Blacksnake does
report that his likeness was "drawn" in Philadelphia sometime after
1785. The likeness can be compared with the images of Blacksnake
later in life, reproduced above. Copyright Yale University Art Gallery.

specticles and hurd him on his eyes little & the cornplanter use
to ware a pease of Shilver mildtle under his chin or on his Breast
Rather that threw to his face and Stroke on his Brow on the left
eye that was cut considerable gash at that time probable Same of
you took Notice of him if you ever Seen him when he was life his
Brow was lop Down Nearly covered over his eye, this was only
had some bad luck on a way of our Journey But Did not Great
Deil handed about our carriages hurd it injured and our Determination is to get to Newyork this Day, So our Driver had to go and
get other carriage to with therefore we Did not get to Newyork
until Next morning after Blackvest than cross the River after 2
Days after arrival in the Town before washington appeared before
us made himselfe Known to us and wanted us [210] made himselfe Known to us and wanted us to come to his office and to let
him know our objects &c and Some of his officers give us orders
to go to any Groceries & Provision Store and got what we want to
Eat while we Stay with him &c I for one that after the Provision
and the order and Several others went with me and got the things,
&c the Next Day morning, the chiefs and others all went to
washingtons office, there I saw three officers Stood one Side
another on another Side one on the middle with well armes with
gun and Swords for to guard washington and would not let us in
for a few manints till Some other officer came to Door invited us
into the house so we all went in and Saw more an hundred and
fifty men in the one Large Room and they gave us a Seats

The Washington got up and said who are you all, and who are
the head chief among you and what are the Nation you all belong
to or what tribes, and how many tribes are you have and what are
your business are here &c and wishes you now presented before
this assambly with my people, and gave us all your object and I
will give you the answered said, the washington

Cornplanter, J. Obail got up and Said you are white man wanted to known who is the head chief among us and what Nation we
belong and what tribes are we and how many are we this Delegation and what business are we here and you wish me to tell before

your people assambly and you will give the answered whatever we wish for &c firstly I am the head and Redjackett & I chief warriors [?] the head chiefs of the Six Nations of the Seneca tribe and Several other chiefs of the same tribe and other chiefs are with us belong to other tribes, that who are was appointed by our people in our General council this Delegation are legal and just proper person to Dail [211] with you, our object is to see you concerning Difficulties you & great Britain and I understand By the commissioner that who held a council at fort Stanwix, that he said that you Sent him there to make a treaty withe the Indians that who are fought against american, for you have now Ready Sittled the Difficulty between you & Great Britain and the British chief hs given up a certain purpostion of this continent from the ocean to ocean and half on lake ontario So on up Niagara River also on lake Erie & also on lake Huron & lake Superior So Direct on Southwest Cours to the ocean these, Discription, British King gave you on South Side of these lakes above mentioned that he gave you a title and establish your own Government and you also provided for us all the Six Nation to Remian on, a certain purportion of tract of Lands Sufficient for us to occupied and Descriped Laid Down on pease of Skin with plain written and together with the treaty for us to Signed upon these Ground be no more war with you and Decleared peace for all Nations &c if so our people are not satisfied in Relation to the Size of land calculated for the Six Nation, the land yet Remains on our hands till we Ratified the treaty or whatever it is for we not given up yet if this Great Britain is we care him nothing now for he is coward, the offer my people will not Excepted unless you Do Better &c say no more at Present,

I cannot be able to give you answered you must Remained here till I be Ready to give you answered said the washington So we had Remained 30 Days before washington gave us answere on the subject,

Said he, my people has been taken a Deep on the consideration, of your affairs and they had come to conclosion, on the

Best sense and their Determination, is to let the wars be Done a way and Drop under the ground to See no more, and they therefore would maken the [212] addisions of the offered that has been made in the 1771 [1784]—and they have made the Best thing for all of us and all the Nations that are yet life throught the Dreadfull Effliction and Now we will make your certisfied for our treaty, and you may have a choice and give us the Discription and we will a granted according to your wishes from Beginning to End, and any quantity of lands, as you See Sufficient for the Six Nations to Remained on and be contented live by yoursilves

Said the washington

Cornplanter, J. Obail than got up and Said unto them, you white man come from on the other Side of the big waters, where your Brother Great Britain live, and you have Fought withe him, for you to again Liberty and you a gain a Day, and it is Right for he is Deciver, as he has Decive the Six Nation of Indians as you called the Red men But we are tru american we live here this continent, our God created us here the lord gaven us all this lands have I had a Right to make Reserve now for my people to live on while the land is belonging to the Indians if I had I shall make Reserve land for my people, and to our Satisfaction and I Shall now commenced to make the Discription we will commenced on the South corner on the South side of the Allegany River about 5 or 6 mile the River which has been made in the 1771 Page 28 the addision to commenced to Run Down, on the Same District from the River to the State Line Newyork and Pennsylvania and following on the line westernly to the cannonwango creek and follow up in the middle of the Stream we will Reserve for our fishing ground So Run up to the lake chautangue and we will reserve one Half of that lake So Direct on north west [213] to the lake Erie and thence on Down to the adge of the water to the other corner about 8 miles from the mouth of Buffalo creek which has been made in the year 1771   Page 28 [i.e., 16-F-202] on this Book, and if you Grant this Discription which are made before you, we would be satisfied

Washington than got up and Said unto us, we will Grant this Discription you made before us, you Shold have this lands if you are satisfied if this lands is Sufficient for the Six Nations to make Residence and injoyed by yourselves, and it Shall not be a lowed to any of my people to Reside on your Reservation or atempted to intercourse with you or to Reside within the Boundy you Shall have authority to Remove them and take his goods or any men hantige [hunting] for you Shall live by yourselves and be independent Nation and act you own Government and I shall act my own Government for the Best for my people and you Shall Do the Same and be peace for all Nations and you Shall obtained for your children and childrens forever and also With your land will Remained it in your hands forever as long as the Sun Rises and Water Runs and the Grass grew on Earth this is the Bargain is now made as good as this if you might kept it as long as I have mentioned, But you may Sale any time when you See fit or any quantity of your land to you Satisfaction I Shold not interfered,   if Sale to my people not foreigner

[157] Cornplanter Rose and pass his gladness for the Garintees of our lands—By the united States Washington

than tell us to stay till the written of the contract and treaty Stipulation compiled and Signed By the Six Nation and

George Washington in be half of the united States in During 12 Days which we has to stayed longer Washington use to called us to Sit together and telling Storys and the character of humanature of Diffrence Nations all what little he has larnt, he was than about 38 or 39 years of his age he only tell from his youth up till than &c Redjackett use to be machine with Washington tellings storys Both understood the Business Well &c in During this time Washington made me a chief of the Six Nations am made me Present of Shilver maddle & Disignate of my sake and wars commander office which I had that office the time commancedment, and the armsnanisions and other things that Represents in the number of office which I hold, and so I was qualify By the Six Nations and Washington &c

after the Stipulation of the treaty was completed and other Businiss Done what we was authorise to Do we than started for home washington gave us a tickett to go on skoner or great canoe up thc Rivcr as far as Albany there we Stoped one Day and also washington gave us a Draw on some trasury of one hundred Dollars in money By the assistaince of the unnida Indians agent So we got the one hundred Dollars money and started on toward home and travaled on as fast as we could go conveniently made no more Stoped only Nights till we arrived at now called Buffalo Creek where we have made homes after the Bloody wars was over and got cold in Eastern Part of the United States,

Chapter Five

Ambassadors to the Western Nations

"we are Sent here
for the purpose of to talk"

INTRODUCTION

Conflict in the Ohio Region

As described in the previous chapter, the Americans were able to come to terms with the Senecas and others of the Six Nations who remained in New York State. Others of the Six Nations retreated to new homes in Canada. In contrast to these Iroquois, the Indians of the Ohio region were unwilling to surrender claims to their territory and were ready to back up their own assertions of sovereignty and ownership with force. The continued presence of the British Indian Department and British troops at posts in the upper country gave these peoples hope (which tragically proved false) that their old ally the king would support their cause.

The new American republic first sought a military solution to the problem of Indian ownership of lands north of the Ohio. However, military operations in the west did not go well for the Americans. In the fall of 1790, Josiah Harmer led an invasion into Ohio. He burned several towns, but his fifteen-hundred-man army met strong opposition on October 18, 19, and 22. Over two hundred were killed and Harmar withdrew, although he claimed to have inflicted equal losses on the Indians (Coe 1968:297–98).

Harmar's losses made it clear that any attempt to dislodge the Ohio Indians from their homeland would be costly, so the Americans began to explore diplomatic solutions. Long before the

American Revolution, the Six Nations (particularly the Senecas) had acted as intermediaries between the western nations and colonial officials. It seemed logical to the Americans to again cast the Senecas in this role. In the summer of 1791 efforts were made to persuade Cornplanter to go into the west as an ambassador for the Americans, conveying a message of peace to the Indians of the Ohio region. Cornplanter was otherwise occupied, however; he had his own political fences to mend at home. Many Senecas needed to be convinced of the wisdom of his actions and the validity of Washington's guarantee that the Senecas would not be disturbed and that their lands would not be taken without their consent. In an effort to spur Cornplanter to the west, the American secretary of war, Henry Knox, sent Colonel Thomas Procter to the Seneca country. Procter was to convince Cornplanter to go on the embassy and to accompany him. As commander of the artillery on the Sullivan expedition, Procter was perfectly familiar with the Seneca territory.

Procter reached the Seneca villages and talked at length with Cornplanter and other Senecas. Although he found a delegation of Senecas was willing to accompany him farther west to deal with the Wyandot, Delaware, Wabash, and Miami Indians, he did not proceed. His excuse for not trying to meet with these nations was that the British at Niagara refused to provide a boat to transport him and the Seneca delegation to Sandusky. Possibly because his mission was classed as secret, Procter had no proof of his official status, so Colonel A. Gordon, commandant at Niagara, refused to give him use of a craft. Procter returned to Philadelphia (ASP, IA, 2:145–65).

In the meantime, Colonel Timothy Pickering met with some Senecas at Newtown, asking their neutrality and requesting that they send delegates to Philadelphia the next spring (Smith 1946: 98).

The autumn of 1791 proved even worse for the American military than the previous fall. General Arthur St. Clair met with disaster on November 4, 1791, suffering "perhaps the worst defeat ever inflicted on a white army by Indians" (Coe 1968:307).

He lost 630 killed, including Major General Richard Butler, who had accompanied Cornplanter and Blacksnake to New York in 1786, and numerous other officers of field rank (ASP, IA, 1:136–38).[1]

Although the task of rebuilding the ravaged United States military force on the frontier was given to Anthony Wayne, the government continued to work at a diplomatic solution using the Senecas and others of the Six Nations as intermediaries. Special efforts were extended to bring Joseph Brant into the peacemaking activities.

Conference at Philadelphia

The Americans raised western matters when they met with the Six Nations in Philadelphia in the spring of 1792. The Indians had agreed to come to Philadelphia to talk of schools and farming. On March 13, 1792, fifty representatives of the Six Nations arrived in Philadelphia. Washington spoke to them on March 23 and again on April 23. Both Timothy Pickering and Henry Knox also dealt with them there. Members of the Indian delegation were given presents for their wives and families at home and were "well fed, well lodged, and well clothed" (ASP, IA, 1:231) while in Philadelphia. Besides these "abundant presents" a $1,500 annuity was granted to them "for the purpose of attempting to civilize them" (ASP, IA, 1:229).

Accompanying these presents was a request that the Six Nations carry the United States position to the western Indians. They were "to assure these Indians of the sincere disposition of the United States to make peace with them" and to inform them of "an unhappy mistake prevailing among them, relative to the claims of the United States to the lands northwest of the Ohio." The Six Nations were told, "As you have in your hands the map of the country, you can explain it to them; and show what parts the United States have purchased at the treaties at fort M'Intosh and Muskingum [Finney], and at the mouth of the great Miami, which runs into the Ohio. That we claim no lands but what belong to the nations who sold to us, that we claim not a foot of the lands of any nation, with whom we have yet held no treaties. That if, at the treaties held with other nations, there has been any wrong doing, the United States will do what is right, and make ample compensation" (ASP, IA, 1:232). Pickering asked that the Six Nations meet with the western Indians at Fort Washington (now Cincinnati, Ohio), but the Senecas pointed out that it would be easier to meet away from the American military. This was agreed to, and the Senecas and others of the Six Nations left, "eager to work for peace" (Coe 1968:312–13).

Blacksnake's narrative captures the spirit if not the letter of these proceedings. The meeting with the Americans he describes took place in Philadelphia rather than Pittsburgh, and Joseph Brant was not there. The Mohawk chieftain was wooed separately, however, and he too agreed to aid the cause of peace at the proposed conference (Coe 1968:314). It is also possible that the episode mentioned in the previous chapter—Blacksnake's having his portrait painted in Philadelphia—took place while he was part of this delegation in 1792. It has been suggested, but not proved, that a portrait by John Trumbull, *The Young Sachem*, is of Blacksnake (Abler 1987). Despite his lapses of memory on these points, Blacksnake exhibits credible recall. Washington's initial speech as Blacksnake remembered it is remarkably close to the record we have of that address (see appendix 4). Blacksnake also recalls the food and gifts presented at this meeting. The Captain Cass who gave him five dollars is probably Captain Jonathan Cass, of the Second United States Infantry (later Second Sub Legion) (Heitman 1967:147). Cass appears to have had close contact with Cornplanter and other Senecas in 1792 (Knopf 1975: 47–48, 67).

Meeting the Western Nations at the Glaize

The Six Nations delegation did not leave for the conference until September, "owning to their frequent counselling, and dilatory manner of conducting business" (ASP, IA, 1:229). The delegation went in great force. This was not unwarranted. Both Anthony Wayne and the old Seneca chief Kayáhsotha? had voiced the opinion that Cornplanter's life was in danger (Coe 1968:317).

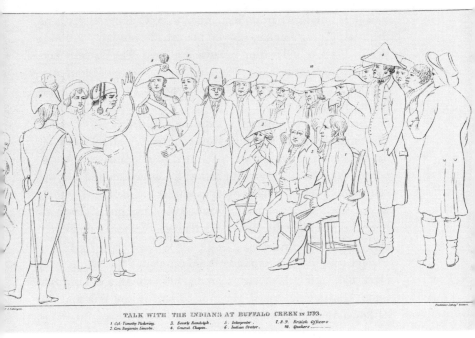

TALK WITH THE INDIANS AT BUFFALO CREEK IN 1793.

1. Col. Timothy Pickering.   3. Beverly Randolph.   5. Interpreter.   7. 8. 9. British Officers
2. Gen. Benjamin Lincoln.   4. General Chapin.   6. Indian Orator.   10. Quakers

Council at Buffalo, 1793 (Lincoln 1836, facing p. 176). Although no
event in Blacksnake's narrative can be ascribed to this council, the
drawing serves to represent these events. Henry Dearborn was told in
1838 that the orator was Cornplanter and the seated Indian with the
pipe was Farmer's Brother, but his informants (Captain Strong, Captain
Pollard, and Blue-Eyes) later changed their minds and indicated that
the orator was a Mohawk from Canada, "a particular friend of Capt.
Brant," named Flying Sky (Dearborn 1904:43, 143–45). Courtesy of the
Massachusetts Historical Society.

The council met from September 30 to October 8, 1792, on the Glaize (now Auglaize) River. Brant had been late in joining the Six Nations delegation because of illness. The peacemakers were not successful. The western Indians showed great contempt for the Six Nations and their subservience to the Americans (Smith 1946:106).

The Shawnees pointedly told the Iroquois delegates, "General Washington sent an army into our country, which fell into our hands. . . . The President of the United States must well know, why the blood is so deep in our paths." It was understandable, the Shawnees observed, that peace messengers could not make their way on these bloody paths. They noted with disdain that the path from the president to the Six Nations was "smooth and easy" (ASP, IA, 1:323–24).

Venturing on this diplomatic mission into the wilderness, Blacksnake fell in love with a young girl in the western Indians' camp. His uncle advised him not to pursue the relationship. Although in the manuscript she is identified as "osage," it seems likely that she was Shawnee. The Shawnees played a prominent part in these matters (they had become spokesmen for the western confederacy), yet curiously they are not mentioned in the manuscript. Since the "osage" are named in the narrative, and since it is not likely that the Osages were present, or that if present that they would have dominated the discussion, it is reasonable to conclude that "osage" refers to Shawnee. This is probably Benjamin Williams's error, not Blacksnake's.

The ill will that then clouded Shawnee–Six Nations relations was doubtless the reason Cornplanter advised Blacksnake to forget the girl.

Language was a problem at this council. The Six Nations and the Wyandots all spoke languages or dialects of the Iroquoian family. The rest of the participants (if the "osage" are really Shawnees) spoke Algonquian dialects. Blacksnake suggests that some of the Wyandots were bilingual and formed the link between the two linguistic groups.

Blacksnake is correct in the important role he ascribes to the rising young orator Red Jacket at the Glaize, but Brant did not arrive in time to participate in the council (Smith 1946:107).

Violence on the Trail to Ohio

Despite the failure to negotiate a peace at the Glaize in the fall of 1792, and despite the insults received there from the Ohio Indians, the Senecas continued in the role of intermediary, attempting to bring peace between the western nations and the Americans. Several conferences were held in an attempt to establish peace, but to no avail.

In July 1793, after a preliminary meeting at Niagara, the Shawnees, Wyandots, Miamis, and Delawares demanded at a conference on the Maumee that the Ohio River serve as the boundary between Indians and whites. Joseph Brant was there, and it is possible that this was the meeting Blacksnake was going to attend. An American delegation at Detroit demanded not only that the Stanwix, McIntosh, Finney, and Harmar treaties be upheld, but that more land cessions be made (Smith 1946:118–19; ASP, IA, 1.352–54). When the United States commissioners stated that they could not remove the whites already settled north of the Ohio, the Indians replied, "We know that these settlers are poor. . . . Divide, therefore, this large sum of money, which you have offered to us, among these people" so that they might remove themselves from the territory north of the Ohio (ASP, IA, 1:356). The American commissioners did not see this as a possible solution. Other councils in fall 1793 and spring 1794 similarly did not reach a peaceful settlement (Smith 1946:129–36).

Blacksnake does not seem to have attended these councils, probably because of the violent encounter with western Indians, whom he identifies as Delawares, while on his way to the peace conference. After this affair the Seneca party he was with probably saw no point, and considerable danger, in continuing their journey to meet with the western Indians.

These negotiations all came to naught in any case, and the western question reached a violent conclusion with Anthony

Wayne's victory at Fallen Timbers on August 20, 1794. The battle "was not an overwhelming or crushing defeat for the Indians," who suffered fewer than fifty deaths (Downes 1940:335). Wayne suffered comparable losses. However, the myth of British support that the optimistic Indians had been cherishing was destroyed. To be sure, a company of militia from Detroit fought beside the Indians, but when Indians retreating from the battle sought shelter in the British post, Fort Miami, its commander locked the gates (Downes 1940:335; Horsman 1964:102–4; Allen 1975:52). The Indians in the Ohio country could carry on the fight only if supplied with British arms; hence the ultimate doom of the Indian campaign to hold the west was settled with the Jay treaty of January 1795, in which the British agreed to give up their posts in the region. The next summer a peace treaty and major land cession was signed by the western Indians at Greenville, Ohio (Downes 1940:337).

[160] the Indians then commence to make homes all quarters with in the Bondies Before Cognized our form and Rule customs washington had send for us to come to his council at Pittsbourgh if I Regulected Right, it was in the year 1773 [1792]

Suposing for the purpose of asociate the western Indians So the Delegation was appointed 7 chiefs was appointed and one hundred and fifty warriors ingage with us to gaurd us from Dangers, while we was making preparation for going arrivel a messenger from Canada, the Indians of the canada wishes us to visit it them But as for us could not go, for we just engage for the invitation of the general washington, and we wishes Brant to go with us, and Sent for by his messenger So he went back with in ten Days Brant was to be present or appeared the country, So he was appeared in the 8th Day from the time was Sent for him he was then Ready to go, 25 more warriors on his side, So making in all the warriors 175 & 8 chiefs So we Started about the middle of the summer before we come to the Small village called Erie 15 more Indians over [161] took us who are engage to go with us, there was 12 onandagas Tuscaroras 2 Cayuga 1 with the adision making 199 Souls, from State of Newyork

So we treveraled on the same old path we use to treveraled on the away to Pittsbourgh, and took us Several Days to get there after we came within 3 miles we camp out about a middle of the Day for to Retired, till we larnt more from washington or some of his commissioner for the purpose and the objects of calling us together with him &c after we eat our Dinners, uncle cornplanter Send me and Some others to go with me to go Down town & see washington in the after noon when we come to the Public house I have to Showed my paper for the Recommandation and want it to see washington, the landlord tell us what house washington was in, So we went on & See him I had white young man for our interpreter when I came to the house, where man Directed us to go, man Standing on the Door with well armed, I ask to my interpreter to ask the Door keeper whither the washington was in the house—he wanted to know what we want of him Replied I told him I want it to see him on Busniss we was soon called in to the house & Saw him was glad to See Each other he ask me how many was in our company I answered him 199 Souls of the five Nations Delegations on Expressed of his Request coming here very well Said he be contained, about 3 days I will meet with you at court house at 9 oclock A.M. Said he, he then give us order on provision Store to get all we wanted to eat So went out after we got through talking, went to the Provision Store and got all we could carried on our backs with flour & pork tea Chorklaw [chocolate] & sugar &c and Started for our camp— after we Back to the camp, Some the Boys was gone out to woods to hunt Some fowl for us to eat for supper, So we injoyed very well During the 3 days our health was good, the Experation of 3 days up we went at the time appointed hour, there was Several carriages met us on the a way, chiefs had to Ride as well as any gentlemanship Althought our clothes was Dirtty the carriages stoped at clothing Store there we got Each [162] of cloths, after got New Dress we went on to the court house, washington then with us when we went in to the court house all most one half the house we occupied Washington wanted the chiefs to sit together to face to face the Seneca chiefs was seated by themselves we was 5 of us chiefs of the Seneca Nation

Washington asks theirs names to be called

So went on tell, Cornplanter John obaile, Redjackett gov Blacksnake Captain Strong & [Young stroked out] chiefs warrior was the Senecas,

Joseph Brant on Mohawk & gr go Da nr yeh onanda—and the 2 chiefs of the Tuscarora Nation & the Cayuga Chief of their Nation I could not mentioned their english names—

our men was seated behind us

Washington called to order, he Says to us

I have called upon you for assistant making Peace and treaty with the western Indians of the Several tribes of Different Nations of Indians, for they are Determined to continue war with us, we Do not want it to Shed Blod any more with them if posible, I have Sent a Small company to make treaty with those Nation But Refuse to Receive the offered to them, But they Distroyed the company But afew escape I therefore thought would have you to try & see whither you could make apeace with them with out any more firghting and Shed Blood, if they Receive you offered come Back to me I will appointed a commissioner to make a treaty with them and be peace war no more among the North america people be peace all Nations, and give you a letter for them and Stipulation of written and with the united States Sealed and I will furnish you all Necessary to take long with you, you Shall not Suffered on my account tryed to make peace every Nation of Indians you will come to, if they threatened you, get out their a way if you cant, if you could not be able to got out their away you must Defaned yourselves and be prepared for that purpose or gave [163] me a Notice as soon as possible if Requirer more men with you to get long with, I will Sent you men as many as you want and Naval force &c

this is all I have to say at Present, if you wanting things more let me Know it

after he got throught talking we consulted Each other and we concluded hold a council By ourselves in Regard to what washington Says to us, So Brant Rose and said unto washington that we will give him answered in Next Day in the afternoon So adjourned

after we arrive to our camps we then held privit metting concerning the Request by washington, we all agreed that we Should obeyed him as friendship that we thought it Should be our Duty to try to make peace with the human race the same our own collored Red men that we might be able to make peace by the help of the great Spirit, that God is able to help any case to Do good &c Next Day we went Down to Pittsbourght at the time of hour to meet washington at court house, we found him on hand—cornplanter then Rose and Says answered that we come to conclusion that we should go where he ordered us to go, if Danger or no Danger, we Shall Do the Best in our own abilities, for to Do good every Nation that we might talk with, for to Declared peace to Shed blood no more, for all this we feel Doutful, they granting us, if they Do not Receive our Disirious it will not be a fualt to laid on our heads & we also wishes to go as soon as we could get Ready, and back again as Soon as posible and bring the News from them and Shall be faithful, Serventship &c

Washington than Rose and says

I feel happy for you Exceptant of my wishes I will furnishes you all Necessaries to take long with you as I told you before, money & provisions and if you want Saile Down stream I furnish you boat to go Down on as far as you See fit any time you got Ready to Start and you Shall be prepared all thing before [164] you Departure, with in three hours the Stipulation will be ready for you to take long with you to Show those Indians whatever Nations you meet with as I told you yesterday, and if you want any more arms I will give order on gun shops and get what you want or I go with you &c

Mr Brant Requested Washington he Should go with us to the Shop, So Says not much more only we all went Down Stairs with washington and lead us to the gun Shops, Redjacket was Next to washington as we went along on Side walk I was far behind, after the chiefs got all they wanted I went in washington ask me why I was not long with him when he went in that I might have my choce before got out many I told him I Did not want put myself too far for I am younger the Rest of the Chiefs, he took my hand and lead me to another Shop and took his own choce to give to me 2 good pistols and Rifle and all what belonging to the Rifle and an Sword, and Captain Cass while we was in the Shop he hand it me five Dollars in pieces, the chiefs and warriors was Satisfy what they want and Returned to court house the written of Stipulation or Recommendation of our object was about Done in the afternoon Brant & Cornplanter Redjacket and myselfe went in and Brant tooke the paper and went back to camp for the Night

Next morning we start Down Town for to go on Down the River, on a way going in the town 3 captains met us for the purpose of let us know where to fined the Boat for us to Rid Down on, on monongahella Shores there was five boats was Ready for us to get into to hold about 220 men and with the baggerst So we Start it, took us Several Days before we got Down to little Muskingum River and went upon that River Several miles where we placed our Boat & camp out there 3 Days before we pursued on the Indians trail, yet see no Indians family or hunting men [165] first Day travel from this place we Expecting them to see Some the Indians settlement long the adge of the prairies, Some Distance from the River of Muskingum, Something like 15 miles travel that Day before we come to the Indians Settlement Something like 8 families together into one place, that appeared there was 2 Distant Nation joined together in wondering about their country, as we approach them the Squaws came out their tents met us in Friendship wanted us to supper with them or to Rused corn or Stayed till their men Return from hunting So we considerate might be Effect the influance of them in our object to communicated with in good manners So we went on and Built tents for the Night, long Side of their tent, we Soon see their men coming home During while our men was fixing tents for us and it look thought that might have a Rain that Night I Stayed with the Nearest Niethbor of these Strangers, I have been wishes I could talked their Language, that I might courted of the Squaw which took it a like to her truble on is that I could not understand what She Says to me She appeared that She feels the Same my feelling in Relation to talking with me, very friendly way of their using with me I wanted to know whither She is

married or promiss or not But truble we could not understand
Each other what we talking about it, I feel Desirious to larnt
Something about her, for She was the handsomes that I never See
among my own people—

I ask Captain Hudson to go and talk with her if he could
understand their language I told him in Secret that should like to
merry her ıf posıble could be Done without interfered our Businiss and camping if She wanted go with us throught journey
& home, in During this conversation with Hudson this young
Squaws father had just come in to our tent he appointed at me
with fore finger wanted me to come over their tent, I felt concern
about it Right off and wanted it to knowe what it was miant
called me to their tent, I then ask capt [166] hudson to go long
with me over to their tent he Says he would So we went over, it is
not But a very few Step between our tent and their, after we was
Set Down in their tent, Capt Hudson than talk with the old man I
Suppose this tribe of Indians they was what they called osage
Indian But Hudson could not understand But little of their language, most of the conversation they had by motions of their
hand we got long that way in order to find it out of all the mianing
of what we Says to them and what they Says to us, and at last we
understant they want it us to go to a certain place that Evenings
for to show us their council tent with some of our company
might go with us So I went Back to our fire and called several of
our men to go long with us to see these osage Dannsing tents So
them started with us when we come to the long tent it was made
of Some Stem of weeds something like 10 foot long of these
Stems made the tents off and covered the same Stuff, this osage
chief he made by Signs for wanted to Dance that Night we agreed
that Some of us might come and See so we went Back again when
we got back to their tent where this young Squaw live I talk with
old man about his Daughter By Signs asking him whither She is
married or promiss for her husban Near I could Larnt that she is
not married and Never was I said no more to him or her about it
till uncle cornplanter I ask him advice concerning of my having

lover to that young Squaw he Says to me that I had better let her a
lone and Speak no more about it, &c I than said no more about it
marriage I have felt sorrow

Redjacket was then, Speaking, and Notifying his companions
that we will have communication with these Osage Indians immidiately we Raisen in the morning concerning of our objects
making peace with all Indians Nations and washington wishes to
firght no more, and we was sent by him for that Businiss [167]
this Night have great Deal of green corn to Rused on fire Side,
Some of us went back to the Dance, as they wanted us to come So
we went on to their Dance and Saw their perform Differant as we
Do and Regulations Seem much strictly attention of their man-
agers on Dancing party and the Squaws also Seem they had as
much to Do as than an man to Regulate on feemal party, then on
the part of make man commanded them During in their Dance,
we have Stayed 3 hours in their Dance we want it to go back we
wanted to Sleep in order for to Rised early in the morning

Next morning Sun 3 hour High we got together Brant tooke
the paper and Read it to them by Signs and motions in order for
them to understand the language of the paper and they understood it well and they give answered that they would go home to
the council for the purpose of getting fully understanding, after
closed we took up our pagages and and Start it on our course, the
osage Indians Start on after us, we Did not see any more Indian
that Day, and the Next Day in afternoon we come to the thick
Settled of Indians where we made a Stop & Brant Redjacket Cornplanter went among the Different Nations to inquire whither
could be found interpreter of Different languages, they found
one of the wyantot Indians that could talk our language well
also found kikapoos could understand wyantots also found chippewas could understand kikapoos also found Pottawatameh understand chippewas also found osage could under Pottawatameh
all these 13 Nations are talk and use Difference languages we
have to transfered one to another in order to understand it all
what we have to say to them in councils &c

Notice was given out a mong them to hold a council opened by us on the Next Day morning yet they Did not know what object is Several of their chiefs come to us made Some inquiries of our object or what our attented to Do, they was Expected to imbraced to carried out plain of our war fair, and they was quit Friendly to us and gave us vensions and corn bread to eat for our suppers, after Suppers they begin to tell their wars with the whites and how [168] they manage Such battle took place, and so long time and So many time within the year how many they kill and how many they lost life &c and where, and what Nation is the most in their number and who least of their number and who the most brave man among the officiers and who is the most cuccessfull in Different times previous During 8 years &c this is if I Regulected Right in the year 1778 [1792] { in the fall

Next Day about 10 oclock AM the people begin gether together, Chief has ordered their man to built a fire Near big Ellem tree where Sheded fine green grass under the Shed tree after the fire was built

old chief called the interpreter to order their Seats between Six Nation & the 13 Nations 1 Mohawk 1 wyantotes 1 kikapoose 1 chippewas 1 Pottawatamehes 1 Osages was Several languages that they could talked and understanded So given us anabled to understanding the whole communications &c

Redjacket a Rose and Said unto the Public, Friends & Brothers it was the will of the Great God that we Should meet together this Day he orders alt things, for his kindness given us anabled to spend this our council he has taken his garment from before the Sun, and caused it to Shine with brightness on us, our eyes are opened, that we See clearly; our ear are might unstopped, that we might be able to understand Distinctly the words that we may Spoken to you for all these favours we thank the Great God, and him only—

Joseph Brant Rose and tooke the Decuration of the peace and Readed to them throught interpreter one to another and after one after in order to understand to every Tongue, after Reading throught he then went on and Speak in behalf of the Six Nation we will now Speak as one united of the six Nations, and Battle field and in the forests and valleys wars is now closed with america and made Reserve large tract of land sufficient for all the Six Nation to Remained and hunting ground and [169] traping pons and fishing Rivers and we are Satisfied what Remians in our control we are Decerve from great Britain in transution in our Bloody wars with our whites Neithbors on north america and we found that we Shall have to Exchange fathers, we have one on this Island hereafter for our protection If we only Submitted to entering a treaty with all Nations for peace war no more to Shed Blood no more God will granted and will give us in future prosperity, we therefore would Say to you all that we had Better to think about what it could be Done to continue war gainst the whites and then to Droped where now are and Save life, and same from Frighten to our women & children, we are Sent here for the purpose of to talk all with you to see whither you will agreed with us which we feel Desirious that you would agreed with us without controversary among you, whatever you given us answered we Shall Return with the tidings to washington I will Repeat, your war fires, covered up with Earth to See no more, an we created new father Near at home for our protection all for foregners people may come unto us if to be any Danger to be another contest, between great Britain & america hereafter we therefore beg you all to come to conclusion to be agreeable with us in our object

we considered this is impartand object to settled up all the Difficulties and Efflications and Sevire feellings Sores hearts we say to washington we asked Each other, what have we Done to Deserve Such Severe Chastisement, our Hacked & tomehawks & nifes, to Barried up under the ground to Rase agrainst any Nation no more or to be both pursuant By the great Britain government, for all we have been helping him, he now gave up to washington

washington bring So kindniss to asked us for Settlement to firght no more, immidiately after the British Defeated and Delivered his Red children to america people, that they may Do as they see fit with us, or to Distroyed or Save [170] them to be Slave or to set us free So we are yet free from Bondage to Day, although we have not completed or to closed with all the treaties we attended to with the town Distroyer that was washington and we are intended to finished which is undone with washington our Six Nations of Indians Residing Eastern continent of the america I will now leaved with you own Judge concerning of it &c ———

one of the osage chief got up and Said we will considerate on the Subject, we shall Returned ourselved tomorrow morning and you must Remained when we Do Return

Second Day about 8 oclock A.M. met together on the Same ground and the fire was Builted early in the morning this assembly more people got together than it was yesterday men and woman and children as far as I could See with half a mile from Each a way on all Directions, it appeared to moving toward the mids of the assembly, in one hour and ahalf time got all Seated and quited

The old chief of Osage Indian

A Rose and saw we are now Ready given you our view on the subject you Said before us yestaday God has given to his western of you Red children to united once more all agreed of the 13 Nations and 13 Different languages of the Red man God made us all and Earth and made men upon it to multiply the Earth and animals given all to his Red children, he said no more Set Down another one got up and Said I am one of the kikapoos war officer for Several tribe of adjacents &c

Friends and Brothers I was Requested to ask you to let me have that Stipulation was Read to us yestaday in which intended for us to Received—[171] I therefore now wanted So I might be able to give you a Short work in answered, &c

he made a few Steps toward us for to take the paper

Brant Rose he says to us,

Shall we give up the written to him Redjacket Say yes, I Speak
no till we further understood, But then Brant thought himself
Best to give up the written to the warrior, handed it him, and
the warrior took it and step back to his place afew feet from the
fire side, they passed afew words amongst themselves, he soon
turned Round toward us and Said Solato River on the head quarters of waters

Brother this paper was written by Town Distroyer, and we also
understand that he wanted to make treaty with the Red man to
firght no more for he has already settled with the Red Coat man
and also we understand that you are the Six Nations is already
Settled with washington I will called you very coward Red men
you may tell washington that I have tooked this paper and cast
into fire, we will continuly Stand firmly protected—for our lands
and Rights we will Die before we would give up to our enemy we
have felling toward our people and Rights, which God given us
and we feel it was honour by the sight of the almighty—Remember how the whites Serve us the time first white man Discovered
our Island how they cheat us, not only cheat it us in Drade, but
all even in Policy, they found us Ignorant, we thought them they
are good people and they was very small and we have amerciful
upon them and gave them good things they gave us poison in
Return—you Deserve punishment you outh to cut off, for fall in
with white man, But we conclute you Should go Back home and
mind your own Businiss and we will Do the Same, So he no more
to say

the assembly arise this afternoon they look thought they are
anemy to us, So we got away Best a way we [172] could from this
place for home Straight way to franklin creek made no stop
before we got franklin only Nights and getting vension fried up
for provision on the away nothing els for Several Days traval

nothingels But vension to eat as we went a long these 13 Nations of Seloto River threatening our lives Considerable before we left them, But cornplanter told them that we Did not come here to firght with them, But if they see fit, to begin upon we Shall try to Defented ourselves as far as we was able, But first Disirious to get away in peace So got a way without firghtin,

after we came to franklin creek we Stayed a rested a few Days, then started in upon this creek followed till got up midfield now called So, on to Erie on the lake Shore we travaled on the lake Shore to Buffalo at home and we all got home Save But one Died on the away coming home, we than had nothing to do this about counciling Businiss only what Suprise to think what we have been in to it being our object was objected By the western Indians, our people thought to let it Rest, till Next Spring in June 1774 [1793?]

Nothing Done in our Regulations amongs the Several Nations of Indians Residing within the State of New York in the winter 1773 [1792?] { in the Spring 1774 [1793?]

A council held at Blackrock near Buffalo, opened by the United States commissioners for the purpose of communicating with the Western Indians once more for us to go to western Indians to make peace with them, of Several tribes of Indians kept anoying to their enemy or to the whites, after the Six Nations was make a treaty with washington &c about at this time our people was making the preparation a Small part of Each Nation to go over to canada, and upon this, washington would have us or the Six Nation of the Iroquois to go west once more to make peace &c So we have taken the consideration of the Desirious and the Request of washington, the consult is [173] of the Six Nation that we would tried once more, So Return the Request favour the following proceeding, So the commissioner Represented a written of Recommendation of Businiss and the Stipulation peace of washington, so finish completed on the part of the united States & New York Indians agreed that they would got Ready within a month, So closed ——

at this time the Indians people that who was swayed to go over to canada, they was about Ready for Starting, But so happen that washington wishes us to go to upper part the lake Erie, put them out from going over at present, I was then Ready any time called But the Rest of the enage [engaged] indians going to the western called for peace with them, General of the Six Nation agreed to let them Remained that who are enage to go over to Canada

about twenty Day after this, the company got Ready to go 200 men in the company Started, I have took it 50 men to my commanded in company, John Docker has took 50 men in his command cornplanter & Brant took charge of the Rest of the company of what we called common company those that the other two companies was choce one, generally good hunter on the a way journey, for the Support the whole compenion, our journey took the old path which we use to travalled Before Several time and know Every part of the country, when we came to franck creek Near allegany River, I think about 100 of us stoped for the purpose of Dressing Deer skins for making their Markinsus, we the hunter fellows went to the River, as we approaching the village of franklin, we come cross a large Drove of Elks, we parsued them and killed about fifteen of them, there we camp out to Dress our vension and Dryed, So we would easily carried with us on the away, But however we had to stayed till the other company over tooke us, So we might get help carring long with our vension which we Exspect when ever we Do go, not stop again till we Reached to upper sandusky, we had to stay at this place two Days before the other company Reaches us, on the third [174] day all got together again, and went on for head quarter of now called Big Beaver creek, the calculation is the striaght course to our appointment as we on the away toward Evening come cross Several of Indians camp out before us or has been for some times, as we approach them, about 10 or 15 Rods from them, they Begin 2 Indians Run, as we continue toward them very soon other Run So one after another I begin to Step lifly toward them, when we come to their fire, them was four

Stayed Near fire side Siting on the ground as we come Surounded them, one of our company took guns & other arms, they appeared to be willing to be taken as prisoner of war they soon whispered one another an instance they Jump against our men and cut throught and Run all their might and fired at them 2 fall 2 got a way from us I followed a Short Distance till I was satisfied they are not wounded or hurd them and wheel back again, as I was Returning, first I know gun fired on the laft side of me they made 3 shots at me never touch, and they give Indians hoobs [whoops] and they out I had fired at them I brok one fellow leg he fall as I came to him he spoke in Deleware language I cannot understand as took Examinate his wound in his leg I Discovered no cure, I just took my hatchet over his head, and say nothing more about it, and I Dragg him toward the other ones, and Barried them that Evening and Retire for the Night, these Indians near could larnt according to what he spoke to me in Deleware language So I should considerate they must be Deleware Indians from the west they are anemy to us and they know it too before we come Near to them Else they would not Run as they Did I suppose that they have been at this place for some time they have had considerable of good venison on hand So we have agood Dish out of it, for our suppers and also Suppose was on their a way to attack the country families to ward Pittsbough we Stayed two Nights at this Place, and our captain ordered us to Return Back

Chapter Six

The Revelation of Handsome Lake

viously held by the Senecas. Land sales were made easier, for under severe pressure the principle of unanimity in council was abandoned. Blacksnake's home village of Conawagus had been included in the lands sold in the Phelps and Gorham purchase of 1788. One cannot know what caused Blacksnake and his relatives to move to the Allegheny, but as thousands of acres were surrendered to land speculators, the Senecas retained only four reservations with land enough to support a large population. These were Allegany, Buffalo Creek, Cattaraugus, and Tonawanda. Undoubtedly kin ties and political allegiances were important in the decision as to who settled where, and Cornplanter played a key role in drawing followers beyond the Allegany Reservation to his personal grant in Pennsylvania a few miles downriver. For whatever reason, Blacksnake was there, on Cornplanter's own land, in the decade when most of the Senecas' land base disappeared.

The continual pressure white authorities were placing upon the Senecas to give up land was the cause of considerable tension between the Indians and the American officials. The treaties of Fort Stanwix and Fort Harmar had ceded lands outside the state of New York and also lands west of Buffalo Creek. Within New York State, the right to purchase lands lay, strange as it may seem, with Massachusetts. Although the new federal government had sole right to purchase Indian lands outside the territories of the founding thirteen states, the states retained the right to purchase lands granted them in their prewar colonial charters. Both New York and Massachusetts had claim through their original colonial charters to the territory owned by the Senecas. Their dispute over which body had the right to purchase and govern this territory even threatened the union of the thirteen new American states. The compromise worked out gave sovereignty to New York but gave to Massachusetts the preemptive right to Seneca lands. In other words, if the Senecas chose to sell land, they could do so only to Massachusetts, which in American law possessed the sole right to purchase.

A group of private citizens tried to circumvent Massachusetts's preemptive right by leasing Seneca lands, but these leases were declared invalid. Massachusetts elected to obtain cash by selling speculators its right to Seneca lands. Oliver Phelps and Nathaniel Gorham purchased the preemptive rights from Massachusetts for $1,000,000 in the currency of that commonwealth. In July 1788 Phelps negotiated a sale of land (known as the Phelps and Gorham purchase) at Buffalo Creek. The Senecas complained to Washington that they were swindled in the transaction (see chap. 4 above and appendix 3).

In 1794 the Senecas at Burnt House were visited by the government surveyor, John Adlum. Complaints about land transactions were at the forefront of Seneca thought, and some advocated war. It is possible that Blacksnake was among the young men who gave their opinion of surveyors and the message from the secretary of war that Adlum read: "When the interpreters, had finished translating the first paragraph—The young indians on the beams

above, saluted me with an univer[sal] roar, *vulgarly called farting.*
I heard several of the elderly woemen exclaim Yaugh-ti-Yaughti
which was as much as to say—*shame, scandalous*—I made a
pause, ruminating within my self how I should act, and concluded to read another paragraph, and received another salute of
the same kind" (Kent and Deardorff 1960:304–5).

General Anthony Wayne's victory over the western Indians at
Fallen Timbers that year and the refusal of the British to aid their
former allies in that battle did much to quell the hostility so
openly expressed by the Senecas. In addition, the Senecas obtained some concessions from the United States. The two sides
came to agreement in the fall of 1794 at Canandaigua, with
Timothy Pickering negotiating for the Americans. This Canandaigua treaty guaranteed the Senecas lands in New York State
west of the Phelps and Gorham purchase (thus returning to them
some lands relinquished in the treaties of Fort Stanwix and Fort
Harmar). The United States acknowledged these "to be the property of the Seneka nation; and [that] the United States will never
claim the same, nor disturb the Seneka nation nor any of the Six
Nations, or of their Indian friends residing theron and united
with them, in the free use and enjoyment thereof: but it shall
remain theirs, until they choose to sell the same to the people of
the United States, who have the right to purchase" (Kappler
1901–41, 2:35).[1]

When the Canandaigua treaty was negotiated in 1794, peace
was not yet firm on the western frontier, although the handwrit-
ing was on the wall following the battle at Fallen Timbers. Three
years later, however, there was no danger of a continuing Indian
war. Hence the Senecas were not in nearly as strong a position
politically as they had been. The famous American financier
Robert Morris had obtained the Massachusetts preemption right.
He exercised his right to purchase lands west of the Phelps and
Gorham purchase in 1797. The Americans insisted that the Senecas abandon their old principle of unanimity and instead accept
the will of a majority of chiefs. Thomas Morris, the son of Robert
(the elder Morris was locked in his home to escape creditors),

skillfully manipulated the meeting and bribed key Senecas (see Wallace 1970:179–83). Of the 4 million acres the Senecas held at the opening of negotiations, they retained fewer than 200,000. These 311 square miles consisted of eleven reservations, the four largest being Buffalo Creek, Tonawanda, Cattaraugus, and Allegany.

Other lands in Pennsylvania were held personally by Cornplanter. Pennsylvania, "to fix his attachment to the state," had granted him 1,500 acres. The three tracts he chose were surveyed in 1795. One was sold that year. Another, near Oil City, Cornplanter is said to have sold in 1818, although the transfer of title is clouded. The third tract, surrounding the village of Tyonoh-sate·keh or Burnt House (see map 1), was where he and his followers, including Blacksnake and Cornplanter's half-brother Handsome Lake, chose to live (Wallace 1970:171–72). Important events in the religious history of the Senecas (and the Iroquois generally) took place in that settlement on the Allegheny River.

Handsome Lake's Vision

Submitting to American dominance must have been a humiliating experience for the proud Senecas. Their British and Loyalist allies had recently lost a bitter war, and the Senecas and Cayugas had seen their homeland invaded. Sullivan's expedition was a severe economic blow, destroying most of their substantial homes, their fields, and their orchards. Once a dominant political force in the northeast, they now saw themselves subject to the dictates of the Americans. Their settlements were essentially refugee camps that have been somewhat overdramatically termed "slums in the wilderness" (Wallace 1970:184). When the British surrendered at Yorktown in 1781, their military band played "The World Turned Upside Down"; the state of affairs must have seemed far worse to the Senecas.

To help the Senecas move from this deprived social situation, the Society of Friends began work near Cornplanter's settlement. Through personal contact with Quakers in Philadelphia, Cornplanter convinced members of that denomination of the desirability of helping the Senecas on the road to "civilization." Quakers had served as observers at the Canandaigua treaty of 1794. Cornplanter had sent his eldest son, Henry O'Bail, to school with them. In 1798 the Quakers began taking schooling to the Senecas (Deardorff 1951:85).

The Quakers were present, then, when Handsome Lake, the half-brother of Cornplanter, fell ill, recovered, and reported a vision. These Quakers provide us with a description of those significant events (see Wallace 1952). An oral history of what happened is still recited in Iroquois longhouses in New York and Canada, the text being called in English the Code of Handsome Lake (Parker 1913). Blacksnake too was a witness and participant in these events. His own description is found here.[2] Wallace notes (1970:359) that these sources agree on the essentials and disagree only on details.

It was on June 15, 1799, that Handsome Lake's daughter sought out Blacksnake to tell him that her father was dead. Blacksnake rushed to the house and found a warm spot on the man's chest, and Cornplanter confirmed this. Handsome Lake ("good lake" in Blacksnake's narrative) recovered and related what he had seen and been told while he was dead.

Handsome Lake's doctrine of religious and social reform, based on this and later visions, forms a classic example of a revitalization movement (see Wallace 1961, 1970). The sachem, who had led a drunken existence in the past, repented his sins and preached the "new" religion, which quickly took root and flowered among the Iroquois. This new religion combined Christian elements with traditional practices, social revolution with ritual reformation, and it was adopted by the demoralized Indians. Handsome Lake preached against such evils as alcohol, land sales, and birth control and advocated male participation in agriculture and the strengthening of the nuclear family.

In his teachings Handsome Lake received considerable support from the Quakers and other whites. Letters expressing President Thomas Jefferson's approval of Handsome Lake and his teachings did much to raise the prophet's status among the Senecas. "The Indians regarded them (and they still do) as the Government's endorsement of Handsome Lake and his teachings. . . . These official endorsements elevated him to a position above even that of Cornplanter, up to then about the only Seneca able to command such credentials" (Deardorff 1951:95).

Handsome Lake was not without opposition from conservative Senecas. Foremost among his opponents was Red Jacket. "The angels then conveniently revealed that Red Jacket was a schemer and a seller of land and an unhappy wretch doomed to carry burdens of soil through eternity as a punishment for perfidy. This was enought to create a prejudice among the Indians and one that lasts to this day among all classes of the reservation Iroquois" (Parker 1913:11).

The competition between the old religion and the "new way" of Handsome Lake was short-lived, and soon the Senecas fell into two religious camps—professing Christians and followers of Handsome Lake. They still do today.

Handsome Lake preached on Cornplanter's Grant until he quarreled with his half-brother. Then, in 1803, he and his followers moved to Coldspring on the Allegany Reservation. A worsening political situation at Coldspring led Handsome Lake to move to Tonawanda, where he served as spiritual leader. Blacksnake remained at Allegany. After unsuccessfully opposing Seneca entry into the War of 1812, Handsome Lake died on a visit to the Onondagas in 1815. He is buried on that reservation.

The narrative describes how Handsome Lake was stricken, demonstrates the community's concern for the ill sachem, and tells the message Handsome Lake gave when he came out of his trance. That the narrative moves to the third person in reference to Blacksnake leaves open the possibility that Blacksnake himself may not have dictated the text to Williams. However, the important role Blacksnake played in these events and the importance of the Code of Handsome Lake in later Iroquois history makes it imperative that this early fragmentary version of the code be included here in Blacksnake's story.

The Seneca condolence belt (NYSM Catalog no. 37431). Harriet M. Converse reported that this belt once belonged to Governor Blacksnake (Clarke 1931:97; Fenton 1971:458). The belt is approximately 1 meter long and 5 centimeters wide. It has been suggested that purple wampum suggests mourning and that it was used in councils when new sachems were raised up to fill the positions of those who had died (Clarke 1931:97). This belt has been on exhibit loan for the past decade from the New York State Museum to Seneca-Iroquois National Museum, Salamanca, New York (George R. Hamell, personal communication, March 4, 1988). Photograph courtesy of the New York State Museum, the University of the State of New York.

[226] The year (1799) Certifies that from a personal Aquanted called good lake—that year he was Sick Confined on his bed he was not able to Rise from the bed and it hapen one morning He was called to Door and the momont he felt So that he is able to Rise and go to Door. he Did So—Saw three [or four?—both have been written] person Standing by the Door and And Take hands with him all—and comminced That he felt vend [faint] and fall Down on the ground By theirs feets and lost his Senses—one of the person That uncle to him Saw this hapen and Saw these Three [again, "Four" seems to have been originally written, then "Three" written over this] person But in the momont they are gon and He went where the good lake is laid, and when He came onto him ask if he is Dead had no answered And he took Examination and Discovered his blath are Gon—and he went nears Next Neighbour Notivefied them That his uncle is Dead and got them to help to take the Body into the house and Did So layed Back to his bed. And give all the Rest notice in the morning and they Gather together and watched the Dead one—and the Council conclud that they Shall put into his grave Next Day at noon— and when the next Day Did come about Seven olock before noon they took his body ento The coffin and they Examinate again and put theirs Hands on to his bosum and they Did feel little wram But Still had no bit of the heart, and the Council Conclud again to let it till Next Day—that is the thirt Day the time called to Death upon good lake, the Thirt Day Did Come, But Still his bosum continues Wram and than the Council Desids that shall put off Till the fouth Day morning come to his Senses again— immediately heard Sound from Him—Saying I have been Dis-dress Every Sence four years Ago, the year (1705) [1795] (Sick and painfull till I am called To Death and Now I came to life again— and I have Been with the happy Company for the angel of The Lord Descended from Heaven—and came to us To teach the Disobedience children—four Days ago Morning I Saw three an-

gel came to my Door [226¹] And Nock and Called upon me to
come to them I Did So—and handed theirs hands to me and I put
Myself Down on the ground for theirs beautifulness Countenance that they was all like and the Raiments Difference corrious and Beautifuls Fearas [tiaras?]—Difference corrious also
wore on Theirs head and Spoke to me Saying go with us and they
took my hand and went with Them when we Came to the beauti-
ful garden and they say to me here is the garden Seat that we will
take Sat and Rast and give More Notice what we presended for To
you for almighty See all Wacked [?] the world and teach ye the
truth and Duties and a right to Do in your countenments on the
Stringh of the world Which your occupied and all affect which
will be Seen in Broad—and taken the outh of the people on
Earth—and the Judgment Seat—and now we Will Say to you, you
will go Back and teach The people where in to your nation for
their great Complaint is now in their hearts—that must be Altered for Sake of our god above

1 Commandmints³ Concering of the ardent Spirit use That
has been known that has been Said By the Prophet & the angel
that Descended from heaven—Saying The ardent Spirits made
for the great King over the Great waters, therefore ye the Nation
Shall not use for ye have had many good people Desstroyed by
using the ardent Spirit in your nation and leading you to Destruction and missary—for verily I say unto you layed side that article
for our lord given you an opportunity to Repend for you Shall
Receive the wise Discended from almighty

2 Commandments⁴ it is Enormous things and believe Such
animals amongs the human being that is What called wicthes,
Evil act, which has been Enormous things [226²] This is the
person Cleips behind the houses and watching The opportunity
to which he or The Enemies to person To wicth or give pision—
again ye have heard that It hath been Said by them of old for-
fathers, that is Truth it is Such practice amongs the Nation and
whosoever practice that Enormous article⁵ and not Repend Shall
be perish all that members according The Lord Son of god will
Direct—and you will have two Sickness in your time—But the

angels which Descended from heaven Saying to you Repend using that article and you Shall be Recieved again

3 Commandments,[6] it is truth that it hath been Said Enormous Things and believe as Such article amongs the people that Is what Called Evil false between male and female That it hath been prove that hath practice amongs The Nation, and hath many Souls Distroyed by Evil false between wife and husband— Whosoever uses the article between the wife or Husband Distroyed the person constitution of Minde and Discorded Sensible, whosoever uses the Article and not Repend and Shall be perish according to the almighty god will Direct—But the angels Which Descended from heaven Saying to you—whosoever Uses the article Repend that practiceing for having Yet an opportunity to Remove that article you Shall Received the offored of our god above and Do as your Promises for theirs is the Kingdom of heaven

4 Commandments[7] that Whosoever marry lawfully and bind them Seff to live together as long as They leive for this is the law of god, for Sake of Multipling the world But whosoever Break one These Commandments—and it hath been commited Such things—to put away his wife for little a cause, and leave his family Sometimes for Sake him to get him a new wife, and She Did also and the children Suffored for the consequence of their Doing it so—god seen all these things [226[3]] and he feels Sorrow—and anger to them, and He will put them out of comfortable of leaving And they Shall be put into punishment in hell fire But the angels which Descended from heaven Saying yet your have an opportunity to Repend and use all your Stringht and all your minde and Do all your promises and think of your god for his kindness, for he will give you a Room in the heaven

5 Commandments[8] male practice for the angels teach us Saying you must fulfiled all your promises for to a Wrong and commited to wrong to female by male after they are married—that is a man gose away from home—for Some Business over Cross the Woods over hills to othe Nation or tribes when that he meeted

with them—and he is Ready looking after Woman, by telling
that he hath no wife—But he is telling a false to her But I say unto
you this man Telling false to his own heart and to god and
whosoever Dose that things, he is not consider the almigthy Seen
over him and the angels also when he to commit adultery—and
Sin it before god—But here is the angels which Descended from
heaven Saying yet you have an opportunity to Repend With all
your Stringht and all your minde and think of your god, for he is
kind and will give you a Room in heaven

6 Commandments[9] female practice to Service to Words to
husband that hath been Said the old time It is truth on the Subject of using to words for husband, and we have acknownladge
that Sush thing among the Nation to a wrong her Husband—live
pracably as family and genaly the Notice of living By hunting to
port his family with gam and when he is off from home Savel
Days Sometime Savel months away from home while the husband is out Side from home then She is Ready [226[4]] and willing
to have if a male Should ask For her to wrong her husband while
he is away From home and if offort by man to be with her or to
marry her the fellow all he wants to See what She Say and Ex-
cases that he will have from her and female Is not a hard minded
and we have had heaved that has been pass Such a woman will
concent to Do So for her husband is gon away from home Now
woman you just look in that principle and considerate the almighty Seen you and all Thought and all what you See and your
mind Therefore you cant not hid, Say unto you if you Dont
Repent that practice you Shall Recd the punishment untill you
pay all the ademus for thing But here is the angel teaches what to
Do for you to Save your Soul—master Say to you Repent and
layed Side all what wrong you Done upon the Earth think no
other But love the lord thy god With all thy heart and with all thy
Soul and with all thy Strength and with all thy mind and thy
Neighbor as thy self

7 Commandments[10] Children Service toward thy parents
your parent has Race you up till you growning person, you are
satisfied for you parent Doing toward you when you childhood

But when you growing up and then you consider you are able to take Care youself and you begin to think about leaving your parent and your keep a Runing about with your friends and Care nothing to your parent and you Began to think something about taking up a wife—Sometime you have taking two or three times before you would Keep on for you wif and the Rest you wrong them and you forfited you agreed But the angel Say to you Wrong yourself and lied to youself and Say to you Return go to your parent again and beseck them and provide for them and Do as they tell you to Do and the lord thy god will Bress you for you Kindness to you parent and love thy god as youself

[226⁵] 8 Commandment[11] female growing person geting a husband, the angels teach us Saying Duties is for female to not Denied whatsoever But not forgotton you parent and Do as you promis With you husband in marriage and love him as yourself be obasiend, as you want to be Done, By if your husband ask to go to his parent go, and if he ask you to liven with his parent go and live with them peacably as you want to be Done By you own parent and the lord thy god will Bress you

9 Commandment[12] the old folk Service for theirs grand Children when the Chil Disobey, Speak lo to them and talk to the Chil and tell good things for the Chil is aughto Do—and the chil keep continue Disobey and tell the chil what you will Do if the Chil Don't Do any Better that you will take a wip to the chil and the chil thirt time Disobey and then take the Wip high and punish the Chil as you own Chil

10 Commandment[13] peace maker to the family when they growing up teach them be a good behavior to to Neighbors as you own Brothers and Sisters talk with Neighbors with good manners if you has Enemy But the angel say unto you love your Enemies for they Shall be cut them off But love thy parent for they are old and love your Brothers and Sisters for they love you and love the lord they god for he is find you foot tools and food live upon for your Strength

11 Commandments[14] Keep with they Neighbor and with theirs Children as you own family if you hear any wrong word from your Neighbor not give no answered Back again the Same But think of thy god forbid you to have any Enemy with you or any other person where Ever you go and you feel more containded throught the world and you will see god for the angel will Direct you

[226⁶] 12 Commandments[15] Dont Carryed with Bad news to your Neighbor, if any one of you Neighbor Should Bring to you Bad news against your other Neighbor your Dudy is to not Say notting or give any answered Any Evils word layed side [?] and Keep yourself not Tell any of you Neighbor when you Do telling a things to your Neighbor tell the truth for you Shall not be ashamed

The angel Shall be witness for you Promises

We are made Separate from the great King people From over great waters and Diffient believing In our Eternal life

Epilogue

"and called to his grand children
to his bedside"

Blacksnake's Support of Handsome Lake

Blacksnake was to live another sixty years after first hearing the revelations of the prophet Handsome Lake. Unfortunately none of this period is treated in the narrative dictated to Benjamin Williams. Throughout the remainder of his lifetime, Blacksnake remained true to the religious doctrine espoused by his uncle, Handsome Lake. In the initial stages of the preaching of that doctrine, Blacksnake provided considerable political support to the prophet.

Handsome Lake was the focal point of a delegation of Senecas and Onondagas who journeyed to Washington, D.C., in January 1802. The mission had secular goals. Uneasiness over land title was again at the forefront of Indian consciousness. In addition, Handsome Lake claimed that the Oil Spring Reservation near Cuba Lake had been reserved for him as a personal grant at the treaty of Big Tree in 1797, and he wanted recognition of that. As a result of the consultation with federal officials in Washington, Handsome Lake received a letter from the president, Thomas Jefferson, which was a strong endorsement of his teachings. The prophet later used this letter for political and evangelical purposes (Deardorff 1951:94; Wallace 1970:266–72).

Blacksnake may have been with his uncle on this journey to

Washington. The chief had possession of the letters from Jefferson to Handsome Lake a quarter-century later (Deardorff 1951: 94–95). We also know that Blacksnake retained in his possession a pass issued by Jefferson's secretary of war, Henry Dearborn. This pass, in its published text, is dated February 14, 1803 (Donaldson 1892:29), but it does remain possible that the date is an error and that Blacksnake, then still known as "the Nephew," received it from Dearborn when Handsome Lake was in the United States capital in 1802.

Blacksnake has been mentioned as one of Handsome Lake's key supporters in a Seneca council held at Burnt House in January 1803. It was determined that the Seneca council fire should burn there rather than at Buffalo Creek (which was dominated by Handsome Lake's rival, Red Jacket), and a delegation was sent to Philadelphia and Washington to negotiate on land issues and press for economic aid (Wallace 1970:285). It is possible that Blacksnake was one of these delegates and that that was when he obtained the pass mentioned above. However, I believe it is unlikely that Blacksnake would have attended a January council at Burnt House and been in Washington to receive a pass from Secretary Dearborn in mid-February.

A strong source of support for Handsome Lake among whites came from the Society of Friends. The Quakers had started a school on the Cornplanter Grant at the time of Handsome Lake's initial visions. Quakers aimed at altering behavior rather than capturing souls, so the goals of Handsome Lake's teachings, with a few exceptions, were compatible or identical with those of the Quakers themselves. Hence members of the Society of Friends viewed the prophet as a strong positive force in the Indian community. In the autumn of 1803, with the approval of a council at which Handsome Lake presided, the Quakers announced that they would move from the Cornplanter Grant to their own lands at Tunessassa, on the Allegheny River just below the Allegany Reservation inside the Pennsylvania border.

A dispute between Handsome Lake and his half-brother Cornplanter soon led most of the Senecas from the Cornplanter Grant to follow the Quakers upriver.[1] The location of sawmills was at least one issue, and a council met and deposed Cornplanter from political office. Handsome Lake, Blacksnake, and their followers moved off the Cornplanter Grant to the Allegany Reservation, where they established the community of Coldspring. There, with Quaker tools, they built a longhouse where the traditional religious ceremonies could be celebrated (Wallace 1970:275, 287–88). Here at Coldspring Blacksnake played an increasingly visible political role, being characterized as Handsome Lake's "privy Counsellor" (Wallace 1970:289, quoting an 1804 observation). When a visiting party of Quakers arrived at Coldspring from Philadelphia in 1806, Blacksnake gave them a lecture on the congruence of aims of their teachings and those of the prophet (Deardorff 1951:96; Wallace 1970:289).

A growing number of the Senecas who resided on the Allegany Reservation began to question at least some of Handsome Lake's teachings, however. One aspect of his religious fervor was the execution of individuals he identified as witches. This appears to have led at least some of the relatives of the convicted and executed witches to withdraw support from the prophet. Witches were a menace, in Iroquois eyes, because they caused disease, and epidemics like that of 1807 led to witchcraft accusations. At least a portion of the community viewed these outbreaks of disease not as a result of witchcraft but rather as the result of neglect of ceremonies traditionally practiced by the secret (or medicine) societies—ceremonies Handsome Lake himself had banned in his teachings. Those in favor of returning to the medicine societies as a mechanism of fighting the widespread sickness in their community also withdrew support from the prophet or questioned at least part of his teachings. Handsome Lake's position at Coldspring deteriorated to the point that in 1809 he suddenly and dramatically moved from that community to the Tonawanda Reservation (Wallace 1970:291–94).

Blacksnake did not go with his uncle. Instead he remained at Coldspring. Wallace (1970:363–64) notes that this important historical episode in Allegany Reservation history is undocumented in conventional historical records but survives in the oral tradition. From the evidence presented in Wallace's lengthy study of Handsome Lake there is no indication what role, if any, Blacksnake played in the erosion of Handsome Lake's power at Coldspring.

The War of 1812

When conflict again broke out between the British Crown and the United States, Handsome Lake vigorously preached against participation by his followers. His attempt to prevent the spilling of more Indian blood in another white man's war had little effect.[2] Considerable numbers of Senecas from all four major reservations—Buffalo Creek, Tonawanda, Cattaraugus, and Allegany—served the American cause (Parker 1916), while residents of the Six Nations Reserve took the field on the side of the Crown (Stanley 1963; Johnston 1964:193–228; Norton 1970). Thus members of the Iroquois Confederacy spilled each other's blood while serving as allies to the white governments of their homelands. The Senecas, under the leadership of Farmer's Brother, fought at Black Rock, Fort George, Lundy's Lane, and Chippawa. The American commander in the engagement at Fort George on August 17, 1813, praised the Senecas for fighting with "great bravery and activity" (Ketchum 1864–65, 2:375). Among their opposition, John Norton, the Scot turned Mohawk chief, noted that the presence of the Senecas in the American forces there "spread no small Dismay among the Warriors attached to the British Army," particularly alarming the Ojibwas because of the reputation the Iroquois still enjoyed as formidable fighting men.

Despite his sixty years, Blacksnake was in these battles (Ketchum 1864–65, 2:326). He had volunteered his services at Buffalo in July 1813 (Kent and Deardorff 1960:455) or perhaps even earlier. In September 1812, 140 Senecas from the Allegheny River danced a war dance in the streets of Buffalo, indicating their willingness to fight for the Americans (Ketchum 1864–65, 2:275). Unfortunately we lack details of his actions in the war on the Niagara frontier. The old chief later told Lyman Draper that he killed two British soldiers and a Delaware Indian in this conflict (DM 4-s-81–82).

Later Life

As a chief of the Seneca Nation Blacksnake continued to be active in political matters, but the Iroquois were no longer at center stage in the drama of white-Indian politics. He was a signatory of the treaty that sold the Gardeau Reserve (named after the husband of the famous white captive, Mary Jemison) on the Genesee River in 1823 (Kappler 1904–41, 2:1034). The sale of the Genesee River lands left the Senecas four major landholdings—Buffalo Creek, Cattaraugus, Allegany, and Tonawanda.

Of the four remaining Seneca reservations, the most populous, Buffalo Creek, was by far the most valuable in white terms, for it lay directly in the path of southward expansion of the growing city of Buffalo. The right to purchase Seneca lands that had originally been held by Massachusetts now lay with the Ogden Land Company. That company negotiated the sale of all Seneca lands in New York at the Buffalo Creek treaty of 1838. These proceedings have been labeled "blatantly corrupt," with lands appraised at over $2,000,000 being sold for $202,000 (Abler and Tooker 1978:511; see also Society of Friends 1840; Manley 1947). The Ogden Company claimed that forty-three chiefs signed the treaty and that this constituted a majority of the Seneca chiefs. The actual number of legitimate chiefs was one of the disputed aspects of the negotiations; claims ranged from eighty-one to ninety-one. Sixteen of the chiefs who did sign the treaty seem to have been bribed to do so, while others claimed their signatures were forged or obtained by threat.

Blacksnake did not sign this infamous treaty, and his name appears on the petitions and lists of those opposed to it (Society of Friends 1840:126, 133, 138, 153, 184, 246). Despite the frequent appearance of his name, at this point in history Blacksnake was not taking a leading role in Seneca affairs. Leadership had fallen to younger bilingual chiefs.

Controversy and factional strife raged for some time. For the

Senecas on the Buffalo Creek, Cattaraugus, and Allegany reservations, it ended with the signing of the "compromise" treaty of 1842. Ownership of Cattaraugus and Allegany was retained, but Buffalo Creek, by far the most valuable of the Seneca reservations, went to the Ogden Land Company. Blacksnake's mark appears on this treaty (Kappler 1904–41, 2:541). The Tonawanda Senecas refused to accept this "compromise" and continued to fight for their reservation home. Prominent in this fight, which was finally won in 1857, was the educated Seneca informant of Lewis Henry Morgan, Ely S. Parker (see Parker 1919; Armstrong 1978; Tooker 1978b).

Even though Blacksnake did not play a leading role politically in his declining years (or at least did not play a visible role vis-à-vis the white community), he still appears to have been important and recognized in the local community. A white, Charles Aldrich, recalled the impact Blacksnake had on those at the funeral of one of Aldrich's Indian playmates that Aldrich attended in the late 1830s:

> With grave and solemn mien, Governor Blacksnake stepped to the top of the mound of earth, and began a half-hour's address to his Indian friends. He spoke slowly and with great deliberation. Some one who understood him informed us that he spoke most kindly of the little boy who was gone, depicting the joys of the new existence upon which he was to enter. He urged his hearers to so order their lives as to be prepared for the better existence in the life to come. I do not remember, I was but a child myself, that I was ever more impressed by the appearance of an orator, except by Abraham Lincoln at his first inauguration. Blacksnake's figure was tall and commanding, his delivery slow and distinct, his appearance graceful, earnest, full of dignity, his sympathy for the bereaved family evident and touching. They paid his words the tribute of fast-flowing tears, except the [dead boy's] father, who looked on unmoved. (Quoted in Donaldson 1892:29)

Aldrich remembered Blacksnake as "a splendid looking Indian. . . . He wore a long blue overcoat, which came nearly to the ground, which was studded with small smooth brass buttons in the old-fashioned style of that day" (Aldrich 1905–7:381). As he addressed the gathering at the boy's grave, Blacksnake was described as "a most striking figure, tall and erect, with hair of snowy whiteness, wearing the blue overcoat" (Aldrich 1905–7:382).

At this time Blacksnake was living in "a small framed house, on the river a mile and a half above Cold Springs." It was said that he "travels a good deal, spends most of his time visiting his numerous descendants, and giving his people the benefit of his counsels" (Turner 1849:509).

Although Blacksnake may have "retained his influence with the Senecas to the end of his life" (Aldrich, quoted in Donaldson 1892:29), he lost whatever formal political power he had with the Seneca Nation "revolution" of 1848. This movement replaced the chiefs as the government for the Allegany and Cattaraugus reservations with an executive of president, clerk, and treasurer and a council of eighteen members, all elected annually by males over the age of twenty-one. Many of the chiefs attempted to stop the "revolution," and the factional struggle in the years after 1848 was heated (see Abler 1969:105–49). During this struggle Governor Blacksnake signed petitions supporting the old form of government, but republican government prevailed and the chiefs were unable to reinstitute the traditional political system.

Blacksnake played one last important political role in 1856, testifying in the Seneca Nation's suit that recovered the Oil Spring Reservation. This reservation had not been included in lands reserved for the Senecas in the treaty of Big Tree in 1797. "Governor Blacksnake . . . testified . . . to being present at the treaty of Big Tree in 1797, and that when the exception was missed upon the public reading of the treaty, Thomas Morris, attorney for Robert Morris, gave to Pleasant [Handsome] Lake, a prominent sachem of the Seneca nation, a separate paper, declaring that the Oil Spring tract was not included in the sale. Governor Blacksnake also produced a copy of the first map of the Holland land purchase, on which this reservation was distinctly marked as belonging to the Seneca Indians" (Donaldson 1892:28).

Epilogue

Blacksnake's Death and Funeral

Blacksnake lived long past his companions of the warpath and council fire. Joseph Brant died in Canada in 1807. Handsome Lake died on a visit to the Onondaga Reservation in 1815. Red Jacket died at Buffalo Creek in 1830. Cornplanter died six years later. But eventually Blacksnake too was to "take the long trail."

On December 26, 1859, Governor Blacksnake died. Benjamin Williams wrote to Lyman Draper about the event.

> I was at his Residant on Day before he Died and Stay most all day with him, and had long conversation with him, for Several Diffirent subjects mostly on his paganism Regious couse & advising to a general people, he was then believed himself that he is not going to live many Days more, although he was not ill, thought he was a weake and low Speach But no Sickness the Next Day eat hardly at dinner and called to his grand children to his bedside and give them good advice, and Remember his advices and to loved theirs father & mother and love to Each other &c. as soon as got through talking, he then went act so he was a Sleep about 15 minutes he was than died about 3 oclock in the afternoon, on the 28th Day he was carried to a council house where a large Number of people Red & Whites people together that Day, preach By Mr Ray an Indian without interpreter after preaching the coffen was then opened again to let the people See him once more But the people did not Seem him all, because So crowd it Confusedly & many followed to his Grave &c. (B. Williams to L. C. Draper, 14-i-1860, DM 16-F-247)

Williams has here described some essential elements of a longhouse funeral. The Senecas feel it is important that the body enter the longhouse and be shown to the people there. They believe that the deceased is still among the people but is passing through the longhouse for the last time on his way to heaven (Shimony 1961:243–44).

Excessive grief is a common motif in Iroquois culture. Handsome Lake is said to have innovated the tenth-day feast as a

Blacksnake's grave and marker, with Deforest Abrams, a resident of Allegany. This entire cemetery was flooded by the Kinzua Dam/Allegheny River Reservoir project in the 1960s (see Abler 1969; Hauptman 1986), so the marker and Blacksnake's remains have been moved to higher ground. Photograph by an unknown Salamanca photographer, ca. 1940.

mechanism for limiting the grief felt by the bereaved. The Senecas believe that the ghost of the deceased remains for ten days;
the tenth-day feast marks his final departure from earth. The
deceased's matrilineal relatives arrange the feast, looking after
the messengers, cooks, and speaker necessary for the occasion.
The property of the deceased is distributed at the tenth-day feast,
and the persons who helped during the funeral and the feast are
rewarded with goods (for details see Shimony 1961:245–51).

Williams told Draper how this ritual was performed for Governor Blacksnake: "From this Day [of the funeral] ten up, was then
made all Kinds of vitted together at council house again, what we
called feast for the Dead that was the Rules among the Natives of
Red people, there was another Preaching of Gov Blacksnakes
funeral, Sermanize manner previous before he died" (B. Williams
to L. C. Draper, 14-i-1860, DM 16-F-247).

The prospect of writing to Draper about the death of Governor
Blacksnake turned Williams's mind, and those of others in the
community, to the manuscript that Blacksnake had dictated,
which Williams had labored over and entrusted to Draper in the
hope of its reaching publication: "One Day I was at his [Black-
snake's] Sons house the old man he mentioned about you when
did I heard from you he inquire and wishing to Know you are to
work at his manuscript I told the last letter was Receive you had a
lame hand" (B. Williams to L. C. Draper, 14-i-1860, DM 16-F-247).

Appendix One

Introduction to the Williams Text

[107]

1 The Birth and of governer Blacksnake or more correctly of Ten, wr, nyrs—for Such was his Real name—interpretation is Chainbraker his last name given to him at the time he became chief warrior—at first commenced Including the Indian wars of the American Revolution—But when Boyhood was then called—Dahgr, yan, Doh—untill he became young man than, Tan, wr, nyrs, as Chainbraker—following to according to the custom of their Rules and traditions—concerning changing their names when became Man—although the Indians have no heralds only what they got into their heads and memory concerning interpretation of the first name given Blacksnake Indian name was a Serval places gambling all it once at one place connected with most Each other or Beting Something when you See all it once you will Say, Da, gr, yan, Doh—that was the meaning of his first name

this can be asurtained fect of the Said Life of governer Blacksnake, and others connected with it and traditions of their ancient history—account of creation of the world and late prophet, and Sanctuary of three times in a year—contains a Sketch of Blacksnake

2 which Idea being handed Down from Generation to generations—we cannot tell the number of years ago for we have no written account, why what we got from the oldest and good man Statements—you will take Notice anything Done wonderfully in Presence of unlarnt Indian will Remember all, as long as he live or become an old age—and it may be some sketch of Iroquois onondagas, when the omission is Supplied by a head from an ancient pipe here after discribed under the class of all the above. [108]

3 Described and Ruler under their confederacy, named Tar, to, tar, ho, he is the first Ruler of Iroquois—

addition of histories

4 Celebrated chief the son of cornplanter charles obail a Sketch of his life and father

and other addition also

5 Life of captain John Dacker one of the chief warrior at the time immediately after Declard Peace, war between Cherokees and Six Nations—

he was a brave man, he was with the Pennsylvanian warriors 2 or 3 years after the American Revolution Break out and figh against his own colour people against western indians

also an account worship

6 of ceremonial of the Seneca nation of Indians residing in western new york

Governor Blacksnake

7 who chief commander in wars with Cornplanter Red Jacket & Brant most principle man Deserves more hard labour During america Revolution till Peace Declared—after this washington and the Six Nation of Indians made treaties and Peace—Blacksnake then became grand Sachem of the Seneca Nation of Indians—

Speech by Philip Schuyler Delivered at German Flats, August 6, 1776

(LOSSING 1872–73, 2:107–12)

Brothers, Sachems and Warriors of the Six Nations:

With this String we open your ears that you may plainly hear what the independent States of America have to say to their Brethren of the Six Nations: with it we wipe away all mists that may interrupt your sight, and let it clear your Hearts from every obstruction and incline them to receive our Words with Brotherly Love.

Brothers:

We thank God that he has been pleased to suffer us to meet you in Health. May sickness never enter into your Country, but may Health and Happiness dwell in your Habitations, and may the Six Nations be a great and happy people. *A String.*

The Council Fire which is now burning at this place has been kindled by a spark taken from the great Council Fire at Albany. We have brought it here in our Bosoms—We have lighted it up here, because we were afraid that the small-pox might infect our Brethren of the Six Nations, if they went farther down the River, and that some of them might go home with Heavy Hearts for the loss of their Relations, and we hope this Conduct of the Commissioners meets with your approbation. *A Belt.*

Brothers, Sachems and Warriors of the Six Nations:

The united Colonies have always been in Hopes that a Reconciliation would take place between us and the King. —To that end they have frequently petitioned the King for Redress of the Grievances they laboured under; but he would not listen to their petitions. —He was deaf and would not give Ear to their Complaints, and instigated by his evil Counsellors he forgot that we were his children, he wanted to make us his Slaves. To accomplish this unjust and cruel purpose he has sent his armies and his fleets to try to destroy and distress us, and therefore the united Colonies, when they found that he had become a cruel and an oppressive Father that hated them, and that he had not only given the Hatchet to the English on the other side of the Water, but had also sent it to the few Friends he had amongst us, ordering them to put it into the Hands of our Negroes and whoever would accept it to strike us, have unanimously left his House, and now no longer consider him as their Father and King, and have accordingly proclaimed to all the World that they will never hereafter acknowledge him or any of his Family to be their King, but that they will always be and remain a free and independent people, and therefore have called themselves the independant States of America, and solemnly agreed always to remain firmly united: we must therefore for the future be called the Commissioners of the United Independant States of America, and that you may remember this great Event we now deliver you this Belt. *A Belt.*

Brothers, Sachems and Warriors of the Six Nations,

now open your Ears and listen attentively to what the independant States of America have further to say to you, for in their Names we speak. Our Speech will be plain as it always has been, for, as we never have been, we scorn to be double Minded. —It will be the Speech of Freemen who will candidly tell you your Faults; you shall know all that is in our Hearts; we will hide

Nothing from you, that you may know our Intentions clearly and fully.

Brothers:

You will remember that soon after the king's warriors had begun to spill the Blood of the Inhabitants of this great Island, that the united Colonies called you together at Albany. —They there rekindled the antient Council Fire and brightened up the Covenant Chain that had bound your ancestors and ours together in Bonds of the purest Love and sincerest Friendship. —It was last Summer that we the Commissioners met you there on that pleasing Business. —We then gave you a full, a fair, and a candid account of the Cause of the Quarrel between us and the King; we did not do it in a dark Corner as those that mean Evil, but in the presence of all that would come to see and hear, that they might witness the Truth of what we said. —When we had related this, we informed you, that as we were unhappily engaged in a Family Quarrel in which the Six Nations were not in the least concerned, either one way or the other, we desired and expected that you should not assist the one or the other, but remain quietly and peacefully at Home and mind your own Business. —We confirmed our words with a large belt.

Brothers:

The answer you made was delivered by Abraham the Mohawk Sachem, whom you had chosen your speaker. —These were his words, we shall repeat them exactly: "Now therefore attend and apply your Ears closely. —We have fully considered this Matter; the Resolutions of the Six Nations are not to be broken or altered. —When they resolve the Matter is fixed. —This then is the Determination of the Six Nations—*Not to take any part, but as it is a Family Quarrel to sit still and see you fight it out.* —It is a long time since we came to this Resolution. —It is the Result of mature Deliberation. —It was our Declaration to Colonel Johnson. —We told him *we would take no part in the Quarrel, and hoped neither side would desire it; whoever applies first we shall think is in the wrong.* —The Resolutions of the Six Nations are not to be shaken."

Brothers:

These Words and these Resolutions pleased us well, because what you declared was what we requested: That you should take no part in the Quarrel, but sit still and see us fight it out, and because we believed that you were sincere; and that you said Nothing with your Tongues, but what you had in your Hearts. —Your Speech was delivered in full Council and in the presence of a Number of people. —We had therefore the highest Reason to expect that you would strictly abide by your Resolutions. But, Brothers, we now ask you, whether you have abode by these wise Words and adhered to these prudent Resolutions? It grieves us to say that you have not. That you have acted directly contrary to your solemn Engagement and broken that Faith which you plighted and which we depended upon, as we shall now plainly make appear by repeating a Number of Facts which are known by you all, and which you cannot contradict or deny.

First. —When our Army went to St. John's last year your people interfered in the Quarrel by joining with our Enemies in attacking our Warriors, and then the Resolutions of the Six Nations were broken and altered, altho' you had said that they were not to be broken or altered.

Secondly. —When our great Council at Philadelphia was informed that Sir John Johnson was inlisting Men, and that he and the Highlanders who lived about Johnstown were preparing to murder our Friends, they sent some Warriors to disarm them, and then you again interfered in the Quarrel. —You were very troublesome, and threatened us, altho' we had sent you Word that no Harm was intended you, for that we had no Quarrel with the

Indians, and thus the Resolutions of the Six Nations were again broken and altered.

Thirdly. —When our great Council in the month of May last had received certain Intelligence that Sir John Johnson was inlisting Men and preparing to join the Enemy, they ordered up a Body of Warriors; but least you should be alarmed, Mr. Douw went up to the East End of the House to inform you that no Evil was intended you. —Yet you nevertheless interfered in the Quarrel. —Mr. Douw was insulted with abusive Language, and Mr. Bleecker the Interpreter was threatened and seized by the Breast contrary to the Custom of all Nations. —For the person of an ambassador and a Messenger of peace is always held sacred, and thus the Resolutions of the Six Nations were a third Time broken and altered.

Fourthly. —Altho' you knew that Sir John Johnson was inlisting Men and preparing to go to the enemy, contrary to the most solemn agreement with us, yet you not only assisted him going to the enemy; but even threatened to kill our Warriors, and actually appeared in arms for that hostile purpose, and thus again interfered in the Quarrel and a fourth time broke and altered your Resolutions.

Fifthly. —Contrary to your Resolutions you have opened your ears, and given ear to the voice of our Enemies, and complied with their Desires. —Butler has prevailed upon you to go into Canada and fight against us. —As we had no quarrel with any Indians; as we had even released those that we had taken prisoners in Battle, we were surprised to find any Indians fighting against us; but when we were told that some of the Six Nations were there and had joined our Enemies; that they had struck the Ax in our Head and covered the Ground with the bones of our Warriors and defiled the earth with their blood, after having but a little Time before promised to remain neuter, we could hardly believe it at first; but upon Enquiry we found it was true. Your ax still sticks in our Heads, and thus you again interfered in the Quarrel and a fifth Time broke and altered your Resolutions.

Sixthly. —You have also lately upon this River, in the midst of the Inhabitants, wickedly and wilfully fired on, attacked and destroyed a Batteau loaded with Flour, which was coming up here for the use of our Warriors and to feed you at this Treaty, and thereby you have again insulted us and interfered in the Quarrel, and a sixth time broken and altered the Resolutions of the Six Nations.

Thus, Brothers, we have mentioned six instances in which the Resolutions of the Six Nations have been contravened, altho' you told us in full Council at Albany that they were not to be broken or altered, and that when you resolved the Matter was fixed, and thus also, instead of sitting still and see us fight it out, as you also told us you would do, you have actually assisted our Enemies and taken an active part in the Quarrel against us, thereby opening your Ears to and listening to the advice of our Enemies by complying with their Request, altho' you expressly said that *whoever applied first you should think was in the wrong.*

Now, Brothers, tell us, if you can, when we have asked you to interfere in the Quarrel? When and where have we desired your assistance? Have we given you a bloody belt? Have we offered you the ax? Have we roasted an Englishman and desired you to drink his Blood? You cannot say that we ever did any of these things, and yet our Enemies have done all this. —You have told us so yourselves, and you cannot deny it. We have always said that we were not afraid of our Enemies; we say so still; we have never asked you to fight for us, and yet some of you have fought for them. —Was this well done? God, who knows all things, knows that it was not. —You yourselves know it was not. —We know it was not, and thus you have unjustly taken up arms against us, and altho' we felt the Blows and altho' the ax still sticks in our Heads, yet we have forborne to take Revenge, because your Ancestors and ours always had a great affection and Friendship for each other and faithfully kept the Covenants they made with each other in such a manner that both were happy both were pleased, and peace dwelt in their Habitations, and because we had resolved to make our Complaint in full Council and lay Grievances before the whole Six Nations, as we now do, expecting that you will speak as plain as we do and remove all Cause of Complaint for the future.

Brothers:

again attend to the voice of all the white people on this great Island. —They say, that they have not injured you, that they wish to live in Friendship with all Indians and in particular with the Six Nations, who are their near Neighbors, and with whom their Ancestors have always lived in peace and Friendship. —They say that you have unjustly injured and insulted them. They say, that as they are Freemen, as free as you are, and are now fighting to preserve that Freedom, that they will not suffer themselves to be affronted, injured and insulted with Impunity by you or any Men on Earth. They will do as you have formerly done; as you still do, and as you have a Right to do, that is, to guard themselves against any Enemy whatsoever by any just Means in their power.

Brothers:

We know that many of you are honest men; faithful to your Engagements; holding sacred the Faith you have plighted and bearing a Brotherly affection to the Inhabitants of this great Island. —These we love, respect and honor, and we call God to witness that we will do them every kindness in our power and never give them the least Cause of Complaint. —We also know who are our Enemies, altho' we do not know why. —We have given them no Cause to be such.

Brothers, Sachems and Warriors of the Six Nations:

—We have spoken plain. —We will if possible speak more plain; open therefore your Ears that you may clearly hear and understand the Declaration of the independent States of America. —It is this, that they mean to live in Friendship and cultivate a good Understanding, and maintain a friendly Intercourse with all Indians, and that in answer to this they do require that all Indians should declare their Intentions, and therefore ask the Six Nations now convened round this Council Fire of peace what their Intentions are? If they mean to live in Friendship, to cultivate a good Understanding and maintain a friendly Intercourse with us, we require that they will take the Hatchet out of our Heads and that none of them will again assist our Enemies, in which case we do most solemnly promise that we will love and cherish them and treat them with the greatest kindess and affection, and that we will forever hereafter rather die than wrong them or suffer others to do it—but if any amongst you should so far forget their own Interest as now to become or continue our Enemies after all the Kindness and Forbearance we have shown, let them say so, that all the white people of this great Island may know what they have to depend upon. —No person shall molest them here or on the way, for it shall never be said that we injured or insulted people with whom we were in Treaty, altho' they intended to be our Enemies.

Brothers:

We have done our Duty; we have spoke plainly—we request you will do the same. —We shall become open Enemies or warm and inviolable Friends. —We wish for your Friendship not out of Fear but out of Love, and that a good Understanding may prevail between the white Inhabitants of this great Island and the Six Nations until the Sun shall grow dim with age. —And it will be your Fault if we do not part as good Friends with the Six Nations, and remain so hereafter, as your Ancestors and ours were in the Time of Quedor, when they fought side by side against the common Enemy.

Brothers:

—We have now spoken our Mind fully. —You cannot charge us with Deceit. Our conduct has been invariably the same from the

Time that we first met at Albany to this Day. We have not said one thing and done another, as our Enemies have, and as you now know all that is in our Hearts, we desire you to think seriously of it and to speak your thoughts fairly and fully and not be double hearted. Do not say one thing and think another, for that is shameful in a private Man and in private affairs, but scandalous in public Bodies and public Business.

This Belt on which our Wishes are described, and which denotes what we hope will take place, that is, a firm Union between the Six Nations and the thirteen united States of America. —This Belt we say confirms our Words. *The Large Belt.*

Appendix Three

Speeches Delivered in Philadelphia, December 1790 to February 1791

[ASP, IA, 1:140–45]

THE SPEECH OF THE CORNPLANTER, HALF-TOWN, AND GREAT-TREE, CHIEFS AND COUNCILLORS OF THE SENECA NATION TO THE GREAT COUNCILLOR OF THE THIRTEEN FIRES

Father:

The voice of the Seneca nation speaks to you, the great councillor, in whose heart the wise men of all the Thirteen Fires have placed their wisdom. It may be very small in your ears, and we therefore entreat you to hearken with attention: for we are about to speak of things which are to us very great. When your army entered the country of the Six Nations, we called you the town destroyer; and to this day, when that name is heard, our women look behind them and turn pale, and our children cling close to the necks of their mothers. Our councillors and warriors are men, and cannot be afraid; but their hearts are grieved with the fears of our women and children, and desire it may be buried so deep as to be heard no more.

When you gave us peace, we called you father, because you promised to secure us in the possession of our lands. Do this, and, so long as the lands shall remain, that beloved name will live in the heart of every Seneca.

Father:

We mean to open our hearts before you, and we earnestly desire that you will let us clearly understand what you resolve to do. When our chiefs returned from the treaty at fort Stanwix, and laid before our council what had been done there, our nation was surprised to hear how great a country you had compelled them to give up to you, without your paying to us any thing for it. Every one said that your hearts were yet swelled with resentment against us for what had happened during the war, but that one day you would reconsider it with more kindness. We asked each other, What have we done to deserve such severe chastisement?

Father:

When you kindled your thirteen fires separately, the wise men that assembled at them told us, that you were all brothers, the children of one great father, who regarded, also, the red people as his children. They called us brothers, and invited us to his protection; they told us that he resided beyond the great water, where the sun first rises; that he was a king whose power no people could resist, and that his goodness was bright as that sun. What they said went to our hearts; we accepted the invitation, and promised to obey him. When the Seneca nation promise, they faithfully perform; and when you refused obedience to that king, he commanded us to assist his beloved men in making you sober. In obeying him, we did no more than yourselves had led us to promise. The men who claimed this promise told us that you were children, and had no guns; that when they had shaken you, you would submit. We hearkened to them, and were deceived, until your army approached our towns. We were deceived; but your people, in teaching us to confide in that king, had helped to deceive, and we now appeal to your heart—Is the blame all ours?

Father:

When we saw that we were deceived, and heard the invitation which you gave us to draw near to the fire which you kindled, and talk with you concerning peace, we made haste towards it. You then told us that we were in your hand, and that, by closing it, you could crush us to nothing, and you demanded from us a great country, as the price of that peace which you had offered us; as if our want of strength had destroyed our rights; our chiefs had felt your power, and were unable to contend against you, and they therefore gave up that country. What they agreed to, has bound our nation; but your anger against us must, by this time, be cooled; and, although our strength has not increased, nor your power become less, we ask you to consider calmly, Were the terms dictated to us by your commissioners reasonable and just?

Father:

Your commissioners, when they drew the line which separated the land then given up to you from that which you agreed should remain to be ours, did most solemnly promise, that we should be secured in the peaceable possession of the lands which we inhabited east and north of that line. Does this promise bind you?

Hear now, we beseech you, what has since happened concerning that land. On the day in which we finished the treaty at fort Stanwix, commissioners from Pennsylvania told our chiefs that they had come there to purchase from us all the lands belonging to us, within the lines of their State, and they told us that their line would strike the river Susqehannah below Tioga branch. They then left us to consider of the bargain till the next day; on the next day we let them know that we were unwilling to sell all the lands within their State, and proposed to let them have a part of it, which we pointed out to them in their map. They told us that they must have the whole; that it was already ceded to them by the great king, at the time of making peace with you, and was *their own*; but they said they would not take advantage of that, and were willing to pay us for it, after the manner of their ancestors. Our chiefs were unable to contend, at that time, and therefore they sold the lands up to the line, which was then shewn to them as the line of that State. What the commissioners had said about the land having been ceded to them at the peace, our chiefs considered as intended only to lessen the price, and they passed it by with very little notice; but, since that time, we have heard so much from others about the right to our lands, which the king gave when you made peace with him, that it is our earnest desire that you will tell us what it means.

Father:

Our nation empowered John Livingston to let out part of our lands on rent, to be paid to us. He told us, that he was sent by Congress, to do this for us, and we fear he has deceived us in the writing he obtained from us.

For, since the time of our giving that power, a man of the name of Phelps has come among us, and claimed our whole country northward of the line of Pennsylvania, under purchase from that Livingston, to whom, he said, he had paid twenty thousand dollars for it. He said, also, that he had bought, likewise, from the council of the Thirteen Fires, and paid them twenty thousand dollars for the same.

And he said, also, that it did not belong to us, for that the great king had ceded the whole of it, when you made peace with him. Thus he claimed the whole country north of Pennsylvania, and west of the lands belonging to the Cayugas. He demanded it; he insisted on his demand, and declared that he would have it *all*. It was impossible for us to grant him this, and we immediately refused it. After some days, he proposed to run a line, at a small distance eastward of our western boundary, which we also refused to agree to. He then threatened us with immediate war, if we did not comply.

Upon this threat, our chiefs held a council, and they agreed that no event of war could be worse than to be driven, with their wives and children, from the only country which we had any right to, and, therefore, weak as our nation was, they determined to take the chance of war, rather than to submit to such unjust demands, which seemed to have no bounds. Street, the great trader to Niagara, was then with us, having come at the request of Phelps, and as he always professed to be our great friend, we consulted him upon this subject. He also told us, that our lands had been ceded by the king, and that we *must* give them up.

Astonished at what we heard from every quarter, with hearts aching with compassion for our women and children, we were thus compelled to give up all our country north of the line of Pennsylvania and east of the Genesee river, up to the fork, and east of a south line drawn from that fork to the Pennsylvania line.

For this land, Phelps agreed to pay us ten thousand dollars in hand, and one thousand a year for ever.

He paid us two thousand and five hundred dollars in hand, part of the ten thousand, and he sent for us to come last spring, to receive our money; but instead of paying us the remainder of the ten thousand dollars, and the one thousand dollars due for the first year, he offered us no more than five hundred dollars, and insisted that he agreed with us for that sum, to be paid yearly. We debated with him for six days, during all which time he persisted in refusing to pay us our just demand, and he insisted that we should receive the five hundred dollars; and Street, from Niagara, also insisted on our receiving the money, as it was offered to us. The last reason he assigned for continuing to refuse paying us, was, *that the king had ceded the lands to the Thirteen Fires*, and that he had bought them from you, and *paid you for them.*

We would bear this confusion no longer, and determined to press through every difficulty, and lift up our voice that you might hear us, and to claim that security in the possession of our lands, which your commissioners so solemnly promised us. And we now entreat you to inquire into our complaints and redress our wrongs.

Father:

Our writings were lodged in the hands of Street, of Niagara, as we supposed him to be our friend; but when we saw Phelps consulting with Street, on every occasion, we doubted of his honesty towards us, and we have since heard, that he was to receive for his endeavors to deceive us, a piece of land ten miles in width, west of the Genesee river, and near forty miles in length, extending to Lake Ontario; and the lines of this tract have been run accordingly, although no part of it is within the bounds which limit his purchase. No doubt he meant to deceive us.

Father:

You have said that we are in your hand, and that, by closing it, you could crush us to nothing. Are you determined to crush us? If you are, tell us so, that those of our nation who have become your children, and have determined to die so, may know what to do.

In this case, one chief has said he would ask you to put him out of pain. Another, who will not think of dying by the hand of his father or of his brother, has said he will retire to the Chateaugay, eat of the fatal root, and sleep with his fathers, in peace.

Before you determine on a measure so unjust, look up to God, who made *us* as well as *you*. We hope he will not permit you to destroy the whole of our nation.

Father: Hear our case

many nations inhabited this country; but they had no wisdom, and, therefore, they warred together. The Six Nations were powerful, and compelled them to peace; the lands, for a great extent, were given up to them; but the nations which were not destroyed, all continued on those lands, and claimed the protection of the Six Nations, as the brothers of their fathers. They were men, and when at peace, they had a right to live upon the earth. The French came among us, and built Niagara; they became our fathers, and took care of us. Sir William Johnston came and took that fort from the French; he became our father, and promised to take care of us, and did so, until you were too strong for his king. To him we gave four miles round Niagara, as a place of trade. We have already said, how we came to join against you; we saw that we were wrong; we wished for peace; you demanded a great country to be given up to you; it was surrendered to you, as the price of peace, and we ought to have peace and possession of the little land which you then left us.

Father:

When that great country was given up, there were but few chiefs present, and they were compelled to give it up, and it is not the Six Nations only that reproach those chiefs with having given up that country. The Chippewas, and all the nations who lived on those lands westward, call to us, and ask us, Brothers of our fathers, where is the place you have reserved for us to lie down upon?

Father:

You have compelled us to do that which has made us ashamed. We have nothing to answer to the children of the brothers of our fathers. When, last spring, they called upon us to go to war, to secure them a bed to lie upon, the Senecas entreated them to be quiet, till we have spoken to you. But, on our way down, we heard that your army had gone toward the country which those nations inhabit, and if they meet together, the best blood on both sides will stain the ground.

Father:

We will not conceal from you, that the great God, and not men, has preserved the Cornplanter from the hands of his own nation. For they ask, continually, Where is the land which our children, and their children after them, are to lie down upon? You told us, say they, that the line drawn from Pennsylvania to lake Ontario, would mark it forever on the east, and the line running from Beaver creek to Pennsylvania, would mark it on the west, and we see that it is not so. For, first one, and then another, come, and take it away, by order of that people which you tell us promised to secure it to us. He is silent, for he has nothing to answer.

When the sun goes down, he opens his heart before God, and earlier than that sun appears again upon the hills, he gives thanks for his protection during the night; for he feels that, among men, become desperate by their danger, it is God only that can preserve him. He loves peace, and all he had in store, he has given to those who have been robbed by your people, lest they should plunder the innocent to repay themselves. The whole season which others have employed in providing for their families, he has spent in his endeavors to preserve peace; and, at this moment, his wife and children are lying on the ground, and in want of food; his heart is in pain for them, but he perceives that the great God will try his firmness, in doing what is right.

Father:

The game with the Great Spirit sent into our country for us to eat, is going from among us. We thought he intended that we should till the ground with the plough, as the white people do, and we talked to one another about it. But before we speak to you concerning this, we must know from you whether you mean to leave us and our children any land to till. Speak plainly to us concerning this great business.

All the lands we have been speaking of belonged to the Six Nations; no part of it ever belonged to the King of England, and he could not give it to you.

The land we live on, our father received from God, and they transmitted it to us, for our children, and we cannot part with it.

Father:

We told you that we would open our hearts to you. Hear us once more.

At fort Stanwix, we agreed to deliver up those of our people who should do you any wrong, that you might try them, and punish them according to your law. We delivered up two men accordingly, but instead of trying them according to your law, the lowest of your people took them from your magistrate, and put them immediately to death. It is just to punish murder with death; but the Senecas will not deliver up their people to men who disregard the treaties of their own nation.

Father:

Innocent men of our nation are killed one after another, and of our best families; but none of your people who have committed the murder have been punished.

We recollect that you did not promise to punish those who killed our people, and we now ask, was it intended that your people should kill the Senecas, and not only remain unpunished by you, but be protected by you against the revenge of the next of kin?

Father:

These are to us very great things. We know that you are very strong, and we have heard that you are wise, and we wait to hear your answer to what we have said, that we may know that you are just.

Signed at Philadelphia, the first day of December, 1790

Cornplanter, his x mark.
Half-Town, his x mark.
Great-Tree, his x mark.

Present at signing,
Joseph Nicholson, Interpreter.
T'y. Matlack

◆

THE REPLY OF THE PRESIDENT OF THE UNITED STATES
TO THE SPEECH OF THE CORNPLANTER, HALF-TOWN,
AND GREAT-TREE, CHIEFS AND COUNCILLORS
OF THE SENECA NATION OF INDIANS.

I, the President of the United States, by my own mouth, and by a written speech, signed with my own hand, and sealed with the seal of the United States, speak to the Seneca nation, and desire their attention, and that they would keep this speech in remembrance of the friendship of the United States.

I have received your speech with satisfaction, as a proof of your confidence in the justice of the United States, and I have attentively examined the several objects which you have laid before me, whether delivered by your own chiefs at Tioga Point, in the last month, to Colonel Pickering, or laid before me in the present month, by the Cornplanter, and the other Seneca chiefs now in this city.

In the first place, I observe to you, and request it may sink deeply into your minds, that it is my desire, and the desire of the United States, that all the miseries of the late war should be forgotten, and buried forever. That, in future, the United States, and the Six Nations should be truly brothers, promoting each other's prosperity by acts of mutual friendship and justice.

I am not uninformed, that the Six Nations have been led into some difficulties, with respect to the sale of their lands, since the peace. But I must inform you that these evils arose before the present Government of the United States was established, when the separate States, and individuals under their authority, undertook to treat with the Indian tribes respecting the sale of their lands. But the case is now entirely altered; the General Government, only, has the power to treat with the Indian nations, and any treaty formed, and held without its authority, will not be binding.

Here, then, is the security for the remainder of your lands. No State, nor person, can purchase your lands, unless at some public treaty, held under the authority of the United States. The General Government will never consent to your being defrauded, but it will protect you in all your just rights.

Hear well, and let it be heard by every person in your nation, that the President of the United States declares, that the General Government considers itself bound to protect you in all the lands secured to you by the treaty of fort Stanwix, the 22nd of October, 1784, excepting such parts as you may since have fairly sold, to persons properly authorized to purchase of you. You complain that John Livingston and Oliver Phelps, assisted by Mr. Street, of Niagara, have obtained your lands, and that they have not complied with their agreement. It appears, upon inquiry of the Governor of New York, that John Livingston was not legally authorized to treat with you, and that every thing he did with you has been declared null and void, so that you may rest easy on that account. But it does not appear, from any proofs yet in possession of Government, that Oliver Phelps has defrauded you.

If, however, you have any just cause of complaint against him, and can make satisfactory proof thereof, the federal courts will be open to you for redress, as to all other persons. But your great object seems to be, the security of your remaining lands; and I have, therefore, upon this point, meant to be sufficiently strong and clear, that, in future, you cannot be defrauded of your lands; that you possess the right to sell, and the right of refusing to sell, your lands; that, therefore, the sale of your lands, in future, will depend entirely upon yourselves. But that, when you may find it for your interest to sell any part of your lands, the United States must be present, by their agent, and will be your security that you shall not be defrauded in the bargain you may make.

It will, however, be important, that, before you make any further sales of your lands, you should determine among yourselves who are the persons among you, that shall give such conveyances thereof as shall be binding upon your nation, and forever prevent all disputes relative to the validity of the sale.

That, besides the before mentioned security for your land, you will perceive, by the law of Congress for regulating trade and intercourse with the Indian tribes, the fatherly care the United States intend to take of the Indians. For the particular meaning of this law, I refer you to the explanations given thereof by Colonel Timothy Pickering, at Tioga, which, with the law, are herewith delivered to you.

You have said in your speech that the game is going away from among you, and that you thought it the design of the Great Spirit, that you should till the ground; but before you speak upon this subject, you want to know whether the Union mean to leave you any land to till. You now know, that all the lands secured to you, by the treaty of fort Stanwix, excepting such parts as you may since have fairly sold, are yours, and that only your own acts can convey them away. Speak, therefore, your wishes, on the subject of tilling the ground. The United States will be happy in affording you every assistance, in the only business which will add to your numbers and happiness. The murders that have been committed upon some of your people, by the bad white men, I sincerely lament and reprobate; and I earnestly hope, that the real murderers will be secured, and punished as they deserve. This business has been sufficiently explained to you here, by the Governor of Pennsylvania, and by Colonel Pickering, on behalf of the United States, at Tioga. The Senecas may be assured, that the rewards offered for apprehending the murderers, will be continued, until they are secured for trial; and that, when they shall be apprehended, they will be tried and punished as if they had killed white men.

Having answered the most material parts of your speech, I shall inform you that some bad Indians, and the outcasts of several tribes, who reside at the Miami village, have long continued their murders and depredations upon the frontiers lying along the Ohio. They have not only refused to listen to my voice, inviting them to peace, but that, upon receiving it, they renewed their incursions and murders, with greater violence than ever. I have, therefore, been obliged to strike those bad people, in order to make them sensible of their madness. I sincerely hope they will hearken to reason, and not require to be farther chastised. The United States desire to be the friends of the Indians, upon terms of justice and humanity; but they will not suffer the depredations of the bad Indians to go unpunished. My desire is, that you would caution all the Senecas, and Six Nations, to prevent their rash young men from joining the Maumee Indians: for the United States cannot distinguish the tribes to which the bad Indians belong, and every tribe must take care of their own people. The merits of the Cornplanter, and his friendship for the United States, are well known to me, and shall not be forgotten; and, as a mark of the esteem of the United States, I have directed the Secretary of War to make him a present of ———— dollars, either in money or goods, as the Cornplanter shall like best; and he may depend upon the future care and kindness of the United States; and I have also directed the Secretary of War to make suitable presents to the other chiefs in Philadelphia; and also, that some further tokens of friendship be forwarded to the other chiefs, now in their nation.

Remember my words, Senecas! Continue to be strong in your friendship for the United States, as the only rational ground of your future happiness, and you may rely upon their kindness and protection. An agent shall soon be appointed to reside in some place convenient to the Senecas and Six Nations. He will represent the United States. Apply to him on all occasions. If any man bring you evil reports of the intention of the United States, mark that man as your enemy: for he will mean to deceive you, and lead you into trouble. The United States will be true and faithful to their engagements.

Given under my hand, and the seal of the United
States, at Philadelphia, this twenty-ninth day
[L. S.] of December, in the year of our Lord one thousand
seven hundred and ninety, and in the fifteenth
year of the sovereignty and independence of the
United States.

Geo. Washington.

By the President:
Th: Jefferson.

By command of the President of the United States
of America:

H. Knox,
Secretary for the Department of War.

◆

THE SPEECH OF THE CORNPLANTER, HALF-TOWN,
AND THE GREAT-TREE, CHIEFS OF THE SENECA NATION,
TO THE PRESIDENT OF THE UNITED STATES OF AMERICA.

Father:

Your speech, written on the great paper, is to us like the first light of the morning to a sick man, whose pulse beats too strongly in his temples, and prevents him from sleep. He sees it, and rejoices, but he is not cured.

You say that you have spoken plainly on the great point. That you will protect us in the lands secured to us at fort Stanwix, and that we have the right to *sell* or to *refuse* to sell it. This is very good. But our nation complain that you compelled us at that treaty to give up too much of our lands. We confess that our nation is bound by what was there done; and, acknowledging your power, we have appealed to yourselves against this treaty, as made while you were too angry at us, and, therefore, unreasonable and unjust. To this you have given us no answer.

Father:

That treaty was not made with a single State, it was with the thirteen States. We never would have given all that land to one State. We know it was before you had the great authority, and as you have more wisdom than the commissioners, who forced us into that treaty, we expect that you have also more regard to justice, and will now, at our request, reconsider that treaty, and restore to us a part of that land.

Father:

The land which lies between the line running south from lake Erie to the boundary of Pennsylvania, as mentioned at the treaty of fort Stanwix, and the eastern boundary of the land which you sold, and the Senecas confirmed to Pennsylvania, is the land on which Half-Town and all his people live, with other chiefs, who always have been, and still are, dissatisfied with the treaty at fort Stanwix. They grew out of this land, and their fathers' fathers grew out of it, and they cannot be persuaded to part with it. We therefore entreat you to restore to us this little piece.

Father:

Look at the land which we gave to you at that treaty, and then turn your eyes upon what we now ask you to restore to us, and you will see that what we ask you to return is a *very little piece.*

By giving it back again, you will satisfy the whole of our nation. The chiefs who signed that treaty will be in safety, and peace between your children and our children will continue so long as your land shall join to ours. Every man of our nation will then turn his eyes away from all the other lands which we then gave up to you, and forget that our fathers ever said that they belonged to them.

Father:

We see that you ought to have the path at the carrying place from lake Erie to Niagara, as it was marked down at fort Stanwix, and we are all willing it should remain to be yours. And if you desire to serve a passage through the Conewango, and through the Chataugue lake and land, for a path from that lake to lake Erie, take it where you best like. Our nation will rejoice to see it an open path for you and your children while the land and water remain. But let us also pass along the same way, and continue to take the fish of those waters in common with you.

Father:

You say that you will appoint an agent to take care of us. Let him come and take care of our trade; but we desire he may not have any thing to do with our lands: for the agents which have come amongst us, and pretended to take care of us, have always deceived us whenever we sold lands; both when the King of England and when the States have bargained with us. They have by this means occasioned many wars, and we are therefore unwilling to trust them again.

Father:

When we return home, we will call a great council, and consider well how lands may be hereafter sold by our nation. And when we have agreed upon it, we will send you notice of it. But we desire that you will not depend on your agent for information concerning land: for, after the abuses which we have suffered by such men, we will not trust them with any thing which relates to the land.

Father:

We will not hear lies concerning you, and we desire that you will not hear lies concerning us, and then we shall certainly live at peace with you.

Father:

There are men who go from town to town and beget children, and leave them to perish, or, except better men take care of them, to grow up without instruction. Our nation has looked round for a father, but they found none that would own them for children, until you now tell us that your courts are open to us as to your own people. The joy which we feel at this great news, so mixes with the sorrows that are passed, that we cannot express our gladness, nor conceal the remembrance of our afflictions. We will speak of them at another time.

Father:

We are ashamed that we have listened to the lies of Livingston, or been influenced by threats of war by Phelps, and would hide that whole transaction from the world, and from ourselves, by quietly receiving what Phelps promised to give us for the lands they cheated us of. But as Phelps will not pay us even according to that fraudulent bargain, we will lay the whole proceedings before your court. When the evidence which we can produce is heard, we think it will appear that the whole bargain was founded on lies, which he placed one upon another; that the goods which he charges to us as part payment were plundered from us, that, if Phelps was not directly concerned in the theft, he knew of it at the time, and concealed it from us; and that the persons we confided in were bribed by him to deceive us in the bargain. And if these facts appear, that your court will not say that such bargains are just, but will set the whole aside.

Father:

We apprehend that our evidence might be called for, as Phelps was here, and knew what we have said concerning him; and as Ebenezer Allen knew something of the matter, we desired him to continue here. Nicholson, the interpreter, is very sick, and we request that Allen may remain a few days longer, as he speaks our language.

Father:

The blood which was spilled near Pine creek is covered, and we shall never look where it lies. We know that Pennsylvania will satisfy us for that which we spoke of to them before we spoke to you. The chain of friendship will now, we hope, be made strong as you desire it to be. We will hold it fast; and our end of it shall never rust in our hands.

Father:

We told you what advice we gave the people you are now at war with, and we now tell you that they have promised to come again to our towns next spring. We shall not wait for their coming, but will set out very early, and shew to them what you have done *for us,* which must convince them that you will do for them everything which they ought to ask. We think they will hear and follow our advice.

Father:

You give us leave to speak our minds concerning the tilling of the ground. We ask you to teach us to plough and to grind corn; to assist us in building saw mills, and to supply us with broad axes, saws, augers, and other tools, so as that we may make our houses more comfortable and more durable; that you will send smiths among us, and, above all, that you will teach our children to read and write, and our women to spin and to weave. The manner of your doing these things for us we leave to you, who understand them; but we assure you that we will follow your advice as far as we are able.

> Cornplanter, his x mark.
> Half-Town, his x mark.
> Great-Tree, his x mark.

Present at signing,
Joseph Nicholson, Interpreter.
Ty. Matlack.
John Dechart, his x mark.
Jem Hudson, his x mark.
Philadelphia, 10th January, 1791.

◆

THE SPEECH OF THE PRESIDENT OF THE UNITED STATES
TO THE CORNPLANTER, HALF-TOWN, AND BIG-TREE,
CHIEFS OF THE SENECA NATION OF INDIANS.

Brothers:

I have maturely considered your second written speech.

You say your nation complain that, at the treaty of fort Stanwix, you were compelled to give up too much of your lands; that you confess your nation is bound by what was there done, and acknowledging the power of the United States; that you have now appealed to ourselves against that treaty, as made while we were angry against you, and that the said treaty was, therefore, unreasonable and unjust.

But, while you complain of the treaty of fort Stanwix, in 1784, you seem entirely to forget that you, yourselves, the Cornplanter, Half-Town, and Great-Tree, with others of your nation, confirmed, by the treaty of fort Harmar, upon the Muskingum, so late as the ninth of January, 1789, the boundary marked at the treaty of fort Stanwix, and that, in consideration thereof, you then received goods to a considerable amount.

Although it is my sincere desire, in looking forward, to endeavor to promote your happiness, by all just and humane treatments, yet I cannot disannul treaties formed by the United States, before my administration, especially, as the boundaries mentioned therein have been twice confirmed by yourselves. The lines fixed at fort Stanwix and fort Harmar, must, therefore, remain established. But Half-Town, and the others, who reside on the land you desire may be relinquished, have not been disturbed in their possession, and I should hope, while he and they continue to demean themselves peaceably, and to manifest their friendly dispositions to the people of the United States, that they will be suffered to remain where they are.

The agent who will be appointed by the United States, will be your friend and protector. He will not be suffered to defraud you, or to assist in defrauding you of your lands, or of any other thing, as all his proceedings must be reported in writing, so as to be submitted to the President of the United States.

You mention your design of going to the Miami Indians, to endeavor to persuade them to peace. By this humane measure you will render those mistaken people a great service, and, probably, prevent them from being swept from off the face of the earth. The United States require, only, that those people should demean themselves peaceably; but they may be assured, that the United States are able, and will, most certainly punish them severely for all their robberies and murders. You may, when you return from this city to your own country, mention to your nation my desire to promote their prosperity, by teaching them the use of domestic animals, and the manner that the white people plough, and raise so much corn. And if, upon consideration, it would be agreeable to the nation at large to learn these valuable arts, I will find some means of teaching them, at such places within your country as shall be agreed upon.

I have nothing more to add, but to refer you to my former speech, and to repeat my wishes for the happiness of the Seneca nation.

Given under my hand, and seal of the United States,
[L. S.] at Philadelphia, this nineteenth day of January,
one thousand seven hundred and ninety-one.

Geo. Washington

◆

THE SPEECH OF CORNPLANTER, HALF-TOWN, AND THE BIG-TREE, SENECA CHIEFS, TO THE GREAT COUNCILLOR OF THE THIRTEEN FIRES.

Father:

No Seneca ever goes from the fire of his friend, until he has said to him, "I am going." We therefore tell you, that we are now setting out for our own country.

Father:

We thank you, from our hearts, that we now know there is a country we may call our own, and on which we may lie down in peace. We see that there will be peace between your children and our children; and our hearts are very glad. We will persuade the Wyandots, and other Western nations, to open their eyes, and look towards the bed which you have made for us, and to ask of you a bed for themselves, and their children, that will not slide from under them.

We thank you for your presents to us, and rely on your promise to instruct us in raising corn, as the white people do; the sooner you do this, the better for us. And we thank you for the care you have taken to prevent bad men from coming to trade among us: if any come without your license, we will turn them back; and we hope our nation will determine to spill all the rum which shall, hereafter, be brought to our towns.

Father:

We are glad to hear that you determine to appoint an agent that will do us justice, in taking care that bad men do not come to trade amongst us; but we earnestly entreat you that you will let us have an interpreter in whom we can confide, to reside at Pittsburgh: to that place our people, and other nations, will long continue to resort; there we must send what news we hear, when we go among the Western nations, which, we are determined, shall be early in the spring. We know Joseph Nicholson, and he speaks our language so that we clearly understand what you say to us, and we rely on what he says. If we were able to pay him for his services, we would do it; but, when we meant to pay him, by giving him land, it has not been confirmed to him; and he will not serve us any longer unless you will pay him. Let him stand between, to intreat you.

Father:

You have not asked any security for peace on our part, but we have agreed to send nine Seneca boys, to be under your care for education. Tell us at what time you will receive them, and they shall be sent at the time you shall appoint. This will assure you that we are, indeed, at peace with you, and determined to continue so. If you can teach them to become wise and good men, we will take care that our nation shall be willing to receive instruction from them.

> Cornplanter, his x mark.
> Half-Town, his x mark.
> Big-Tree, his x mark.

Signed at Philadelphia, 7th February, 1791,
in presence of
Joseph Nicholson, Interpreter,
Thomas Procter,
Ty. Matlack.

◆

◆

THE SPEECH OF THE SECRETARY OF WAR
TO THE CORNPLANTER, HALF-TOWN, AND BIG-TREE,
CHIEFS OF THE SENECA NATION OF INDIANS.

The subscriber, the Secretary of War, has submitted your speech, of yesterday, to the President of the United States, who has commanded him to assure you of his good wishes for your happiness, and that you may have a pleasant journey to your own country.

The Governor of the Western territory will appoint you an interpreter whenever one shall be necessary. The President of the United States does not choose to interfere on this point.

The President of the United States thinks it will be the best mode of teaching you how to raise corn, by sending one or two sober men to reside in your nation, with proper implements of husbandry. It will, therefore, be proper that you should, upon consultation, appoint a proper place for such persons to till the ground. They are not to claim the land on which they shall plough.

The President of the United States, also, thinks it will be the best mode of teaching your children to read and write, to send a schoolmaster among you, and not for you to send your children among us. He will, therefore, look out for a proper person for this business.

As soon as you shall learn any thing of the intentions of the Western Indians, you will inform the Governor of the Western territory thereof, or the officer commanding at fort Washington, in order to be communicated to the President of the United States.

Given at the War Office of the United States, this eighth day of February, in the year of our Lord one thousand seven hundred and ninety-one.

H. Knox, Secretary of War.

Appendix Four

Speeches and Messages
to the Five Nations Delegation,
Philadelphia, March and April, 1792

[ASP, IA, I:229–33]

SPEECH OF THE PRESIDENT OF THE UNITED STATES
TO THE CHIEFS AND REPRESENTATIVES
OF THE FIVE NATIONS OF INDIANS,
IN PHILADELPHIA. —23D MARCH, 1792.

Sachems and Warriors of the Five Nations:

It affords me great satisfaction to see so many of you, who are the respectable chiefs and representatives of your several tribes; and I cordially bid you welcome to the seat of Government of the United States.

You have been invited to this place by Colonel Pickering, at my special request, in order to remove all causes of discontent, to devise and adopt plans to promote your welfare, and firmly to cement the peace between the United States and you, so as that, in future, we shall consider ourselves as brothers indeed.

I assure you that I am desirous that a firm peace should exist, not only between the United States and the Five Nations, but also between the United States and all the natives of this land; and that this peace should be founded upon the principles of justice and humanity, as upon an immoveable rock.

That you may partake of all the comforts of this earth, which can be derived from civilized life, enriched by the possession of industry, virtue, and knowledge; and I trust that such judicious measures will now be concerted to secure to you, and your children, these invaluable objects, as will afford you just cause of rejoicing while you live.

That these are the strong and sincere desires of my heart, I hope time and circumstances will convince you. But, in order that our peace and friendship may forever be unclouded, we must forget the misunderstandings of past times. Let us now look forward and devise measures to render our friendship perpetual.

I am aware that the existing hostilities with some of the Western Indians have been ascribed to an unjust possession of their lands by the United States. But be assured, that this is not the case; we require no lands but those obtained by treaties, which we consider as fairly made, and particularly confirmed by the treaty of Muskingum, in the year 1789.

If the Western Indians should entertain the opinion that we want to wrest their lands from them, they are laboring under an error. If this error could be corrected, it would be for their happiness; and nothing would give me more pleasure, because it would open to both of us the door of peace.

I shall not enter into further particulars with you at present, but refer you to General Knox, the Secretary of War, and Colonel Pickering, who will communicate with you upon the objects of your journey, and inform me thereof.

As an evidence of the sincerity of the desires of the United States for perfect peace and friendship with you, I deliver you this white belt of wampum, which I request you will safely keep.

Geo. Washington.

[On the 15th of March, a deputation of the Five Nations, consisting of fifty, arrived in Philadelphia. They were invited through the agency of Mr. Kirkland, for the purpose of attaching them to, and convincing them of, the justice and humanity of the United States; and also, to influence them to repair to the hostile tribes, in order to use their efforts to bring about a peace. These objects appeared to be effected, and they departed to carry them into execution. Besides abundant presents, fifteen hundred dollars, annually, were stipulated to these Indians by the President and Senate of the United States, for the purpose of attempting to civilize them.

All the various speeches, to and from them, have not been

deemed necessary to be here inserted. The speeches of the President of the United States to them, of the 23d of March, soon after their arrival, and of the 23d of April, before their departure, together with Colonel Pickering's speech to them, of the 30th of April, will show the general aspect of this conference.

They arrived at Buffalo creek in the beginning of June, but, owing to their frequent counselling, and dilatory manner of conducting business, they did not set out from Fort Erie for the hostile Indians until the middle of September, when they were accompanied by the firm friend of the United States, the Cornplanter.

The result of their interference is not yet known, but may, with the determination of the hostile Indians, be daily expected.]

◆

MESSAGE FROM THE PRESIDENT OF THE UNITED STATES
TO THE DELEGATION OF THE FIVE NATIONS OF INDIANS
IN PHILADELPHIA, 25TH APRIL, 1792.

My Children of the Five Nations!

You were invited here at my request, in order that measures should be concerted with you, to impart such of the blessings of civilization as may at present suit your condition, and give you further desires to improve your own happiness.

Colonel Pickering has made the particular arrangements with you, to carry into execution these objects, all of which I hereby approve and confirm.

And in order that the money necessary to defray the annual expenses of the arrangements which have been made, should be provided permanently, I now ratify an article which will secure the yearly appropriation of the sum of one thousand five hundred dollars, for the use and benefit of the Five Nations—the Stockbridge Indians included.

The United States having received and provided for you as for a part of themselves, will, I am persuaded, be strongly and gratefully impressed on you minds, and those of all your tribes.

Let it be spread abroad among all your villages, and throughout your land, that the United States are desirous not only of a general peace with all the Indian tribes, but of being their friends and protectors.

It has been my direction, and I hope it has been executed to your satisfaction, that during your residence here, you should be well fed, well lodged, and well clothed; and that presents should be furnished for your wives and families.

I partake of your sorrow on account that it has pleased the Great Spirit to take from you two of your number by death, since your residence in this city I have ordered that your tears should be wiped away according to your custom, and that presents should be sent to the relations of the deceased.

Our lives are all in the hands of our Maker, and we must part with them whenever he shall demand them; and the survivors *must submit* to events they cannot prevent.

Having happily settled all your business, and being about to return to your own country, I wish you a pleasant journey, and that you may safely return to your families after so long a journey, and find them all in good health.

Given under my hand, &c.

Geo. Washington

◆

THE SPEECH OF TIMOTHY PICKERING, COMMISSIONER,
TO THE SACHEMS AND CHIEFS OF THE FIVE NATIONS.

As some of you propose to attend the great council of Western Indians, soon to be held near the west end of Lake Erie, you are hereby authorized to assure those Indians of the sincere disposition of the United States to make peace with them. That there has been, probably, an unhappy mistake prevailing among them, relative to the claims of the United States to the lands northwest of the Ohio, as though we extended them even to the Mississippi, and to all the country between the lakes Erie, St. Clair, Huron, and Michigan. As you have in your hands the map of the country, you can explain it to them; and show what parts the United States have purchased at the treaties at fort M'Intosh and Muskingum, and at the mouth of the great Miami, which runs into the Ohio. That we claim no lands but what belong to the nations who sold to us, that we claim not a foot of the lands of any nation, with whom we have yet held no treaties. That if, at the treaties held with other nations, there has been any wrong doing, the United States will do what is right, and make ample compensation. That, if they are disposed to treat with the United States, in order to make peace, and settle all matters in dispute, and they will send runners to give notice thereof, to the commanding officers of any of our posts, orders will be given for their friendly reception, and measures taken to conduct the chiefs and all others, who shall come to the treaty, to fort Washington, on the Ohio, near the mouth of the little Miami, where provisions in abundance will be ready for their support. And as the long continued hostilities may have rendered them jealous, the United States will deliver into their hands a proper number of officers, as hostages for the safety of the chiefs, and all who shall attend them at the treaty. Fort Washington is proposed as the most suitable place for the treaty, because it is but a few steps from the country of the Western Indians; because provisions can be got there in plenty; and because there will be commissioners on the spot, to treat with them.

If they enter into a treaty, the Western Indians will experience the friendship of the United States, as you have done; and those who are the instruments in bringing about a peace, will be liberally rewarded, while they will receive the thanks and blessings of many nations.

In behalf of the United States:

Timothy Pickering, Commissioner.

Dated at Philadelphia, the thirtieth of April, 1792.

[The Five Nations, especially the Senecas, manifesting great uneasiness at the proposal of holding a treaty at fort Washington, whither they said the hostile Indians would not come, the passage here written, was added:]

"Although the Western Indians would be perfectly safe, in attending a treaty at fort Washington, yet, if they are unwilling to go to that place, we will meet them at some other, convenient to them and to us; as on the Muskingum, or Big Beaver creek, or twenty or thirty miles up French creek, above Venango, at places where there are no forts."

Notes

Introduction

1. The Draper Manuscripts are grouped into a large number of document series that bear the designations given them by Draper, possibly relevant to his plans for writing and publication. Hence within the collection one can examine the George Rogers Clark Papers, the Joseph Brant Papers, the Kentucky Papers, and so forth. In fact many of the documents filed in this manner have only a slight connection to the personality or geographical region whose name designates a series. As an alternative to the names, each document series also has a letter (or two-letter) designation. Each series consists of several volumes of documents. Convention demands that one cite materials in the Draper Manuscripts by volume number (within the document series), document series letter designation, and page number. The Joseph Brant Papers are designated by the letter *F*, and Blacksnake's narrative is found in volume 16 of that series, mounted on pages 107–219; hence the citation is to 16-F-107–219.

2. "Reservation English" is a term ethnographers use for unique aspects of English as spoken by native people on reservations and reserves. For previous generations of ethnographers it was a "broken" English spoken by a community whose first language was not English; today reservation English among the Senecas, based on my own observation (I have neither extensive linguistic training nor a "good ear"), does not deviate far from dialects of English spoken in surrounding white communities, but it does encompass some sound shifts and a specialized vocabulary to deal with native social, political, and religious institutions.

Chapter One

1. The testimony of Governor Blacksnake was crucial to the case in which the Senecas reclaimed title to the Oil Spring Reservation near Cuba, New York.

2. Examination of Indian Department records from the late eighteenth century provides fascinating lists of goods passing from European hands to native people, giving us a clear conception of the wardrobe of the typical (and not so typical) Indian of this time (see Abler 1975).

3. There is a large and rich body of ethnographic literature relating to the Seneca calendrical ceremonies. This literature begins with the writing of Morgan (1851), but students of this aspect of Seneca life must consult the writings of both Fenton (1936, 1941b, 1953) and Tooker (1970, 1978a).

4. L. H. Morgan (1851) initially used the word "sachem" to designate members of the confederacy council. Although the word is Algonquian rather than Iroquoian, it is useful to distinguish members of the league council from other political officials who can be designated "chiefs."

5. As superintendent of Indian affairs Johnson was on the campaign to lead the Six Nations contingent. The expedition's commander, Brigadier John Prideaux, was killed in an artillery accident. The assumption of command by Sir William was not without controversy (see Hamilton 1976:251–53).

6. Draper's notes state that Blacksnake had no knowledge of the forts at Venango and Erie, but he refers to the fort at the mouth of French Creek as Franklin. Venango (later called Franklin) was at the mouth of French Creek, and the circumstances described fit what little we know about that action (Parkman 1851:337; Peckham 1947:167–68). Clearly Draper erred and meant Le Boeuf when he wrote Venango.

7. The portraits of Blacksnake included in this volume show eyes that are far from small.

8. It is tempting to suggest that the Iroquois put on their leggings one leg at a time just like the rest of us.

9. Obviously a euphemism used by the missionary Heckewelder. For unexpurgated speeches relating to this question see Weslager (1944).

10. Page numbers from this volume of the Brant Papers in the Draper Manuscript (16-F) are enclosed in square brackets.

11. In the seventeenth century the usual Iroquoian residence was a multifamily dwelling known as a longhouse. The one that housed a chief and his kinsmen was often larger and used for meetings and ceremonies. When the Iroquois residence pattern changed and most nuclear families lived in separate houses, it was (and is still) usual for each community to maintain a longhouse both for religious ceremonies and for political councils. Seventeenth-century pole-and-bark longhouses were replaced in the eighteenth century by similar buildings made of logs and still later by frame and clapboard construction. Aluminum siding covers one contemporary structure. Photographs of contemporary longhouses from modern Iroquois communities, now used primarily for religious ceremonies, can be found in *Northeast* volume of the *Handbook of North American Indians* (Tooker 1978a:455).

12. It was not unusual for the chiefs to refuse to decide a contentious issue and instead to pass it to "the warriors" for an opinion. This ensured that the decision would reflect the will of the entire group.

Chapter Two

1. Before the American Declaration of Independence in 1776, participation by Indians in the conflict was limited to a few encounters. The Cherokees did attack whites who were squatting on their lands in 1776. The officers of the Southern Department of the British Indian service in fact tried to prevent these attacks, for they knew they had no military resources to coordinate with Cherokee actions. The attacks were clearly the result of Cherokee initiative because of very real grievances. In the north there were two actions before July 4, 1776, in which Indians participated. As a result of the American invasion of Canada, the native population of Caughnawaga, just outside Montreal, participated, with the help of some of their Mohawk kinsmen, in the defense of Canada, meeting the Americans before the post of St. Johns (this post was part of the defenses of the approaches to Montreal, not St. John's, Newfoundland, which Wallace [1970:

129] erroneously asserted was defended by Iroquois warriors) in a sharp skirmish in which both sides claimed victory (Graymont 1972:75–76; NYCD, 8:660–61). The next spring again saw Indians in conflict with American armies (who were retreating from Canada) on May 20, 1776, at the battle of the Cedars, forty miles from Montreal. Graymont (1972:94) has corrected the often-repeated assertion that Joseph Brant was at the Cedars (see Stone 1838, 1:153; Swiggett 1933:71–72; Mathews 1965:37; Wallace 1970:131). Brant was in England at the time (Graymont 1972:106).

2. A long paper could be written to refute the widely circulated opinion Wise also expounds, that Indians were ineffective on the battlefield. Suffice to note here that the contents of this volume say much for the mettle of the Indian warriors.

3. Belts of wampum, cylindrical shell beads, were exchanged regularly as part of diplomacy. A belt used to cement an offensive alliance was termed a war belt, and acceptance of such a belt was a commitment to go to war (see Jacobs 1949).

4. At the beginning of the conflict many Loyalist units wore green coats. Some of these, such as the Royal Regiment of New York, raised by Sir John Johnson and sometimes called Johnson's Royal Greens, later adopted red coats like the British regulars. Others, such as Butler's Rangers and the Queen's Own Rangers (commanded by John Simcoe), fought the entire war in green uniforms (Lefferts 1926).

5. The question whether the British paid for scalps during the Revolution is a contentious one (see Sosin 1965). I have seen nothing in British documents from the Revolution to indicate they did, but Blacksnake in his narrative records the offer of a scalp bounty (DM 16-F-125), and Draper's notes of his interview with the chief agree (DM 4-S-18).

6. The British post at the mouth of the Niagara River was Fort Niagara. After the war the British surrendered this fort to the Americans and built Fort George on the Canadian side of the river. Williams used the latter name in translating Blacksnake's story.

Chapter Three

1. Draper believed otherwise. He thought Blacksnake's father, De-ne-o-ah-te, was killed two years later, on 12 August 1779, while fighting against General Sullivan's army traveling up the Susquehanna River. A member of Sullivan's expedition has provided a brief description of the skirmish on that date: "Genl Hand was ordered with the light Infintry to pursue the Enemy and ware one miles above the town, hs Advanced Guard was fired on by the indians Who in Ambush, and at the first fire Killd 3 privets and wonded two offasers, viz Captn Carbury & Adjutant Hutson, one Guide and 3 privets; the Fire was Returned by our people which obliged them to Quit the Ground. The Kild and wounded ware braught of the field" (Grant in Cook 1887:139; see also other journal entries for August 12 and 13 in Cook 1887).

Evidence from his interview with Blacksnake that supports Draper's conclusion is that Blacksnake's father was killed on "a hill in the forks of the Susquehanna and Tioga" (DM 4-S-13–14). The hilltop battle with the light infantry of General Hand took place fifteen miles from the conjunction of these two rivers. But this section of Blacksnake's narrative places the scene of his father's death on the banks of a branch of the Mohawk River—a description fitting neither the Susquehanna nor the Tioga. Either Blacksnake is confused, or he has been misinterpreted by Benjamin Williams or by Lyman Draper and William Crouse.

Support for the Williams version is provided by the testimony of Blacksnake that his father was not present at the taking of Fort Freeland on July 18, 1779—that he had been killed before that date (DM 4-S-33). However, if De-ne-o-ah-te was killed in August 1777, then Blacksnake's testimony, recorded by Draper, that he was at Wyoming (DM 4-S-13) must be in error. Draper's notes, then, are internally inconsistent, and some of them contradict the simplest interpretation of Blacksnake's narrative as recorded by Williams.

I believe one should accept this simplest interpretation of the narrative—that Blacksnake's father was killed on a tributary of the Mohawk River immediately after the battle of Oriskany. Schoharie and the skirmish between the forces of McDonell and Harper fit this interpretation.

2. A skeptic might question the validity of this tale. A secret Masonic sign is also reported to have led Brant to spare Captain John Wood a year later at Minisink (Graymont 1972:201). I am personally convinced that at least one of these stories must be a fabrication and, indeed, think it possible that both are fiction.

3. Chafe (1963:55) gives us ?o?so·ǫt for "turkey" in Seneca.

4. I have argued in this chapter that "general Ducky" in the narrative is a white officer known to the Senecas as Turkey and that said Turkey is John Butler. Draper thought that Turkey was Captain John McDonell (or as Draper, following American practice, spelled it, McDonald) and Walter Butler was Dux,e,a. Support for Draper's position is provided by Blacksnake's report that Dux,e,a and Turkey were at Cherry Valley (DM 4-S-30).

5. The similarity of this account to Blacksnake's description of Red Jacket's behavior at Oriskany is noteworthy.

6. That Blacksnake told Draper he did not fight at the Wells House "but was near by engaged in other destruction of property" (DM 4-S-32) lends further support to the correctness of the identification made here of a large segment of the narrative (16-F-144–47) as the battle of Wyoming rather than Cherry Valley. There is no indication in his interview with Draper that Blacksnake killed anyone at Cherry Valley.

7. The consensus of ethnohistorians is that care for crops was a traditionally female task among the Iroquois. Males did play a not inconsiderable economic role in that they cleared the land and helped in the harvest. However, I think it possible that in the late eighteenth century males were assuming a larger role in agricultural production. The economic distress caused by the war is an indication that males, at this point in Iroquois history, were important in food production. Although, as Graymont (1972:203) points out, females did on occasion accompany war parties, I have no doubt that a sufficient portion of the female population re-

mained at home to have maintained food production if it had been almost solely a female task.

8. Relevant to Draper's conclusion that Turkey is John McDonell rather than John Butler is his report that Blacksnake had "no recollection about *Turkey* being along" (DM 4-S-33).

9. The rebels had begun 1779 with an offensive action against the Onondagas. Until this time the Onondagas had been largely neutral, but distinguishing among various Indian tribes has never been a frontier characteristic. Under the command of Colonel Goose Van Schaick an army of 558 left Fort Schuyler on April 18. With great stealth they managed to approach the neutral villages unnoticed. They killed a dozen Indians, captured thirty-three others, mostly women, and burned three towns. The Indians later complained of the rebel troops "using the Onondaga women for their own purposes" (Graymont 1972:196). The towns were plundered and trunnions knocked off the swivel gun mounted at a council house. By April 24 the army returned to Fort Schuyler "with much spoil and little glory" (Beauchamp 1905:239).

10. Blacksnake told Draper that Dux-e-a and Turkey led the British soldiers, but he "don't recollect about Sag-au-tah." Recall that Draper felt that Sag-au-tah, not Turkey, was the Seneca name for John Butler (DM 4-S-35).

11. Blacksnake notes that Dux-e-a and Turkey were along as well as another British officer known as "*Kah-oon-war-ha* or *The New-Canoe*" (DM 4-S-47).

Chapter Five

1. "Custer's Last Stand" (the battle of the Little Bighorn) has for a century served as a symbol of Indian victory over the white military might. Lieutenant Colonel George Armstrong Custer perished with only 215 of his officers and men (47 of his regiment, the Seventh Cavalry, were killed elsewhere on the field) (Utley 1973:267–68). Thus the number of soldiers who died at the Little Bighorn was less than half the number killed in St. Clair's defeat.

Chapter Six

1. The Senecas were to learn what the American government meant by their promise to "never claim [Seneca lands] . . . nor disturb the Seneka nation." This solemn promise was broken less than two centuries later when the United States dammed the Allegheny River at Kinzua, Pennsylvania, flooding a third of the Allegany Reservation. This taking of Seneca lands, initiated in 1956 and completed in the next decade, was without Seneca consent (Abler and Tooker 1978:515; Wilson 1960:191). Also flooded was the entire Cornplanter Grant in Pennsylvania. The Allegany Senecas were forced to resettle in two new, compact communities (Fenton 1967). A new longhouse was constructed in one of these, Steamburg, so that the Senecas who still followed the way of Handsome Lake could carry on their ceremonies (Abrams 1967). I was privileged to attend the first strawberry ceremony held in that building, in June 1965. Not only the living were disturbed. Cemeteries from both the Cornplanter Grant and the Allegeny Reservation, including the remains of many of the Indians mentioned in this book, had to be relocated on dry ground (see Abrams 1965; Sublett 1965; Lane and Sublett 1972). Both Burnt House on the Cornplanter Grant, where Handsome Lake had his vision, and Coldspring, where Handsome Lake preached after leaving Cornplanter and where Blacksnake continued to reside to his death, are now under the water of the Allegheny River Reservoir.

2. Arthur Parker's published version of the Code of Handsome Lake, from a text provided him by the Tonawanda Seneca ritualist Edward Cornplanter, lays even greater emphasis on the role of Blacksnake (whose name Parker [1913:23] writes as Tää'-wŏnyăs) in these important events. To summarize, Handsome Lake's daughter sent for Blacksnake when she thought her father, who had been sick for four years, was dead. Blacksnake sent for his uncle, Cornplanter. Cornplanter declined to come immediately, however, and continued his work hoeing a field. Blacksnake felt the body, found a warm spot, and told the people that

Handsome Lake might revive. Cornplanter arrived, and he too found the warm spot, but he simply sat silently, saying nothing. The next morning, Blacksnake noted that the warm spot was spreading. When Handsome Lake finally revived, it was Blacksnake who first spoke to him: "Are you well? What think you?" (Parker 1913:22–24).

3. Handsome Lake's visions and teachings have provided the basis for an oral text that is recited yearly in the longhouses of his followers in Canada and New York. The text is long, taking three or four days to recite; since the instructions of Handsome Lake state that this recitation must take place before noon, the meeting adjourns until the next day when the sun reaches the zenith. Parker has provided a published version of this Code of Handsome Lake in English, but efforts of scholars since Parker to record the entire code have not met with success (see Fenton 1978). Parker's text is of sufficient quality, however, that it is used as a reference by contemporary ritualists. The Parker text contains 129 passages, each marked by a formal closing. Parker labels and numbers these as "sections." Some of these sections describe episodes in the life of Handsome Lake, some vividly describe his visions as the angels led him into the next world, but most are messages pointing out sinful or correct behavior. Some of these messages clearly correspond to the "commandments" of the text recorded here. One can compare this passage with "section 1" of Parker's code. One'ga' (which Parker translates as "Whiskey or Rum") "has reared a high mound of bones" and was made not for Indians but for "our younger brethren, the white man" (Parker 1913:27).

4. Compare to "section 2" of the code. Witches, "people without their right minds . . . [who] make disease and spread sickness," must confess their guilt either in public or privately to the prophet or his speakers (Parker 1913:27–29).

5. Williams uses the word "article" in this and the subsequent section to mean substances or practices used in witchcraft—in other words, "medicines" (in the sense that medicine is used by students of the North American Indian) used for malevo-

lent practices. See Shimony (1970) for a discussion of witchcraft in contemporary Iroquois society.

6. Parker's "section 3" forbids the use of charms. Parker (1913: 46n) notes that these "charms" or "Witch-powders" were used as poisons and as love charms. The rather ambiguous text of "3 Commandments" may relate to an injunction against some such use of love magic, or it might be related to the injunction against birth control (that is, the use of medicines to make a woman sterile) in Parker's "section 4" (Parker 1913:30).

7. The text here corresponds closely to the discussion of males' abandoning wives and children found in "section 6" of Parker (1913:31).

8. "Section 12" of Parker's code deals with a husband who falsely claims to be single while away from home. In contrast to the text found here, that of Parker's code adds that although the man is "on his way to the house of the Wicked One" that the wife "is good in the eyes of her Creator" if she ignores the affair (Parker 1913:33). A major concern of Handsome Lake at the time he was making his reforms was the high divorce rate among the reservation population, and many of his messages from the angels support behavior that lends stability to the nuclear family (see Wallace 1971).

9. Compare this text with "section 11" in Parker (1913:32), which deals with a wife who is unfaithful while her husband is away.

10. No section in Parker corresponds closely with this text as is the case for the passages above. However, "section 19" in Parker (1913:35) does discuss duties that the young have toward the elderly.

11. Interestingly enough, there is no passage in Parker to correspond to this injunction in favor of patrilocal residence. As Wallace (1971) has indicated, much of Handsome Lake's preaching involved a social revolution replacing the old matrilineage (which was reinforced by matrilocal residence) with the nuclear family as the primary social institution in Seneca life. Patrilocal residence would certainly weaken the matrilineage as a social

institution. It seems possible that the decline of the matrilineage and of matrilocal residence may have been such that this message was lost (being unnecessary) between the time William wrote this text and the time Parker obtained his text from Edward Cornplanter.

12. This passage is clearly related to "section 14" in Parker (1913:33–44). However, the text in Parker suggests the child should be dunked in water rather than whipped, and Parker in a note states, "Punishment by violence as by whipping or striking was discountenanced."

13. While similar sentiments are found in several of the messages conveyed by Handsome Lake as recorded in Parker, no specific section can be related to this passage.

14. Again, it is impossible to relate this section of text to any specific section in the text published by Parker.

15. Gossip and those who practice gossip are reviled at several points in Handsome Lake's code. This text seems most closely related to "section 23" of the text published by Parker (1913:36–37).

Epilogue

1. Deardorff (1951:95) claimed that there was "no evidence of an open break" between Cornplanter and Handsome Lake. He also claimed Handsome Lake "was still resident at Burnt House in 1809." Generally speaking, Deardorff's scholarship is of the highest quality, but here his findings are superseded by Wallace's later work on the life of Handsome Lake.

2. Here again Deardorff (1951:97) has erred. He has suggested that Seneca participation in the war came almost exclusively from Buffalo Creek, where Handsome Lake had least influence. However, even Tonawanda, where the prophet resided, provided a roster of eighty-nine volunteers to the American war effort (Roster of Tonawanda Veterans, ESPP).

References

Abler, Thomas S.

1969 Factional dispute and party conflict in the political system of the Seneca Nation (1845–1895): An ethnohistorical analysis. Ph.D. thesis, Department of Anthropology, University of Toronto.

1970 Longhouse and palisade: Northeastern Iroquoian villages of the seventeenth century. *Ontario History* 62:17–40.

1971 Moiety exogamy and the Seneca: Evidence from Buffalo Creek. *Anthropological Quarterly* 44:211–22.

1975 Presents, merchants, and the Indian Department: Economic aspects of the American Revolutionary frontier. *National Museum of Man Canadian Ethnology Service Mercury Series* 28(2): 603–21.

1979 Kayahsotha?. In *Dictionary of Canadian biography*, 4:408–10. Toronto: University of Toronto Press.

1982 "The Indians old dradition." *Man in the Northeast* 24:71–87.

1987 Governor Blacksnake as a young man? Speculation on the identity of Trumbull's "The Young Sachem." *Ethnohistory* 34:329–51.

Abler, Thomas S., and Elisabeth Tooker

1978 Seneca. In *Handbook of North American Indians*, vol. 15, *Northeast*, 505–17. Washington: Smithsonian Institution.

Abrams, George H.

1965 The Cornplanter cemetery. *Pennsylvania Archaeologist* 35:59–73.

1967 Moving the fire: A case of Iroquois ritual innovation. In *Iroquois culture, history, and prehistory: Proceedings of the 1965 Conference on Iroquois Research*, ed. Elisabeth Tooker, 23–24. Albany: New York State Museum and Science Service.

Aldrich, Charles

1905–7 Recollections of the Senecas. *Annals of Iowa*, ser. 3, 7:380–84.

Allen, Robert S.

1975 The British Indian Department and the frontier in North America, 1755–1830. *Canadian Historic Sites* 14:5–125.

Anderson, Rufus

1825 *Memoir of Catherine Brown, a Christian Indian of the Cherokee Nation.* Boston: Crocker and Brewster.

Apes, William

1829 *A son of the forest: The experience of William Apes, a native of the forest.* New York: The Author.

Armstrong, William H.

1978 *Warrior in two camps: Ely S. Parker, Union general and Seneca chief.* Syracuse: Syracuse University Press.

ASP, IA (United States Congress)

1823–61 *American state papers: Indian affairs.* Washington: Gales and Seaton.

Beauchamp, William M.

1892 *The Iroquois trail.* Fayetteville, N.Y.: Beauchamp.

1905 *A history of the New York Iroquois, now commonly called the Six Nations.* Bulletin 78. Albany: New York State Museum.

1907 *Aboriginal place names of New York.* Bulletin 108. Albany: New York State Museum.

Black Hawk

1955 *Black Hawk: An Autobiography.* Ed. Donald Jackson. Urbana: University of Illinois Press. (Original edition, 1833, Life of Ma-ka-tai-me-she-kia-kiak, or Black Hawk.)

Bond, Richmond P.

1952 *Queen Anne's American kings.* Oxford: Clarendon.

Boswell, James

1776 An account of the chief of the Mohock Indians, who lately visited England (with an exact likeness). *London Magazine* 45:339.

Brumble, H. David, III

1981 *An annotated bibliography of American Indian and Eskimo autobiographies.* Lincoln: University of Nebraska Press.

Campisi, Jack

1978 Oneida. In *Handbook of North American Indians,* vol. 15, *Northeast,* 481–90. Washington: Smithsonian Institution.

Cartwright, Conway Edward

1876 *Life and letters of the late Hon. Richard Cartwright.* Toronto: Belford Brothers.

Chafe, Wallace L.

1963 *Handbook of the Seneca language.* Bulletin 388. Albany: New York State Museum and Science Service.

1967 *Seneca morphology and dictionary.* Smithsonian Contributions to Anthropology 4. Washington: Smithsonian Institution.

Clarke, Noah T.

1931 The wampum belt collection of the New York State Museum. *New York State Museum Bulletin* 288:85–121.

Coe, Stephen Howard

1968 Indian affairs in Pennsylvania and New York 1783–1794. Ph.D. thesis, American University, Washington, D.C.

Congdon, Charles E.

1967 *Allegany oxbow.* Salamanca, N.Y.: Congdon.

Continental Congress

1904–37 *Journals of the Continental Congress, 1774–1789.* 34 vols. Washington: U.S. Government Printing Office.

Cook, Frederick, ed.

1887 *Journal of the military expedition of Major General John Sullivan against the Six Nations of Indians in 1779.* Auburn, N.Y.: Knapp, Peck, and Thomson.

Copway, George

1847 *The life, history, and travels of Kah-ge-ga-gah-bowh.* Albany: Weed and Parsons.

Cuffe, Paul

1839 *Narrative of the life and adventures of Paul Cuffe, Pequot Indian: During thirty years spent at sea, and in travelling foreign lands.* Vernon: Horace N. Bill.

Day, Sherman

1843 *Historical collections of the state of Pennsylvania.* Philadelphia: G. W. Gordon.

Dearborn, Henry A. S.

1904 Journals of Henry A. S. Dearborn. *Buffalo Historical Society Publications* 7:33–225.

Deardorff, Merle H.

1941 The Cornplanter Grant in Warren County. *Western Pennsylvania Historical Magazine* 24:1–22.

1951 The religion of Handsome Lake: Its origin and development. *Bureau of American Ethnology Bulletin* 149:77–107.

DM (Draper Manuscripts)

State Historical Society of Wisconsin, Madison.

Donaldson, Thomas

1892 . . . *Indians. The Six Nations of New York: Cayugas, Mohawks (Saint Regis), Oneidas, Onondagas, Senecas, Tuscaroras.* Extra Census Bulletin. Washington: U.S. Government Printing Office.

Donehoo, George P.

1928 *A history of the Indian villages and place names in Pennsylvania with numerous historical notes and references.* Harrisburg: Telegraph Press.

Downes, Randolph C.

1940 *Council fires on the upper Ohio: A narrative of Indian affairs in the upper Ohio until 1795.* Pittsburgh: University of Pittsburgh Press.

Drake, Samuel

1832 *Indian biography, containing the lives of more than two hundred Indian chiefs: Also such others of that race as have rendered their names conspicuous in the history of North America, from its first being known to Europeans, to the present period.* Boston: Josiah Drake.

ESPP (Ely S. Parker Papers)

Library, American Philosophical Society, Philadephia.

Fenton, William N.

1936 An outline of Seneca ceremonies at Coldspring Longhouse. Publications in Anthropology 9. New Haven: Yale University.

1941a Masked medicine societies of the Iroquois. In *Annual report of the Smithsonian Institution for 1940*, 397–430. Washington: Smithsonian Institution.

1941b Tonawanda longhouse ceremonies: Ninety years after Lewis Henry Morgan. *Bureau of American Ethnology Bulletin* 128: 140–66.

1941c Iroquois suicide. *Bureau of American Ethnology Bulletin* 128:80–137.

1945 Place names and related activities of the Cornplanter Senecas. *Pennsylvania Archaeologist* 15:25–29, 42–50, 88–96, 108–18.

1949 Collecting materials for a political history of the Six Nations. *American Philosophical Society Proceedings* 93:233–38.

1950 The roll call of the Iroquois chiefs: A study of a mnemonic cane from the Six Nations reserve. *Smithsonian Miscellaneous Collections* 111(15): 1–73.

1953 The Iroquois eagle dance: An offshoot of the Calumet dance. Bulletin 156. Washington: Bureau of American Ethnology.

1956 Some questions of classification, typology, and style raised by Iroquois masks. *Transactions of the New York Academy of Science*, ser. 2, 18:347–57.

1967 From longhouse to ranch-type house: The second housing revolution of the Seneca Nation. In *Iroquois culture, history, and prehistory: Proceedings of the 1965 Conference on Iroquois Research*, ed. Elisabeth Tooker, 7–22. Albany: New York State Museum and Science Service.

1971 The New York State wampum collection: The case for the integrity of cultural treasures. *Proceedings of the American Philosophical Society* 115:437–61.

1978 Northern Iroquoian culture patterns. In *Handbook of North American Indians*, vol. 15, *Northeast*, 296–321. Washington: Smithsonian Institution.

1986a Leadership in the northeastern woodlands of North America. *American Indian Quarterly* 10:21–45.

1986b A further note on Iroquois suicide. *Ethnohistory* 33:448–57.

Fenton, William N., and Elisabeth Tooker

1978 Mohawk. In *Handbook of North American Indians,* vol. 15, *Northeast,* 466–80. Washington: Smithsonian Institution.

Garratt, John G., and Bruce Robertson

1985 *The four Indian kings.* Ottawa: Public Archives.

Graymont, Barbara

1972 *The Iroquois in the American Revolution.* Syracuse: Syracuse University Press.

Hale, Horatio E.

1883 *The Iroquois book of rites.* Philadelphia: D. G. Brinton.

Hamilton, Milton W.

1976 *Sir William Johnson: Colonial America, 1715–1763.* Port Washington, N.Y.: Kennikat Press.

Harper, Josephine L.

1983 *A guide to the Draper Manuscripts.* Madison: State Historical Society of Wisconsin.

Harris, George Henry

1903 The life of Horatio Jones. *Buffalo Historical Society Publications* 6:381–526.

Hauptman, Laurence M.

1986 *The Iroquois struggle for survival: World War II to red power.* Syracuse: Syracuse University Press.

Hayes, Charles F., III

1965 *The Orringh Stone Tavern and three Seneca sites of the late historic period.* Research Records 12. Rochester: Rochester Museum of Arts and Sciences.

Heckewelder, John G. E.

1820 *A narrative of the mission of the United Brethren among the Delaware and Mohegan Indians from its commencement in the year 1740 to the close of the year 1808.* Philadelphia: M'Carty and Davis.

Heitman, Francis B.

1967 *Historical register of officers of the Continental Army during the War of the Revolution . . . with addenda by Robert H. Kelby, 1932.* Baltimore: Genealogical Publishing Company.

Hesseltine, William B.

1954 *Pioneer's mission: The story of Lyman Copeland Draper.* Madison: State Historical Society of Wisconsin.

Hewitt, J. N. B., and William N. Fenton

1944 The requickening address of the Iroquois condolence council. *Journal of the Washington Academy of Sciences* 34(3): 65–85.

Horsman, Reginald

1964 *Matthew Elliot, British Indian agent.* Detroit: Wayne State University Press.

Hubbard, John Niles

1886 *An account of Sa-go-ye-wat-ha, or Red Jacket and his people, 1750–1830.* Albany: J. Munsell's Sons.

Jacobs, Wilbur R.

1949 Wampum: The protocol of Indian diplomacy. *William and Mary Quarterly,* 3d ser., 6:596–604.

1950 *Diplomacy and Indian gifts: Anglo-French rivalry along the Ohio and Northwest frontiers, 1748–1763.* Stanford: Stanford University Press.

Jennings, Francis

1984 *The ambiguous Iroquois empire: The Covenant Chain Confederation of Indian tribes with English colonies from its beginnings to the Lancaster treaty of 1744.* New York: Norton.

Jennings, Francis, et al., eds.

1984 *Iroquois Indians: A documentary history of the Six Nations and their league.* Microfilm edition, 50 reels. Woodbridge, Conn.: Research Publications for the D'Arcy McNickle Center for the History of the American Indian and the Newberry Library.

Jester, Margo

1961 Peace medals. *American Indian Tradition* 7(5): 149–57.

Johnston, Charles M., ed.

1964 *The valley of the Six Nations: A collection of documents on the Indian lands of the Grand River.* Toronto: Champlain Society.

Jones, Dorothy V.

1982 *License for empire: Colonialism by treaty in early America.* Chicago: University of Chicago Press.

Kappler, Charles J., comp.

1904–41 *Indian affairs: Laws and treaties.* 5 vols. Washington: U.S. Government Printing Office.

Kelsay, Isabel Thompson

1984 *Joseph Brant, 1743–1807: Man of two worlds.* Syracuse: Syracuse University Press.

Kent, Donald H., and Merle Deardorff

1960 John Adlum on the Allegheny: Memoirs for the year 1794. *Pennsylvania Magazine of History and Biography* 84:265–324, 435–80.

Ketchum, William

1864–65 *An authentic and comprehensive history of Buffalo, with some account of its early inhabitants, both savage and civilized, comprising historic notices of the Six Nations.* Buffalo: Rockwell, Baker and Hill.

Knopf, Richard C., ed.

1975 *Anthony Wayne: A name in arms. . . . The Wayne-Knox-Pickering-McHenry correspondence.* Westport, Conn.: Greenwood.

Krupat, Arnold

1985 *For those who come after: A study of Native American autobiography.* Berkeley: University of California Press.

Lane, Rebecca A., and Audrey J. Sublett

1972 Osteology of social organization: Residence patterns. *American Antiquity* 37:186–201.

Langness, L. L.

1965 *The life history in anthropological science.* New York: Holt, Rinehart and Winston.

Langness, L. L., and Gelya Frank

1981 *Lives: An anthropological approach to biography.* Novato, Calif.: Chandler and Sharp.

Lefferts, Charles Mackubin

1926 *Uniforms of the American, British, French, and German* armies in the War of the American Revolution, 1775–1783. New York: New-York Historical Society.

Lincoln, Benjamin

1836 Journal of a treaty held in 1793, with the Indian tribes northwest of the Ohio, by commissioners of the United States. *Massachusetts Historical Society collections*, ser. 3, 5:109–76.

Lossing, Benson John

1872–73 *The life and times of Philip Schuyler.* New York: Sheldon.

Lounsbury, Floyd G.

1978 Iroquoian languages. In *Handbook of North American Indians*, vol. 15, *Northeast*, 334–43. Washington: Smithsonian Institution.

Lowenthal, Larry, ed.

1983 *Days of siege: A journal of siege of Fort Stanwix in 1777.* New York: Eastern Acorn Press.

Lydekker, John W.

1938 *The faithful Mohawks.* Cambridge: Cambridge University Press.

McKenney, Thomas L., and James Hall

1933–34 *The Indian tribes of North America, with biographical sketches and anecdotes of the principal chiefs.* Ed. Frederick W. Hodge. 3 vols. Edinburgh: John Grant. (Original edition published 1836–44.)

Manley, Henry S.

1947 Buying Buffalo from the Indians. *New York History* 28: 313–29.

Marshall, Peter

1967 Sir William Johnson and the treaty of Fort Stanwix, 1768. *Journal of American Studies* 1:149–79.

Mathews, Hazel C.

1965 *The mark of honour.* Toronto: University of Toronto Press.

MBPP (Maris B. Pierce Papers)
    Buffalo and Erie County Historical Society, Buffalo, N.Y.

MHC (Michigan Historical Collections)

Collections and Researches Made by the Pioneer and Historical Society of the State of Michigan, Lansing.

Morgan, Lewis Henry

1851 *League of the Ho-de-no-sau-nee* [or] *Iroquois.* Rochester:
Sage.

Newberry Library

1912 *Narratives of captivity among the Indians of North America.* Chicago: Newberry Library.

New York (State Historian)

1929 *The Sullivan-Clinton campaign in 1779: Chronology and
selected documents.* Albany: University of the State of New
York.

Norton, John

1970 *The journal of Major John Norton, 1816.* Ed. Carl F. Klinck
and James J. Talman. Toronto: Champlain Society.

NYCD (New York Colonial Documents)

1853–87 *Documents relative to the colonial history of the state
of New York.* Ed. Edmund B. O'Callaghan. 15 vols. Albany:
Weed, Parsons.

PA (Pennsylvania Archives)

1852–56 *Pennsylvania archives.* Ed. Samuel Hazard. Philadelphia: J. Stevens.

Parker, Arthur C.

1909 Secret medicine societies of the Seneca. *American Anthropologist,* n.s., 11:161–85.

1913 *The Code of Handsome Lake.* Bulletin 163. Albany: New
York State Museum.

1916 The Senecas in the War of 1812. *Proceedings of the New
York State Historical Association* 15:78–90.

1919 *The life of General Ely S. Parker: Last grand sachem of the
Iroquois and General Grant's military secretary.* Publication
23. Buffalo: Buffalo Historical Society.

1927 *Notes on the ancestry of Cornplanter.* Researches and
Transactions 5(2). Canandaigua, N.Y.: New York State Archaeological Association (Lewis H. Morgan Chapter).

Parkman, Francis

1851 *History of the Conspiracy of Pontiac and the war of the northern American tribes against the English colonies after the conquest of Canada.* Boston: Little, Brown.

Peckham, Howard H.

1947 *Pontiac and the Indian uprising.* Princeton: Princeton University Press.

Plummer, Ken

1983 *Documents of life: An introduction to the problems and literature of a humanistic method.* London: George Allen and Unwin.

Prucha, Francis Paul

1971 *Indian peace medals in American history.* Madison: State Historical Society of Wisconsin.

Rose, Richard

1983 *Face to face: Encounters with identity.* Rochester: Rochester Museum and Science Center.

Schoolcraft, Henry R.

1847 *Notes on the Iroquois, or contributions to American history, antiquities, and general ethnology.* Albany: Erastus H. Pease.

1851–57 *Historical and statistical information respecting the history, condition, and prospects of the Indian tribes of the United States.* 6 vols. Philadelphia: Lippincott, Grambo.

Seaver, James E.

1824 *A narrative of the life of Mrs. Mary Jemison.* Canandaigua, N.Y.: J. D. Bemis. (Reprint New York: Corinth, 1961.)

Shimony, Annemarie A.

1961 *Conservatism among the Iroquois at the Six Nations reserve.* Publications in Anthropology 65. New Haven: Yale University.

1970 Iroquois witchcraft at Six Nations. In *Systems of North American witchcraft and sorcery,* ed. Deward E. Walker, Jr., 239–65. Moscow: University of Idaho.

Simms, Jeptha R.

1845 *History of Schoharie County and border wars of New York.* Albany: Munsell and Tanner.

Smith, Marc J.

1946 Joseph Brant: Mohawk statesman. Ph.D. thesis, University of Wisconsin, Madison.

Society of Friends

1840 *The case of the Seneca Indians of New York, illustrated by facts.* Philadelphia: Merrihew and Thompson.

Sosin, Jack M.

1965 The use of Indians in the War of the American Revolution: A reassessment of responsibility. *Canadian Historical Review* 46:101–21.

Stanley, George F. G.

1963 The significance of the Six Nations' participation in the War of 1812. *Ontario History* 55:215–31.

Stone, William L.

1838 *Life of Joseph Brant–Thayendanegea.* 2 vols. New York: Blake, Dearborn.

1841 *The life of Sa-go-ye-wat-ha or Red Jacket.* New York: Wiley and Putnam.

Sublett, Audrey J.

1965 The Cornplanter cemetery: Skeletal analyses. *Pennsylvania Archaeologist* 35:74–92.

Swiggett, Howard

1933 *War out of Niagara: Walter Butler and the Tory Rangers.* New York: Columbia University Press.

SWJP (Sir William Johnson Papers)

1921–65 *The papers of Sir William Johnson.* Ed. James Sullivan et al. Albany: State University of New York.

Thatcher, B. B.

1832 *Indian biography, or An historical account of those individuals who have been distinguished among North American natives as orators, warriors, statesmen, and other remarkable characters.* 2 vols. New York: J. and J. Harper.

Thwaites, Reuben Gold

1903 A memoir of Dr. Draper. In *Collections of the State His-torical Society of Wisconsin, edited by Lyman Copeland Draper . . . being a page-for-page reprint of the original issue of 1855,* i–xxix. Madison: State Historical Society of Wisconsin.

Thwaites, Reuben Gold, and Louise Kellogg, eds.

1908 *The revolution on the upper Ohio, 1775–1777.* Madison: State Historical Society of Wisconsin.

Tooker, Elisabeth

1970 *The Iroquois ceremonial at midwinter.* Syracuse: Syracuse University Press.

1978a Iroquois since 1820. In *Handbook of North American Indians,* vol. 15, *Northeast,* 449–65. Washington: Smithso-nian Institution.

1978b Ely S. Parker, Seneca, 1828–1895. In *American Indian intellectuals,* ed. Margot Liberty, 15–30. 1976 Proceedings of the American Ethnological Society. St. Paul, Minn.: West.

1978c The League of the Iroquois: Its history, politics, and ritual. In *Handbook of North American Indians,* vol. 15, *Northeast,* 418–41. Washington: Smithsonian Institution.

Trigger, Bruce G.

1978 Early Iroquoian contacts with Europeans. In *Handbook of North American Indians,* vol. 15, *Northeast,* 344–56. Wash-ington: Smithsonian Institution.

Tubee, Okah

1848a *A thrilling sketch of the life of the distinguished chief Okah Tubbee, Alias Wm. Chubbee, son of the head chief Mosholeh Tubbee of the Choctaw Nation of Indians.* New York: N.p.

1848b *Sketch of the life of Okah Tubee, Alias William Chub-bee.* Springfield, Mass.: H. S. Taylor.

Turner, O.

1849 *Pioneer history of the Holland purchase of western New York.* Buffalo: Jewett, Thomas.

Utley, Robert M.

1973 *Frontier regulars: The United States Army and the Indian, 1866–1891.* New York: Macmillan.

Vail, R. W. G.

1949 *The voice of the old frontier.* Philadelphia: University of Pennsylvania Press.

Vaughan, Alden T.

1983 *Narratives of North American Indian captivity: A selective bibliography.* New York: Garland.

Wallace, Anthony F. C.

1952 Halliday Jackson's journal to the Seneca Indians, 1798–1800. *Pennsylvania History* 19:117–47, 325–49.

1961 Cultural composition of the Handsome Lake religion. *Bureau of American Ethnology Bulletin* 180:139–51.

1970 *The death and rebirth of the Seneca.* New York: Knopf.

1971 Handsome Lake and the decline of the Iroquois matriarchate. In *Kinship and culture,* ed. Francis L. K. Hsu, 367–76. Chicago: Aldine.

Wallace, Paul A. M.

1945 *Conrad Weiser, 1696–1760: Friend of colonist and Mohawk.* Philadelphia: University of Pennsylvania Press.

Washington, George

1925 *The diaries of George Washington.* Ed. John C. Fitzpatrick. Boston: Mount Vernon Ladies' Association.

Watson, Lawrence C., and Maria-Barbara Watson-Franke

1985 *Interpreting life histories: An anthropological inquiry.* New Brunswick, N.J.: Rutgers University Press.

Weslager, Clinton A.

1944 The Delaware Indians as women. *Journal of the Washington Academy of Sciences* 34(12): 381–88.

Willett, William M.

1831 *A narrative of the military actions of Colonel Marinus Willett.* New York: G. and C. and H. Carvill.

Wilson, Edmond

1960 *Apologies to the Iroquois.* New York: Farrar, Straus, and Cudahy.

Wise, S. F.

1970 The American Revolution and Indian history. In *Character and circumstance: Essays in honour of Donald Grant Creighton*, ed. John S. Moir, 182–200. Toronto: Macmillan.

Wray, Charles F., and Harry L. Schoff

1953 A preliminary report on the Seneca sequence in western New York, 1550–1687. *Pennsylvania Archaeologist* 23(2): 55–63.

Index

Abeel, John (Dutch trader, father of Cornplanter), 19, 24, 120
Abraham (Mohawk), 36, 231–32
Abrams, Deforest (Seneca), 224
Adlum, John, 204–5
Albany, council at (1775), 36, 41
Albany, council at (1776). *See* German Flats council
Albany militia, 122
Alden, Colonel Ichabod (commander at Cherry Valley), 104, 105
Aldrich, Charles, 221–22
Algonkin Indians, 158
Allegany Reservation, 5, 6, 130, 142, 203, 206, 208, 218, 219, 220, 221, 224, 274n.1
Allegheny River, 38, 48, 141, 146, 203, 206, 219, 224, 274n.1
Allen, Ebenezer, 254
Amherst, Sir Jeffery, 29
Army (British-Loyalist) units: Butler's Rangers, 83, 97, 104–5, 106, 108, 121, 270n.4; 8th Foot, 83, 104, 106; 44th Foot, 29; 46th Foot, 29; Jaegers, 83, 120; Queen's Own Rangers, 270n.4; Royal Regiment of New York,

83, 86–89, 120, 270n.4; 34th Foot, 83
Army (rebellious colonies) units: Bedford Rangers, 124–25; 1st New Jersey, 113; Morgan's Virginia Rifle Regiment, 113
Atrocities, 89, 97, 112–14, 130, 133, 141, 146, 149
Autobiographies: of native North Americans, 8–9; early publication of, 10
Avon, N.Y. *See* Conawagus

Bartoli, F., 82
Berry, Jack (Seneca), 106, 108, 119
Big Sandy Creek, 48, 171
Big Tree (Seneca), 111, 255; speeches delivered with Cornplanter and Halftown, 238–47, 250–55, 257–58
Bird, Lieutenant John (8th Foot), 66, 86, 101
Black Rock, battle of, 219
Black Rock, councils at, 167–69, 200–201
Blacksnake, Governor: ancestry of, 19, 24; appearance of, 6–7, 221–22; attacked by Delaware,